THE OMNI
FUTURE ALMANAC

THE OMNI FUTURE ALMANAC

Edited by Robert Weil
Foreword by Ben Bova

An Omni Press Book

World Almanac Publications
New York, New York

Interior design: Cris Graña
Cover design: Lawrence Ratzkin

First published in paperback in 1983.

Paperback edition distributed in the United States by Ballantine Books, a division of Random House, Inc. and in Canada by Random House of Canada, Ltd.

Library of Congress Catalog Card Number 81-52844
Newspaper Enterprise Association, Inc. ISBN 0-911818-39-1
Ballantine Books ISBN 0-345-31034-9

A hardcover edition of this book was originally published by Harmony Books, a division of Crown Publishers, Inc.

Printed in the United States of America

Newspaper Enterprise Association, Inc.
World Almanac Publications
200 Park Avenue
New York, NY 10166

Acknowledgements

A team of *Omni's* editors and contributing writers assembled this *Almanac*, a project far too complex for any single person to undertake on his own. The inspiration behind their work on *The Omni Future Almanac* was *Omni* itself, a magazine that, since its inception in 1978, has taken enormous strides to popularize science and stimulate interest in the future.

Too many people worked on this volume to cite or to thank individually, but the following have made noteworthy contributions: Douglas Colligan, Anthony Connor, Murray Cox, Regina Dombrowski, John Evans, George Goldey, Marianne Howatson, Hildegard Kron, Wendy Lipkind, Nancy Lucas, Francesca Lunzer, Kathleen McAuliffe, Judy McCusker, Robert Malone, Dan Morrill, David Myerson, Beverly Nerenberg, Gregg Ochs, Tim Onosko, David Owen, Marcia Potash, Margaret Richichi, Michael Schrage, Lisa Shapiro, Tom Stinson, Robert Sutton, Michael Weinglass, Gurney Williams III, and Elizabeth Woodson.

A few names must be cited more specifically: Bob Guccione and Kathy Keeton, whose joint dream of a future world created through science and technology is the basis for *Omni*; Dick Teresi, whose helmsmanship of the magazine has provided the fodder for scores of ideas in the *Almanac*; Frank DeVino, the artistic vision behind *Omni*; Ben and Barbara Bova, for their sustaining interest in *Omni* books; and the editorial triumvirate of Owen Davies, Michael Edelhart, and Paul Hilts, without whose efforts this volume would not exist.

Lastly, a word of gratitude to the publishers: editor Patricia Fisher, who has superbly navigated the *Almanac* through its intricate stages; Peter Shriver, an editor with a passion for technology; William Armstrong, a futuristic publisher across the Atlantic; and Jane Flatt, whose unerring support for the book and optimism about the future has seen this project through.

Robert Weil
Editor, Omni Book Division

Contributors to

The Omni Future Almanac

Edited by Robert Weil

Foreword by Ben Bova

CONTENTS

FOREWORD

The American astronomer Harlow Shapley once said, "The urge to know has evolved from an instinct to a profession."

The urge to know. Curiosity. If curiosity is an instinct, it is one that has stood us in good stead for a long time. Fools say, "Curiosity killed the cat," usually in an attempt to prevent you from asking them questions they cannot or will not answer. Wise men say, as Samuel Johnson did, "A generous and elevated mind is distinguished by nothing more certainly than an eminent degree of curiosity."

And what are we most curious about? The future. That unknown territory into which we are heading, whether we like it or not, on a journey that can be stopped only by death.

The future. What's going to happen tomorrow, ten minutes from now, next year, next century, next millennium? Will I find happiness? Will I get that promotion? Who's going to win the next election? Are we going to have a war? When will we have robots to serve around the house? How soon will I be married? How long will I live?

Human beings are time-binding creatures. We can perceive the future. We are intensely curious about it, and for a very practical reason. *The future is the only part of our lives that we can change.* The past is over and done with, immutable. The present is only a fleeting moment, a mathematically one-dimensional dividing wall between the past and the future. But the future has not happened yet. It can be molded, changed, shaped by what we do—and what we fail to do.

Our actions and inactions create our future. How, then, can we decide on what to do? How can we guide our steps along this pathway into tomorrow?

Through knowledge. As Shapley put it, turn the instinct of curiosity into a profession. Learn to predict the future.

Every form of human society has its future-forecasters. Primitive shamans studied the entrails of slaughtered animals or the shapes of clouds. The star-strewn nighttime sky became a forecaster's workshop. Comets boded ill fortune. Eclipses brought terror.

Gradually, as scientific reasoning replaced astrology and palmistry, we began to learn how to predict some parts of the future with great accuracy. The heavens moved according to discernible rules. Eclipses became predictable, so much so that tourists now travel halfway across the world to witness them.

In the twentieth century, the scientific tools for examining the future became formidable indeed. A whole new discipline of *futurism* was born. Scientists now spend careers advising government and industry about many aspects of the future, from population growth to climate change, from trends in technology to public attitudes toward new inventions.

Omni magazine's five-some million readers are curious about the future. So are *Omni*'s editors, who devote their careers to uncovering tomorrow and showing us what the future might possibly be like. In this Future Almanac, *Omni*'s editors and writers have pooled their efforts to present a kaleidoscope of tomorrow: visions of the future based solidly on the knowledge of today, seasoned with a touch of speculation.

Not all of these predictions will come true. Even with all the powers of modern science, much of the future remains hidden from us. But once you have read this Almanac, very little that happens in the next two decades will be a shock to you. From robot servants to enormously lengthened lifespans, from the colonization of space to the defeat of every major disease, the next two decades promise to be the most exciting and rewarding in human history.

And you can get a glimpse of it all, right here. If you are curious enough to read on.

Ben Bova
Editorial Director, Omni

THE OMNI
FUTURE ALMANAC

1 SCIENCE AND TECHNOLOGY

1 SCIENCE AND TECHNOLOGY

The next few decades should be a celebration of scientific and technological discovery. Scientific development comes in waves: a cascade of new discoveries and ideas breaks over the heads of researchers who then spend years exploring the vibrations of that creative swell. The Renaissance generated vital new concepts that kept many thinkers busy for their entire lives. At the time of Newton, a universal view of the world was created that directed scientific inquiry for 200 years afterward.

We seem to be poised on the verge of such a wave today. Scientists are on the brink of breakthroughs that will expand upon Einstein's theories, unravel the genetic tangle of our bodies, and craft new forms of electronic intelligence. In hundreds of other areas, breakthroughs will also be achieved. We have explored the concepts of industrial technology and World War II-vintage atomic science about as extensively as possible. In many cases, we have reached inconsistencies that must be explained or barriers to further development that must be overcome.

At such points in history, science bursts into activity. Research races off in new directions. Fresh ideas come to the fore. Unexpected insights emerge to spur new levels of human exploration in untouched regions of experience.

Electronics, quantum physics, genetic engineering, microcomputing, and space travel were all beyond the imagination three generations ago. Here is a glimpse of what may be commonplace three generations from now.

The New Age of Scientific Discovery

Astronomy

Astronomers will devote themselves to essential questions over the next few decades. How and when will the universe die? Will it regenerate itself? How big is it, and is it really all running away from us?

Black Hole Discovery and Study. Several suspected black holes—pockets of gravity in space so intense that not even light escapes them—have already been mentioned in astronomical journals. Before the turn of the century, a black hole will have been fully verified. Astronomers will undertake an intensive study of the celestial void. Within one decade after the hole's discovery, we will know if the many unsettling characteristics attributed to black holes are true. We will know if they are star gates opening new routes through the universe, or cosmic trash compactors, sucking in everything in their paths.

Census of the Universe. The fate of the universe rests on a simple question that will be answered during the next thirty years. How much matter exists and is the amount constant, or is new matter being made at all times? The giant space telescope that will be launched in the mid-1980s and the enormous space radio telescopes that will follow it will allow astronomers to complete an unprecedented census of the universe during the first decade of the twenty-first century. Astronomers will attempt to measure the total amount of hydrogen in the universe and to detect any sources of new matter. Depending upon what they find, we will discover if the universe we live in is eternal, if it will implode on itself one day and then regenerate, or if a final disintegration into nothingness will be the cold fate of everything.

Explanation of Doppler Anomalies. Since it was first expressed in 1842, the Doppler effect on light from an object that is traveling away from the viewer has held true throughout all scientific tests. The light, it was discovered, shifts toward the red end of the spectrum. This effect indicates that every part of the universe is moving away from earth. Recently, though, studies of distant powerful astronomical features, such as quasars, have challenged the Doppler effect, causing astronomers to question whether something other than motion could sometimes cause the shift on the spectrum. If the suspicion that the effect has alternate explanations is true, our entire view of the universe's activities may need to be revised. We may find ourselves in a smaller, more intimate cosmos, or we may discover that the rules of physics as we know them do not apply everywhere in quite the same way.

Biology

The main arena for biological achievement over the next twenty years is the crowded, complex community of the cell. Before 2000, scientists will be capable of taking cells apart piece by piece and putting them together again in new, startling combinations. It is vital work, because understanding the cell is the basic requirement for understanding all of life.

Genetic Transcription. As the turn of the century approaches, biologists will successfully transcribe all the genetic information in a healthy human cell for the first time. This fully detailed "map" for the coding of human cell operation will allow researchers to consider ways in which the code might be strengthened or protected for better health or longer life. It will also open up the whole new science of genetic markers—clues found in the genes of individuals that detail every biological tendency. Studying genetic markers will make diagnosis of adult illnesses possible at or even before a person's birth, so preventive measures can be applied from the first moments of life.

Brain Code Deciphering. The manner in which the brain encodes, assimilates, stores, and retrieves infomation will be understood within our lifetimes. The implications are enormous. The brain is by far the most efficient and compact information storage system ever known. Understanding the way the brain works could greatly expand people's ability to acquire and retain knowledge, making brain code deciphering as historic an achievement as the discovery of language. The field also holds promise for our ability to "debrief" a human brain before death, giving a person's thoughts and feelings an immortality his body can't achieve. Scientists at Stanford, the University of Missouri, and many other institutions are finding new ways to pick out and decipher individual brain waves, to map the pattern of the brain's electrical charges, and to chart the course of chemicals in brain cells. These are the first steps in reading the secret messages of our minds. Early in the twenty-first century, researchers will achieve the ability to use the electrical patterns of the brain code to communicate directly with our minds.

Genetic Creation of New Plants. Using genetic engineering techniques, scientists will craft new kinds of plants before the end of the century. The first will most likely be nitrogen-fixing grain crops. In nature, only legumes can capture their own nitrogen, a vital plant nutrient, from soil. The technologically advanced farmer must increasingly rely on expensive and destructive fertilizer to get nitrogen to grain. DNA specialists should be able to graft nitrogen-fixing ability onto the actual grain crops, vastly reducing the need for fertilizer and expanding the world's usable agricultural land.

Eventually, genetic engineers may attempt to construct a plant that will build an analogue for complete animal protein. This would be a true "soy-burger," a material grown by a plant that has all the best nutritional aspects of meat.

Chemistry

For chemists, the upcoming decades will be the era of new materials. The diversity of techniques at a chemist's command—lasers, genetic manipulation, and space manufacturing—will allow chemists to create mind-boggling compounds for virtually every area of human experience.

Unlocking Enzymes. If plastics were the key chemicals of the past twenty years, enzymes will assume that role during the next two decades. The uses of enzymes will be an interesting union of chemistry and biology. These biologically derived compounds will fill innumerable roles in nonbiological situations. They will make petrochemicals, digest garbage, form structural materials, and much more. Already companies like Novo Labs, Corning, General Electric, and many major energy corporations are testing enzyme processes for industry. By 1990, enzymes may represent a $500 million market. In addition, understanding enzymes may bring about a greater awareness of the chemical links that may cause some forms of cancer, providing a greater measure of safety in chemical design and production.

Ultimate Glue. A deepening understanding of surface dynamics will enable chemists to create adhesives by the end of the century that can replace virtually all fasteners now used. Airplane bodies, rockets, space platforms, and train rails will be held together by sophisticated adhesives. These materials will also allow engineers to create laminates of widely varied materials to produce an exact configuration of strength, suppleness, long life, and beauty for any task. By the twenty-first century, nails, screws, and rivets may be found only in museums.

Geophysical Sciences

In the physical sciences over the next generation, space will help us understand the earth. Detailed information from satellites, atmospheric probes, and space missions will help bring about new insights into how our planet works.

Successful Earthquake Prediction. A satellite network in space, linked with a computer on earth, can view all the tectonic plates that support earth's continents, seismic zones, and all geological disturbances. Such a wealth of information should greatly improve scientists' ability to predict earthquakes. The first fruits of this work should come by the end of the century, but reliable prediction of earthquakes won't be possible for at least a generation after that.

Early Hurricane and Tornado Identification and Destruction. The combination of infrared, laser, atmospheric pressure, and other monitors in orbit will allow meteorologists on earth to pinpoint incipient hurricanes and tornadoes. Infusion of energy into these forming storms might allow earth scientists to break them up in their early stages, alter their course, or blunt their power, but this is not likely to be achieved much before 2050.

Reversal of the CO_2 Effect. The crucial test for earth scientists in the decades ahead may well be their ability to overcome the warming caused by pollution in the ozone layer and the build-up of carbon dioxide (CO_2) in the atmosphere. This trend, it is generally held, could have a disastrous impact on earth weather, even potentially altering the shorelines of many countries. As the situation worsens toward the end of the century, scientists will undertake a massive research effort, the atmospheric equivalent of the space race, to devise methods of removing the pollutants and rebalancing the atmosphere. The major breakthroughs will come a decade into the twenty-first century and will lead to eventual climate control through manipulation of atmospheric conditions.

Physics

New challenges will emerge in the field of physics where a number of inconsistencies undermine existing theories. New ideas must explain these gaps before a better understanding of the world's building blocks can be achieved.

Unified Field Theory. Sometime between now and the end of the century, physicists will finally construct a mathematical model that will tie together the four basic forces holding the universe's particles together—gravity, electromagnetism, the weak nuclear force, and the strong nuclear force. Einstein's theory of relativity revealed only that gravity was an expression of *space-time*.

Many physicists, however, believe that the three other forces are also expressions of space-time, but have been unable to devise a theory that unites the four forces in a manner coinciding with verifiable experience. Once this is achieved, a new, more accurate world view will be possible that could open vast, conceptual areas for scientific development. With a unified field theory—a model of reality that expresses the relationship of the four elemental forces—we might learn to translate all forms of energy back and forth, and could relate events that occur across the universe that today seem irreconcilable.

High-Energy Particle Anomalies. The existing laws of physics state that information cannot be transmitted instantly; it can only move as fast as light. Therefore, a cause and an effect cannot be simultaneous. Yet, in the strange world of high-energy particles, there are several well-documented circumstances in which cause and effect do seem to be simultaneous.

Another set of situations seems to involve some kind of prior knowledge by one distant particle about what another, seemingly unconnected particle is doing. For instance, there are certain pairs of subatomic particles that always move in opposite directions. If one spins left, the other spins right. When one particle of such a pair is separated and put through a tunnel that spins it randomly, the other particle always immediately begins spinning in the opposite direction. How can this be? The particles are not connected and information cannot travel at such a great speed. Scientists will develop an explanation for these types of phenomena sometime in the early twenty-first century.

Superconductivity. A full understanding of the superconduction phenomenon—the ability some materials attain at low temperatures to transmit electricity without any resistance—will arrive during the next twenty years. It will be soon followed by development of a room-temperature superconductor that will transform energy usage in every aspect of human life. Superconduction is such a significant field of science because it allows electrical operations to take place at incredible speeds without any loss of power. One application already being developed is a superconducting computer that can compress all the memory of the world's largest existing system into a fourteen-centimeter cube.

Macro-Engineering
Projects of the
Twenty-first Century

There are schemes afoot that could end the world's energy shortage, rebuild international cities, provide cheap transportation at supersonic speeds, and turn the North African deserts into farmland. They all have two things in common: complexity and sheer size. They are so sophisticated that they demand new technology, so costly that they could absorb the entire economy of a medium-sized country, and so unwieldy that we can hardly organize the manpower needed to carry them out.

This is the territory of macro-engineering. Macro-engineers take the wildest dreams of science fiction and turn them into reality. The Space Shuttle and the Alaska Pipeline were macro-projects. So were the Pyramids and the Panama Canal. Macro-engineers always build things just a bit more difficult than the rest of us believe possible.

Here are several feasible macro-projects of the twenty-first century and predictions for a few more.

Planetran

A truly modern subway could carry passengers from New York to Los Angeles in less than an hour at a cost as low as fifty-four dollars. The secret is to lift the trains over the rails with electromagnets and run them through a tunnel with most of the air removed. Top speed: 6,000 miles per hour. Yet, energy costs would be only one-tenth those of today's railways. The first Planetran route could be in operation by 2000. By the end of the next century, these routes will connect the continents.

Solar Power Satellite (SPS)

Scientists can already build the first solar power satellite to collect the sun's energy in orbit and beam it to earth as microwaves or laser light. By 2025, a satellite power system could provide most of North America's electricity. All it will take is the decision to go ahead and build the vast network of orbiting solar collectors. It will not come cheap, but American-born SPS inventor Peter Glaser feels that his system is as economical as any other high-energy product. As he says, "Any power system that can provide that much energy will cost a trillion dollars."

ICONN/Erie

World-famous engineer Nigel Chattey wants to transport coal-fired generators, natural-gas storage tanks, sewage treatment plants, and other noxious industries to a series of man-made islands twenty miles out into the Atlantic. Some of the platforms would be twice the size of Manhattan. They would be built of dirt dredged out of the Erie Canal in upstate New York. The coal needed to run the generators would be shipped down the Canal and out to sea. By sending industry safely out to sea, Chattey says, the Island Complex Off New York/New Jersey (ICONN) would dramatically reduce air pollution in the East, while its

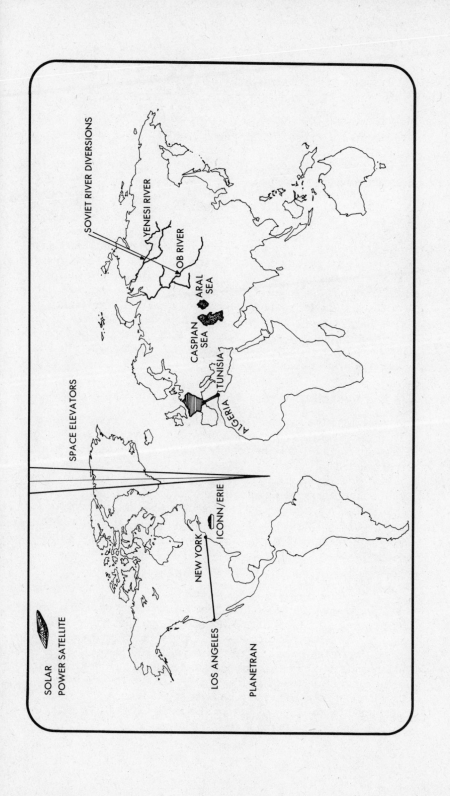

SOLAR
POWER SATELLITE

SPACE ELEVATORS

SOVIET RIVER DIVERSIONS

YENESI RIVER

OB RIVER

ARAL
SEA

CASPIAN
SEA

TUNISIA

ALGERIA

NEW YORK

ICONN/ERIE

LOS ANGELES

PLANETRAN

dependence on coal, rather than oil, would make the region energy-independent. The project would take only forty years to complete.

Space Elevators

By the mid twenty-first century, space could be just a six-hour train ride away. First suggested almost seventy years ago by the Russian space pioneer Konstantin Tsiolkovsky, the so-called skyhook would suspend a crystalline graphite cable from a satellite 22,300 miles up to a mountain top at the equator. The cars, carrying thirty passengers or 100 tons of cargo, would climb the cable by magnetic levitation at 3,700 miles an hour. A new version of the skyhook, the space elevator, would use a shorter cable from a satellite spinning in a lower orbit. Twice during each rotation, one end of the cable would drop into the atmosphere to be met by a shuttle plane carrying cargo or passengers. Hooked to the end of the spinning cable, the payload would be lifted into space in only one hour.

Silicon Revolution

Already, more than half a million homes in the United States contain a computer. Electronic mail systems can send a single message transmission anywhere in the country for less than the cost of an airmail letter. And Britain's "Open University" system enables students to "attend class" by watching television and taking tests by mail. These are the first steps in the development of a worldwide information network that within twenty years will enable us to learn anything and speak with anyone without leaving our homes or offices. The system requires no huge construction projects, just highly developed technology, an enormous investment, and international cooperation.

Pipelines

France may soon export the Rhone River to Libya or Algeria, sending it through a 150-foot plastic pipe under the Mediterranean. Used for irrigation, the water could double the arable land of both Algeria and Tunisia. The aqueduct would cost as much as $30 billion, but it is an expense the oil-rich nations of North Africa could easily afford. In return for the water, France would receive oil—say 100 million barrels a day. A similar tube could carry the Tigris River to arid Syria. Another pipeline could transport the rivers of Northern California under the Pacific to the parched southern half of the state.

Soviet River Diversions

The Caspian and Aral seas have begun to dry up because the rivers that once flowed into them are being used for irrigation. But the Soviets have the answer—just bring in new water. They have devised a plan to reverse the northern flow of the Ob and Yenesi rivers, pump the water—a quantity equal to that in the Mississippi River—up over the Ural Mountains, and run it into the seas through 3,000 kilometers of canals. Environmentalists have charged that the plan could melt the Arctic ice cap, change weather patterns, and perhaps throw so much weight toward the equator that earth itself would begin to wobble in orbit.

Among the other possibilities for future macro-engineering projects are the following:

• Construction of a "Friendship Bridge" across the Bering Strait, connecting Alaska with Siberia.

• A dam project that would tap the water of the Amazon River for enormous reservoirs in South America.

• Shipment of Antarctic icebergs to the African deserts to make the land eventually arable.

Science Meccas of
the Future

As different technologies wax and wane, research and development centers rise and fall. Today, as computers command ever-increasing interest, the science center in Silicon Valley, California, is probably America's best-known hotbed of research. After World War II, the atomic research center at Oak Ridge, Tennessee was pre-eminent, while in the 1950s a cluster of electronics companies near Cambridge, Massachusetts, produced the largest flow of science headlines.

Now a new group of science centers is moving to the fore where scientists are researching vital areas for the future: energy, cosmology, materials, small technologies, and environmental engineering. These locations will appear more frequently in the datelines of tomorrow's science news stories. They will challenge Japan and Silicon Valley for the leading role in applied science discovery and achievement.

Austin, Texas

The University of Texas, backed by oil money and surrounded by wide-open spaces, has attracted some of the best minds in the country, including Nobel Laureate John Wheeler, an astrophysicist. Austin rapidly seems to be turning into a hotbed of technological activity, emphasizing work in astronomical theory and high-energy physics. The Texas center offers researchers big budgets and new facilities. Close at hand are the intense research programs of major oil and chemical companies and a number of well-endowed private foundations, such as the Wadley Institute, which spent millions of dollars to provide interferon for Texas researchers. In all likelihood, the Texas science center will spread across the whole southeastern corner of the state, all the way up to Dallas.

Columbus, Ohio

Columbus's emergence as a science center has been spurred by the growth of Ohio State University. The heart of the private work done here will reflect the university's strengths in the industrial sciences— lasers, welding, materials formation, adhesives, and so on. A few short years ago Columbus might have been considered too far from the East and West coasts for convenient use as a high-tech center, but this era of commuter jets has made the area a virtual suburb of New York and Washington.

Burlington, Vermont

With minimal fanfare, central Vermont is quietly attracting small, high-intensity think tanks and industrial research centers, which will emphasize state-of-the-art sciences: cybernetics, fiber optics, and high speed computers. Leading research companies want their scientists and inventors to have a quiet, undisturbed environment. Vermont is also a focus of development in alternative energy systems and high-tech farming. Science writers of the twenty-first century may find themselves heading for Vermont as often as they used to journey to Cambridge.

Rehovoth, Israel

Discovering and saving water will be a major challenge over the next twenty years, as land grows more dense and desertification increases. The Israelis have one of the world's best desert research programs, and Rehovoth, located in the Negev Desert, is the center of this activity. Solar ponds, magneto-hydrodynamics plants, wind power, hydroponics, and many other environmentally oriented scientific developments will be advanced by work done in the Negev. Genetic engineering and pharmaceutical creations will also receive attention here, and many advances in these fields will first emerge in the Israeli desert.

Riyadh, Saudi Arabia

The best that money can buy will come to Saudi Arabia over the next generation as this geographically and culturally isolated Arab nation tries to improve its desert countryside. The Saudi government will attempt to prolong the wealth of its oil fields and prove that Arabs can maintain the pace with Israeli research. Since energy poses no problem, high-energy experimentation may turn out to be a staple here. Obviously, environmental engineering will also hold a special role in any Arabian science center.

Northern France

The French may be on the verge of returning to a leading role in science and technology. The government has committed itself to technological achievement, and the central authority in France has the clout to make its plans take hold. France is pursuing an aggressive nuclear policy, has a space program independent of the European Space Agency, and has become a leading country in interferon research. Major advances in cancer research may, as a result, come out of France. Experimental music and architecture have also flourished recently in France.

Scientists are already conducting tidal power experiments along the Brittany coast, and Frenchmen can now travel from Paris to Marseilles on a train that averages over 200 miles per hour. Research centers in Paris and its environs may generate some of the most exciting research and inventions of the next generation.

Projected Computer
Milestones: 1990-2010

1990

IBM places the world's first Josephson Junction computer on-line. The device uses super-cold superconducting switches that can work more than one thousand times faster than any previous computer devices. The switches can also be placed more closely together, making the Josephson computer the world's fastest by far.

All the memory storage and computing ability of IBM's largest previous system will be contained in the fourteen-centimeter cube of the Josephson memory. The computer may be leased to the U.S. Weather Service for gathering and evaluating all available weather information from every station in the country together with known historical weather data. The result: weather forecasting of superb accuracy, even for months into the future.

1992

The National Computer Mercantile Network is established. A network of high-speed, superconducting computers is created along lines similar to the Federal Reserve Bank. Specially coded microprocessor units at all checkout counters, bank teller windows, currency exchanges, and other locations where mercantile activity occurs are tied to central processing units in individual cities. These computers then feed data to the regional mercantile computer centers in ten major cities.

These regional centers evaluate mercantile activity in their own areas and pass along information to the federal expert systems computers in Washington. These ultra-high speed systems are designed to work alongside one another with slightly different programming so that each unit can evaluate data outside the range of the other.

The system, which conjures up images of Big Brother in George Orwell's *1984*, records every commercial transaction in the United States, maintains personal income files for tax computation, alerts credit counseling authorities to potential bankruptcies, and maintains a second-by-second account of all essential economic indicators.

1993

Two connected computers, sharing one memory that communicates with both systems, will have the capability of defeating the human world champion at chess.

1994

Perfection of the room-temperature superconducting chip will make possible the first wristwatch computer with a larger capacity than a 64K memory. This device will be able to handle all the computing functions of tabletop home microcomputers. Instead of depending on typed input or a video screen, the device will accept and impart information through vocal instructions in English.

2005

An American firm demonstrates the first commercially viable biochip "interface." In a likely demonstration, a volunteer will be linked by wire with a multilingual interface computer by means of a revolutionary device that averages human brain waves, recognizes the computer-request wave by means of a biofeedback-learned code, and then translates it into pulses the machine understands.

In this manner, the individual can draw on the computer directly by brain waves and receive information in the same way. The subject could conceivably be asked a series of five questions devised and sealed by outside experts. The volunteer, who may have as little as an eighth-grade education, will answer the questions within thirty seconds by referring the questions to the computer and receiving the answers back by brainwave.

2006

A high-density ultra-high speed network intelligent computer system is established. The system will be able to tie together all global economic information for extensive evaluations. As the network develops, the computer, empowered to make monetary decisions, will grant international credit loans, oversee operation of all world markets, and produce raw information for formulation of national and world budgets. Soviet Bloc countries may refuse to participate, creating the need for a team of human experts to simulate and feed Eastern Bloc economic data into the system.

2007

Demand for a global Computer Rights Pact will lead to the signing of such an agreement by most world nations. This document will set forth the rights of humans and computers over authorship of software (including books, movies, economic models, etc.), creation of patentable systems, and mistakes arising from computer recommendations. At the same time, a Computer Appeals Network may be established for countries to air international grievances. Even in the 1980s, questions arising from the theft of computer software and hardware have frequently arisen. American software companies have been particularly vulnerable to theft of material by Soviet agents.

2010

The first portable biochip interface computer model will be demonstrated. A corporate partnership using high-speed computers will develop and patent a biochip interface that may operate with a vest-pocket computer. The chip will be implanted near crucial nerve bundles in one side of the chest with a plug that lies on the skin surface. A thin wire will run from the chip to the computer, which can be kept in any convenient pocket. The chip will pick up, average, and translate brain waves recorded through residual ganglia vibration.

Beyond 2010

The decision-making power of computers will become so awesome that a Computer Responsibility Act may have to be passed in the United States. A possible scenario: In 2035, some seven hundred fifty publicly assisted housing unit residents, deemed expendable by a civic energy balance maintenance computer, will be frozen in their homes. Many of the elderly will die. Upon examination and investigation, the computer will respond that its evaluation revealed that the community was better served by letting the individuals freeze than by saving energy in any other fashion. Resulting protests from computers over the dismantling of the offending machine may lead to negotiations on computer responsibility for such actions. The establishment of a computer court for dealing with ethical problems will be the result.

The Laser Revolution —
at Last

During much of the sixties and seventies, the laser remained a disappointment, a fascinating scientific toy that somehow eluded its promise for practical applications. In the 1980s, however, lasers have begun to come into their own. Uses for lasers have sprung up in businesses as diverse as tire testing and television. Looking ahead, the final years of this century should be the beginning of the laser's long-delayed commercial adulthood. These controlled, powerful light beams will become ubiquitous, replacing many other tools and processes.

Here are some of the areas where lasers will achieve predominance over the next generation.

Internal Information Handling

Fiber optics is the transmission of information with a laser through an incredibly pure strand of glass. Already, phone companies are turning to fiber optics for carrying phone messages and digital information for phone equipment. A number of sociologists have written about "the fibered society," a landmark development to occur over the next fifty years. In this society, the massive information-carrying capacity of fiber optic strands will link every home and business so freely that few people will need to travel to their work-places anymore. They will simply communicate with their offices using fiber optics.

The more certain, short-term growth area for information transmission on laser beams lies inside machines and buildings. In Detroit, for example, auto manufacturers are experimenting with using fiber optics inside car engines for diagnostic tests and communications with fuel control and dashboard microprocessors. Other short-range fiber optics applications include information processing in robot "brains," internal office data networks—a kind of high-tech computer-to-computer intercom—and high-speed, high-resolution television and digital stereo units.

Irrigation and Crop Control

Water conservation will be one of the major issues of the next twenty years, and lasers will take on an ever greater role in preserving water supplies and protecting previous crops in the fields. At the University of Oregon, experimental laser systems are being developed to assure that a field is absolutely flat at planting time. Uneven fields lead to run-off, which wastes water and harms crops. From the heights of space, laser scanners can tell, with the precision of a few acres, where crops are too dry and where they are being overwatered. This system can give farmers vital information about what's going on in the fields. By 1985, lasers may be a vital component of efficient agriculture.

Optical Computers

Computers are close to the point where they can make calculations faster than their wires can carry information. So, engineers are working on new computers that use fiber optic cables rather than wires for speedier informational transmission. The laser can handle information far faster than magnetic tape because the data becomes part of the laser beam itself and can be stripped from the light as fast as it passes. Also of interest to computer designers is the possibility of using lasers to create a computer that can handle interchangeable analogue picture information and digital numerical information. Fiber-optic computers, being researched at Bell Labs, IBM, and elsewhere, may appear as early as 1990.

Space Power Transmission

If power plants are built in space during the twenty-first century, lasers are one likely way their energy will be beamed down to earth. Unlike other energy forms, the laser spreads only slightly, so an energy-enriched laser beam could be collected in a relatively small area. Also, lasers are totally self-contained; they don't wander and they don't create radiation or other unwanted side effects. Finally, even a massive laser presence in the atmosphere shouldn't ruin radio and television signals, which a microwave beam from space could easily do. This laser space plant could use the power it gleans from the sun to power a massive laser gun, which could then create a beam of virtually limitless force. Since the laser light waves are packed tightly together, incredible power can be concentrated in a beam over a brief time span. A laser could deliver at least ten times more power than any other wave in a given period of time.

Chemical Reactions

In the future, lasers will help chemists handle tasks that flames and pressure chambers do today. A laser, or group of lasers, focused on a crucible under the proper conditions, can heat materials with incredible speed, control, and precision. Heat could even be varied at different times or in different parts of the vessel. If material is enclosed in a collapsible container or pellet, an array of lasers can generate incredible pressures by causing an implosion under precise, specified conditions. Lasers could form high-temperature plastics that are now impossible and could create strong alloys that would be unstable if blended in a furnace. We may see laser chemical apparatus at major industrial corporations within twenty years.

Stereo and Television

Already, lasers have made an inroad into television with the large screen video models that use three beams of colored light to form the picture. Laser videodisc machines are also in limited use. Next to come are digital-audio players, whose grooves are cut by lasers into an exact replica of the sounds produced in a recording studio. When read by a small laser within the home disc player, these grooves generate music of total fidelity and clarity without any hiss or hum, and without any aural distortions. Sony, MCA, EMI, and other electronic giants will be heavily involved with this market during the next decade.

Lasers will turn up inside television sets during the 1980s, producing cleaner pictures and leading the way toward three-dimensional video. Soon, laser-based home information systems, where polarized light brings in signals and cheap, small semiconductor lasers decode them for all home entertainment functions, will cost no more than old-fashioned television sets.

Industrial Forming

In Columbus, Ohio, a small company was recently established to produce lasers for welding, cutting, shaping, and other industrial processes. As materials become more scarce and expensive, as requirements for sophisticated technology applications grow more precise, lasers will become increasingly important for industrial-forming operations. Laser beams can cut far more intricately than any blade because they have virtually no thickness. This also means that they waste no material during processing; a saw always wastes at least its own width, an expensive loss with lumber or rare metals. Lasers can also shape objects under computer control without leaving scratches or tooling burrs on the product, without ever needing sharpening, and without wearing out. Laser welds can be stronger than traditional ones and can be made much faster, thereby improving productivity. Best of all, almost every laser process can be adapted for robotics development. The laser can be built into a robot so that the worker and the tool become one mechanism. As robot operations expand, so will industrial laser use.

Archival Storage

Dense or long-lived informational material can be stored more efficiently by laser than with any book or microfiche. A single laser videodisc can store the information from hundreds of books on a surface no larger than a record album. A similar LP-sized computer laser disc can store 10^{11} bits of data, as much as twenty-five magnetic computer tapes. In addition, laser storage media are as durable as they are compact. They don't fade or wear out with use; they don't scratch or get bent. Because of these advantages, libraries will use laser-based information storage systems enthusiastically over the next decade. By the turn of the century, laser storage will predominate. Major libraries will put their huge archival files on laser discs, freeing up space and improving user access to the files.

Weapons

In recent reports, lasers have been endowed with the force of every weapon ever made. Other laser weapons have taken on capabilities possible only in science fiction. In truth, laser weaponry will not supplant other tools of war within the foreseeable future. Laser weapons will, however, become an important adjunct to today's arsenal. In space, lasers will knock out enemy satellites and possibly even missiles flying through the atmosphere below. Laser bursts from earth could blind spy satellites at a crucial instant. Laser beam weapons could become important in air-to-air battles both between planes and guided missiles. In today's world, the Russians appear slightly ahead in the race to perfect laser weapons, but the United States is forging ahead with its own development. Both countries should have laser arsenals by the turn of the century.

More importantly, though, lasers will allow for improved accuracy of many weapons through pinpoint guidance and control systems. Lasers will also provide astonishingly precise information to troops on the ground about enemy locations. These tasks are at least as important as the potential of beam weapons.

Load and Site Leveling

Future carpenters will not rely on bubbles to tell them whether foundations are level; they'll use lasers. Structural engineers will use lasers to determine how much an old bridge is sagging. Lasers may also take over balance functions in ships and airplanes. At highway truck weighing stations, a laser could determine overweight conditions faster and more accurately than today's spring scales. Lasers are so precise that they can detect variations in size and weight faster and more accurately than any other measuring system.

Coming Technological Flops

Into every era of development, a few technological flops must fall. Remember quadraphonic sound? The years ahead will have their share of vanishing technologies, too. Here is a selection.

Video Games

One of the great boom and bust stories of technological history will be the rise and fall of the home video game, as these hot-selling technological marvels of the early 1980s plunge to obscurity during the middle years of the decade. Ironically, the fall of video games will be the result of increased consumer interest in games play, rather than indifference.

The TV game systems will disappear because the prices of home computers will keep falling quickly. Personal computer software will become so ubiquitous and varied that families that once would have bought games will now buy computers that not only play games but can do many other things as well.

By 1985, computers offering the power of today's IBM-PC will cost considerably less than $1,000. They will allow users to play games far more intricate than virtually any video game system available today. These new computers will be modified to the user's skill and interests.

The final blow for video games will be the emergence of interactive game "networks" over cable TV systems in the mid-1980s, providing an endless library of the latest in games without the need for cassettes.

Nuclear Power Plants

By the turn of the century, most of the problem-plagued nuclear power plants already built will be shut down. Most will grind to a stop on their own because of broken pipes, leaks, or assorted fuel problems. The rest will be closed by economic necessity. They will be expensive white elephants, unable to generate enough power to outweigh related mechanical difficulties.

The poorly conceived and designed nuclear power plant that was once touted as the answer to our energy woes by virtually every major utility is almost certainly the biggest technological boondoggle ever perpetrated on the public. Nuclear power, in itself, is not a bad energy form, but the manner in which it was developed was clumsy and poorly planned. Plants took years longer and millions of dollars more to build than estimated, worked less efficiently, and cost far more to operate. Safety, as illustrated by the leakage at Three Mile Island in Pennsylvania, was also suspect. One can only hope that this string of disappointments will be instructive to future planners and designers.

Breeder power plant reactors, which make their own fuel, may very well be regarded more favorably in the near future. The world needs fuel almost as much as it needs energy. Closed systems—those processes that feed off themselves or that link smoothly with other needs—will be the desired energy form for the future. Breeder reactors are such closed systems.

Artificial Heart

From time to time, science develops a technique that, while it works, does not seem to fulfill a public desire. The heart transplant operation was such a case. It worked, but few patients wanted transplants. The price of the operation, in human terms, seemed too high.

The artificial heart, recently tested in Barney Clark, may suffer a similar fate. The heart kept Clark alive for several months, but at a great cost. He had to cart around a rolling support system of power packs and electronic controls. Few people will want to be so vulnerable and dependent. Even if support functions can be miniaturized and implanted in the body, many people may have trouble living with the knowledge that a plastic pump over which they have no control is singlehandedly responsible for their survival. It may prove psychologically impossible for a human to live without a heart. Life under those circumstances may seem empty to some people, an unfair fraud against nature. The artificial heart may not find wide acceptance for many years.

MX Missile

The MX is the Pentagon's answer to Russia's growing nuclear might. According to the original plan, the huge missiles were to be mobile, constantly ferried around on trucks in vast underground labyrinths. The hostile nations presumably would never know where the missiles were, so they would not be able to knock them out. The system's deployment was scheduled for the 1990s.

During its initial development, the MX's various inconsistencies and drawbacks—buying the vast land tracts, building the highways, maintaining safety, testing—caused the project to be scrapped.

President Reagan tried to sell a "dense pack" concept for MX deployment and lost. Few Congressmen believed Russian missiles would destroy themselves while converging on the MX sites. The next step for MX is a Presidential Review Commission that will try to come up with other possible configurations for this ill-fated defense system.

Techno-Farming of
the Future

Tomorrow's farmer is as likely to wear a lab coat as a pair of overalls. Growing food will become a highly sophisticated, technological operation. From genetically engineered seedlings to computer-controlled fields and space monitors for weather and water patterns, every step of the farming process will draw upon new scientific techniques. The techno-farmer will be able to grow more food on less land than today's agriculturalist, and the produce may be markedly different from today's wheat and corn.

Genetic Engineering

By 2000, genetic engineering will have made enormous strides. While perhaps not making good on a quip by agri-businessman Martin Apple, who said that "we're going to make pork chops grow on trees," this second Green Revolution will increase crop yields, help preserve farmland, and ease hunger in the Third World.

Among the advances genetic manipulation of agricultural components will produce are:

• Crops that fix their own nitrogen, making expensive, dangerous fossil fuel fertilizers obsolete.

• Plants that can grow in salty ground, staving off disaster in the American Southwest and other lands where too much irrigation has left the earth saline.

• Corn that automatically blooms each year, like a perennial flower, without replanting or refertilizing.

• Potatoes and tomatoes that grow on the same vine.

• Livestock immune to hoof-and-mouth disease and most other common ailments. Genetically engineered vaccines to combat hoof-and-mouth disease have already been created.

• Crops that contain all the basic nutrients in one food.

• Plants that can be tapped for the electric production of their photosynthesis, as well as artificial chemicals that can imitate photosynthesis for production of oxygen and elimination of pollutants.

• Crops that can be harvested three times a growing season.

Aquaculture

Intensive aquaculture—fish farming—will become a major source of the world's food in the twenty-first century. The leader will be the Chinese, who will vastly expand the 2.5 million acres of fish farms that produced more than 16 million tons of fish in 1980. Other nations will follow suit.

American aquaculture, a fledgling business in the 1980s, will provide much of the nation's food in 2000. Americans will double the annual consumption of fish to an average of forty pounds. With little or no cholesterol or fat, fish will become a favorite food of a public that has become increasingly concerned about health and diet. More importantly, anti-erosion laws and strip mining in the West will cut down on land available for grazing cattle and growing corn, the preferred livestock food of the 1980s. These measures will drive the prices of beef and pork so high that fish will be the only animal foodstuff most people will still be able to afford on a regular basis.

Closed Systems

In the future, plants that stand in a farm field will be only one part of a carefully controlled agricultural chain. The husks will be used after harvest to make gasohol that will run the machines that preserve the harvested crop. The water that nourished the plants will be carefully recaptured and used again the next season. Nutrients lacking in the soil will be provided by farmers growing genetically engineered plants in off seasons that spew the needed nutrients from their roots into the soil.

The farm will be a self-contained ecosystem. It will create the basic ingredients for harvest within its confines and utilize the leftovers of agriculture fo feed other parts of the system. The future farmer will be more concerned with monitoring the system than in watching the weather or sitting on a tractor. He will run an operation with minimal waste and total efficiency.

Computer Control

Today, if a farmer wants to know whether a field is dry, he goes out and looks at it. In the future, his computer will automatically tell him if any of the hundreds of sensors in the field detect a deficiency. The computer will also suggest possible solutions to the problem and implement whatever plan he chooses. In short, the computer will serve as the foreman and the field hands.

Some agricultural theorists even imagine a scenario in which the computer actually runs the farm machinery, directing the harvesters around as it senses each section has achieved optimum ripeness.

Several dozen experimental computer-controlled farms already exist on government research acres all across the country. The technique will spread to commercial factory farms by the end of the century and will be nearly universal by 2050.

The Arsenal of Tomorrow

The greatest arms suppliers in the world are the United States and the Soviet Union. Most of their weapons are delivered to other nations, but in Europe they meet face to face. Europe is, therefore, the most closely watched and heavily armed area in the world, a battleground of words, a saber-rattler's paradise. All along the frontier between East and West Germany, soldiers peer across the barbed wire and wonder, "What if...?"

It is difficult to assess America's readiness to fight a war, because it is nearly impossible to get straight answers about the military sophistication of its potential adversaries—who has what weapons, where they are, and how well trained are the soldiers who will use them. The United States Department of Defense paints the Soviet military as the biggest, toughest, best-equipped fighting force in the world. The Defense Department booklet, *Soviet Military Power*, quoted by Defense Secretary Caspar W. Weinberger at Congressional hearings on the defense budget, says, "The Soviets have a larger array of general purpose submarines, surface warships, and combat naval aircraft than any other nation."

This sounds very impressive. However, of the 1,300 ships that the Defense Department cites, all but 276 are smaller than frigates. (A frigate is roughly equivalent in speed and armament to a World War II destroyer escort.) Most are minesweepers and coastal patrol craft. Of the 276 destroyers and frigates, more than 160 were built before 1965. The Soviets actually have about 50 modern warships in these classes.

Of those combat naval aircraft, more than 1,000 in all, only the Forger vertical-take-off-and-landing fighter (VTOL) can fly from an aircraft carrier. There are fewer than 50 Forgers in service, and the Soviets have only three carriers equipped to use them. All other "combat naval aircraft" must fly from shore bases. The United States Navy has more than 1,800 aircraft, with 1,100 based on thirteen carriers.

The Red Army hardly fares better. Though it has 2.5 times as many men as the United States Army, the Soviet army is in terrible shape. Its alcoholism rate approaches 40 percent, according to leading U.S. reports. In the newest Soviet tank, the shell-ejection mechanism has a tendency to malfunction, throwing spent shell casings back into the tank at high speed, killing the tank crew. And though the Soviet army is staffed by Russian officers, most troops are Asians. It is estimated that only half of the troops speak Russian.

Whose military is stronger? That depends on your point of view. The following tables compare the military might of the United States and Soviet Union over the next twenty-five years. They are based on information from the United States Department of Defense and assume that there will be at least one war using conventional forces before 1995.

MILITARY PERSONNEL (in thousands)

	1982		1995		2005	
	U.S.	USSR	U.S.	USSR	U.S.	USSR
Army	774	1,825	800	2,000	700	2,000
Navy	528	433	620	500	550	575
Air Force	555	475	600	510	550	530
Marines (vs. Soviet Naval Infantry)	189	12	210	22	180	25

Though the Soviet Army vastly outnumbers the United States Army, it is the only Soviet military force that is now even as large as its U.S. counterpart. At only 12,000 men, the Soviet Naval Infantry is hardly a credible fighting force. These figures reflect the tendency of American forces to grow in times of emergency, then shrink to a relatively stable size. The Soviet military, by contrast, has a tendency to expand continuously. In the 1990s, this may well reflect growing internal unrest.

ARMY AND AIR FORCE HARDWARE

	1982		1995		2005	
	U.S.	USSR	U.S.	USSR	U.S.	USSR
Tanks	7,000	19,500	15,000	25,000	12,000	27,000
Artillery	5,000	20,000	7,000	22,000	6,000	23,000
Tactical fighters	2,600	4,800	4,000	6,000	3,300	6,100
Strategic bombers	490	880	650	1,000	500	1,000

This comparison is misleading if one looks at numbers only. The Soviets seem to own a commanding lead in every area. However, much of the Soviet equipment is archaic. Almost half of their strategic bombers are propeller-driven. Many of their fighters, MiG 19s, were built between 1953 and 1962, and more than half of their tanks are T-62s with external fuel tanks. Both countries must do a lot of building in these areas to meet the demands of desert warfare.

NAVAL VESSELS

	1982		1995		2005	
	U.S.	USSR	U.S.	USSR	U.S.	USSR
Aircraft carriers	13	3	15	8	12	10
		(VTOL only)		(4 VTOL only)		(5 VTOL)
Cruisers	28	38	32	45	27	43
Destroyers	70	68	84	72	66	80
Frigates	5	168	80	155	78	160
Submarines						
Nuclear missle	41	62	50	79	44	75
Torpedo attack	78	220	75	225	70	230

These estimates clearly show the changes in Soviet naval strategy. They will continue to build the nuclear missile submarines already on order, but older nuclear submarines will not be replaced. Instead, the Soviets will add to their stable of aircraft carriers to extend the reach of their military power. They will also let the smaller coastal defense frigates fall into disrepair and replace them with larger frigates, destroyers, and cruisers to strengthen their image as a "blue water navy," not just a coastal defense force.

NUCLEAR WEAPONS SYSTEMS

	1982		1995		2005	
	U.S.	USSR	U.S.	USSR	U.S.	USSR
Land-based ballistic missiles	1,054	1,398	1,054	1,398	1,250	1,600
Submarine-launched missiles	656	950	825	1,100	850	1,300
Bombers	396	215	425	300	400	325
Total warheads	9,000	5,000	10,500	8,000	13,500	11,000

Note that while the Soviets have more missiles in every case, the United States has more total warheads. U.S. missiles carry an average of ten warheads, Soviet missiles only three.

Who's Got the Bomb?

Every nation that has tried to make an atom bomb since 1945 has succeeded, so far as is known. More than 1,700 bombs have been tested by the United States, the Soviet Union, Great Britain, France, China, and India. There is strong evidence that South Africa has tested a bomb and that Israel has the components to manufacture one. Israel, in turn, claims that Iraq has an active bomb-development program and the Central Intelligence Agency predicts that Pakistan will produce its first nuclear weapons by 1985. Over the next twenty years, it is quite possible that Libya, Brazil, Argentina, Taiwan, and South Korea will also obtain nuclear weapons. By 2020, it is likely that Saudi Arabia, Nigeria, Iran, Cuba, Venezuela, Zaire, Spain, Indonesia, and Angola will all have atomic weapons.

Each of these countries will have bombers capable of dropping atomic weapons on any nearby enemy. By 2000, all nations with nuclear bombs except Taiwan and South Korea will have ICBMs, or at least intermediate-range ballistic missiles (IRBMs). All nuclear powers by 2020 should have at least IRBMs.

Future Weapons: The Personal Gear of the Soldier

The individual fighting soldier will not change in the next twenty years, but his—or her—gear certainly will. Lighter, stronger metals, plastics, and textiles will enable the infantryman to carry more equipment farther and faster, yet be in better shape to fight when he gets there.

There is little here that is truly new. The next war is always fought with the weapons of the last one. The materials and basic technology for these weapons have been with us since the Vietnam war. What is presented here are likely new combinations of the ideas and technology that could become the standard weapons of the United States armed forces.

Rifle. The M-22 Assault Rifle of the future will weigh 5.6 pounds with Razerscope sniper sight attached. It will be made mostly of plastics, with a titanium subframe to withstand the stresses at high rates of fire. The M-22 will be capable of firing single shots at 30 rounds per minute, fully automatically at 100 rounds per minute, or in short bursts at 750 rounds per minute. With slight modifications, it will be able to be loaded with 30-round clips, 100-round magazines, or belt-fed ammunition. Cooling may be a problem in rapid fire. Prolonged firing without allowing time to cool could jam the load-eject mechanism.

There will a wide choice of ammunition for the M-22. The bullets, which will all be NATO-standard 7.62 millimeter, will be available in high-explosive, light-armor piercing, fragmentation, and ordinary lead-tipped varieties. Standard lead ammunition will most often be used, but light-armor piercing rounds will be useful against trucks and personnel carriers, and the shock of high-explosive ammo will mean that even

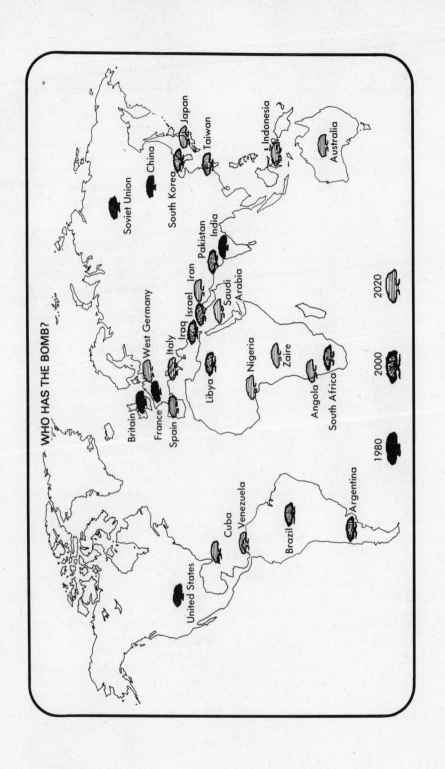

WHO HAS THE BOMB?

a graze to the hand or foot could be fatal. The M-22 will have a muzzle velocity of 3,900 feet per second and a range of 600 yards.

The Razerscope will be a combination radar-laser-infrared sight with a microprocessor to provide accurate aiming and range-finding even in very bad conditions, such as a moonless night. The scope will take bearing and range readings on the target, then give aiming instructions through a digital display.

The prototype of the M-22 already exists in the Stoner 63 rifle, which saw action in Southeast Asia with American Navy and Marine assault teams. The Stoner weighs 6.6 pounds with its ammo clip, fires bursts of 600 rounds per minute at a muzzle velocity of 3,750 feet per second, and has an effective range of 500 yards. The laser-infrared scope is already used by Army artillery units and could fit into a normal rifle with only a little miniaturization.

Body Armor. The soldier's battle fatigues will become protective outfits as well as camouflage. The cloth will be mostly bullet-resistant Kevlar. (President Reagan took his oath of office in a bullet-proof Kevlar suit; he was not wearing it when shot two months later.) On the back, chest, thighs, and the straight parts of the arms and legs, strips and discs of high-impact plastics will be sewn into the garment, making it nearly as impenetrable as a suit of armor. The plastics will stop a .25 caliber bullet at twenty paces, yet the fatigues will weigh no more than ordinary cotton-and-wool clothing. Early experiments with these materials were conducted in Vietnam in 1968.

Helmet. It, too, will be plastic—the same plastic as the inserts in the fatigues, but thick enough to stop a .38 caliber bullet at twenty paces. To prevent injury in case of a shock to the head or neck, the helmet will be suspended not by webbing, but by foam cells like those used in football helmets. Built into it will be heating wires for cold weather, a radio transceiver with a range of 400 yards, and fittings for a nuclear blast shield. With the shield in place, the helmet will weigh only three-fourths as much as a standard steel helmet with liner.

Chemical-Biological Warfare Equipment. Chemical warfare poses a special problem to the armies of the future. Everyone has weapons as potent as they will ever need; no one has an effective defense against them. As the Duke of Wellington said when he was advised to use poison gas in 1814, "Two can play at that game." You cannot afford to use a weapon until you can defend against it.

Modern plastics can shield against chemical and biological weapons, but no one has figured out how to protect a soldier while he eats, drinks, and performs other bodily functions. This is one area in which no great advances are likely in the next two or three decades.

Life Support. The modern soldier's bivouac outfit would be very familiar to backpackers and other outdoorsmen. In a turnabout of the traditional order where equipment moves from army surplus to sportsman, most of this gear was first developed for backpackers and mountain climbers, then adapted for military use. Superlight backpacks, self-erecting tents with rigid frames and flooring, and small, safe, bottled-gas stoves are all standard issue for the twenty-first century foxhole.

Other Weapons

• Hand-held rockets will be more important in the guerrilla wars of the coming decades. Yard-long missiles that weigh only eight pounds each and that can pierce all but the thickest armor are available even today.

• Armored cars with rockets and Gatling-gun style Vulcan cannons will be more valuable than tanks because they are much faster and use less fuel. The Vulcan fires twenty-millimeter ammunition from seven rotating barrels at 6,000 rounds per minute.

• Drones and robots will be adapted for special purposes within thirty years, but they will probably not make up the main force of any army in the next half century. Drone airplanes and armored vehicles will be used most often to draw fire away from real missions.

Innovations in Transportation

The years of the near future in transporation will see increasing competition between Americans' desires for comfortable personal vehicles and the growth of new high-tech public transport systems designed to do away with urban traffic.

The compelling need for energy conservation will lessen somewhat over the next decade as the world oil glut continues, the strength of OPEC weakens, and the steady use of synthetic fuels increases. The dominant issue in transportation will be a greater concern for traffic safety and control, as computer technology will be applied more extensively in the construction of vehicles.

As the emphasis in transportation development shifts, several once promising systems will fade away. Most of the so-called alternative engines—Wankels, Sterlings, and such—will fall by the boards as the fuel crisis dims in memory. The electric and solar car movements will be abandoned, as researchers realize the drawbacks of these technologies simply aren't worth trying to overcome.

The impact of computers will be to create much smaller vehicles with the same passenger space and power of today's cars and busses. The micros will also make it possible to design incredibly intricate traffic webs with many systems interlocking to move people about smoothly.

The union of computers and new space technologies will create new vehicles that bring the look of spaceships down to earth—or at least into earth's sky. Here are some innovations that lie ahead.

Urban Transportation

Compucars. The wedding of cars and computers will create a vehicle with increased operating efficiency under normal driving conditions of 60 miles an hour or less. By 2000, computer-assisted fuel flow and engine control will produce cars that average 100 miles to the gallon.

The use of computer-controlled cars in urban centers will create further saving by lessening traffic jams, reducing stopping to a minimum, dramatically decreasing accidents, and increasing the life expectancy of a car to nearly twenty years. A reduction in pollution levels and a smoother flow in urban traffic patterns will restore quiet and order to the city.

Moving Sidewalks. Moving sidewalks will not gain widespread acceptance as urban transportation until the Variflex Moving Sidewalk is developed for practical use in the early 1990s. This particular sidewalk functions under a variable width, variable speed system. It travels at slightly faster-than-walking speed on approach and departure, but accelerates from about two miles an hour to over ten miles at maximum speeds. Cross walks will have slow zones. More complex systems will add speed lanes, creating multiple-sidewalk highways. They will replace sidewalks in shopping areas, airports, and large public buildings.

TrolleyBuses. Highly efficient, low-profile TrolleyBuses will make their debut for long range urban transit in the early part of the twenty-first century. They will be the size of jitneys and will move along track-less rights-of-way using electronic guidance. Their electric/diesel motors will have solar-assist batteries and fuel cells to propel them. The trolleys will be so quiet that they will have to emit computer-controlled musical notes to warn pedestrians of their approach.

Robobuses. By 2000, van-sized Robobuses will provide personalized mass transit in smaller urban areas. These "thinking" vehicles will have their own computers that will be programmable by riders for different locations and most traffic situations. The buses will not require a driver, except as a safety measure when transporting school children. Robobuses will improve airport connections and will be used for the aged and the handicapped.

People Assists. Infirm and handicapped people will wear computer-assisted, hydraulic mover systems of endurable weight to provide them with increased mobility. These units will be rented in various sizes and will come with powered arms if so ordered. "People assisters" will develop from manned, maneuvering units first invented by NASA and from small-scale robotics research companies.

Hydrofoil Buses. The small-scale (thirty passenger) hydrofoil bus, already in the developmental stage, will offer alternative transportation to city commuters dependent upon urban waterways. Capable of fifty knots in fair weather and forty knots under bad conditions, the hydrofoil bus is attracting attention because of its variable-foil varieties, but will not be employed extensively for at least another fifteen years. Likely urban areas for use are New York's southern harbor, Puget Sound and San Francisco Bay. The hydrofoil bus would cut down the commuting time between Staten Island and Manhattan from twenty-five to ten minutes.

Long Haul Transportation

Private Rockets. Aerospace maverick Robert C. Truax is developing a small-scale rocket that will in the 1990s greatly expand the building and use of private rockets for sub-orbital, orbital, and even extended space flights for shipping goods or for establishing objects in space. Launch and recovery systems will be offered to companies and individuals on a share basis, making the cost of private rocket development feasible. World government efforts to regulate private rocket flight will be unsuccessful, despite the dangers of unregulated flight and payloads.

Thermoskyships. The use of gas-lifted devices with helicopter rotors for saucer-shaped vehicles will create the Thermoskyship. Such a carrier could become the workhorse truck of the commercial world by 2025. Its ability to rise directly from a platform while hauling great loads will make it a viable alternative to ground transportation for carrying grain, ore, and other heavy, high-volume cargoes.

Trisonic Jets. The introduction of a Trisonic Jet will balance the setbacks plaguing the development of supersonic aircraft since the late 1970s and early 1980s. Flying at 2,500 miles per hour, the Trisonic Jet will make transcontinental flights more quickly and efficiently than ever before. There will probably be three sizes of Trisonics: 650-passenger, 450-passenger, and the minitrisonic 150-passenger. Boeing will develop the first Trisonics for the United States government by 2050.

Special Purpose Transportation

Manned Maneuvering Units. The demands of space travel will create new forms of transportation. Personal maneuvering units for spacewalks may become very popular early in the next century. These pressurized, mobile, and radiation-proof suit-capsules will fit all body sizes and specific atmospheric needs. Vacuum suits for weightlessness and empty space, moon suits for modified walking and jetting, and dense atmosphere suits will be most frequently used. Some suits may even be fitted with solarsail kites for extended travel.

Submersibles. Deep and surface water-diving units with long-range power capability are opening up otherwise-unreachable areas of lakes and oceans. There are two basic forms: Remote Operating Vehicles (ROV), which will be controlled from a mother ship, and Controllable Operating Vehicles (COV) with onboard control. Units will be built to accommodate one to ten individuals, while others will transport cargo. The need for oil exploration on a long-term, sustained underwater basis will force rapid research in this technology. Both ROVs and COVs will operate regularly between shore stations, rigs, and underwater stations. The individual units can achieve a top speed of fifteen knots underwater and twenty on the surface.

Moon Bugs and Mars Rovers. Wheeled vehicles will be heavily used on the moon and on other planets for future exploration. The smaller Moon Bug has since 1969 been the ''mule and horse'' of moon travel, and will continue to be used for pleasure and work. A larger, enclosed Mars Rover, to be developed for exploration on Mars, will be able to circle the planet on one power charge. The extendable arms of the Rover will make it extremely functional for survey work on other planets as well as on their moons. Short hauls for both vehicles are possible using large-scale, photovoltaic power, which will provide energy for life-support systems.

New Forms of Aviation

In 1981, the United States had 800,000 private airplane pilots, 300,000 private planes, and 14,000 landing strips. Twenty years from now those numbers will seem unbelievably small. Air travel will become a common means of personal transportation in the years ahead. It's not that there will be many more airplanes; rather, the future will see development of whole new families of air vehicles that will take us and our cargoes around the skies in ways we can barely imagine today. Some of the forms the upcoming revolution in aviation will create include:

STOL and VTOL. These two names stand for "short-take-off-and-landing" and "vertical-take-off-and-landing." They refer to a pair of new airplane designs that will bring airports back into the heart of cities. STOL craft will be able to take off and land on runways only one-half as long as today's. This means big airports will be able to get more planes in and out of the same space, and small airports will be able to open on tight city spaces. VTOL planes can land and take off like helicopters by using rotor engines that tilt to any angle desired, making it conceivable that a future passenger plane could take off from a rooftop or from a depot in the heart of downtown.

Skyships. The stately, massive outlines of lighter-than-air skyships should be in the skies within thirty years. These craft will be vaguely similar to the grand zeppelins, such as the Hindenburg, and to the Goodyear blimp, but much more sophisticated and varied. Airlifters will combine the aerostatic buoyancy of a dirigible—generated by helium gas—with the aerodynamic lift of an airplane. These acrobatic hybrids of the air will be able to lift enormous loads quietly and efficiently from small airfields or even from factory loading docks. They will hover or fly like a plane. Much larger passenger-freight liners will transport thousands of people and millions of tons through the air at extremely low cost. Longer than three football fields, they will land and take off with swiveling rotors, and then float through the air like dirigibles.

Human-powered Fliers. Throughout history, one of man's most fervent wishes has been to fly under his own power. In the late 1970s, Paul MacCready brought these dreams closer to realization with his Gossamer Condor and Gossamer Albatross human-powered airplanes. While MacCready's craft were simply demonstration models, continuing advances in lightweight plastics and the mechanics of converting human motion into force, such as super bike pedals, will make human powered flight a commercial possibility by 2000. We are unlikely to use small human-powered vehicles to fly short distances for grocery shopping and local commuting, but they will be pure pleasure on sunny weekend afternoons.

Hand-made Planes. In the 1990s, pint-sized aerodynamic forms will emerge from the work of aircraft design pioneers. These innovators will design modifications in all areas of the aircraft, creating a vehicle the size of a lounge chair with the speed of a commercial prop plane and many built-in safety features. These planes will be so simple that any reasonably handy person will be able to buy a kit for a few thousand dollars—possibly even a few hundred—and build the plane at home.

The Automatic Plane. Although as early as 1965 it was possible to fly a commercial plane in mid-flight by automatic pilot, it may not be until the early 1990s that regular airline flights become totally automatic in nature with a pilot aboard merely as a backup safety system. Telecommunication control by ground controllers will add to the safety factor of automated planes.

Invisible Planes. Radar-absorbing materials combined with new design configurations will make possible a series of aircraft nearly undetectable by ground or airborne radar. At the turn of the century, these planes will galvanize military aviation development. Since these planes will require the use of plastics as structural materials, they will encourage new aircraft ideas. The new plastic materials will, in many cases, be stronger than the original metal, allowing planes to be larger and fly faster. They will also be lighter, thereby saving expensive fuel.

Flatbed Aircraft. The concept of the flatbed truck will be extended to the design of freight-bearing aircraft early in the twenty-first century. Freight will be hauled on open container platforms between the wings and aft of the cockpit and forward of the tail assembly.

Computer-Assisted Air-Traffic Control. Just as the aircraft itself will be further enhanced by computer assistance, so will ground control. Since the amount of aircraft data flooding control towers already overwhelms human controllers, the use of computers to store traffic patterns, list priorities, and warn of impending disasters will increase dramatically. Automatic message generation will assist the controller in communicating with aircraft and other controller stations. The controller will be able to generate a message by simply punching a computer keyboard. The use of voice-activated computer instruction will also increase the capabilities of controllers and pilots.

Unmanned Aircraft. Several military developments, such as the cruise missile and the unmanned spotting aircraft, have emerged in the 1980s. These will lead to the use of unmanned aircraft for freight delivery, particularly in remote regions such as deserts, the polar caps, and between distant ocean oil rigs. These craft will be controlled from their point of origin and will have modular freight containers that can be unloaded automatically at the destination. Unmanned aircraft will gain much from robotics development such as visual sensing, computer-controlled equipment operation, and remote control.

Mars-flight Airplane. A Mars-flight airplane to be used in the thin atmosphere of Mars is a combination product that owes its creation to advances in man-powered flights and to the technology of high-flying surveillance aircraft (such as the famous U-2). Using very long, swept-back wings and a very light airframe of composite materials, the Mars flyer will arrive on that planet being capable of sustained exploration flight without a pilot. Extremely sophisticated imaging and sensing devices will enhance exploration and mapping of the Martian surface. Development of this plane should begin in the early part of the twenty-first century.

Multibeam Security System. The dream of erecting a deflecting screen around aircraft, or in science fiction around a spacecraft, will become a reality though the fan-beam technology originally designed for aircraft spotting. The microwave fan will be extended into a fully protective array around the craft to warn against air-to-air collisions and other similar disasters and to trigger automatic evasive maneuvers.

Civilian Aircraft Carriers. Skies crowded by personal planes, along with increased need for corporate material delivery and energy control, will make civilian aircraft carriers a necessity. These carriers will, like their Navy prototypes, be a form akin to a floating city. The civilian version will offer various forms of flight service: local helicopter, VTOL flights of longer range, and small jets to distant points. They will have their own fleets of planes, their own control towers, flight decks, hangars for hire, sleeping and eating accommodations, entertainment centers, and repair facilities.

2 MEDICINE AND THE BODY

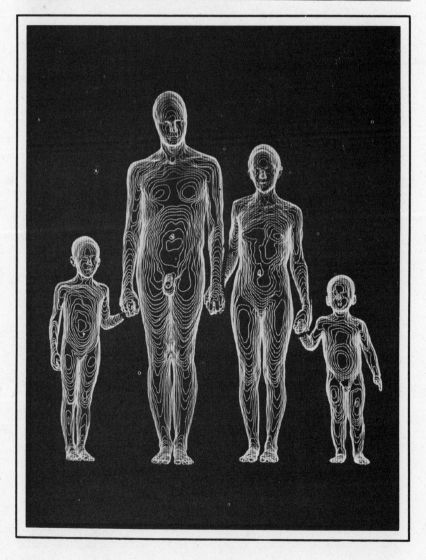

2 MEDICINE AND THE BODY

Some of the developments forecast in the field of medicine sound more like fantasy than science, yet all are well on their way. Many, possibly most, are closer to realization than we think. Perhaps it will help to know that an organization as renowned as the British Royal Society of Medicine has made the following predictions:

1980s:	New generations of antibacterials perfected
1983:	Dental caries conquered
1985:	Male contraceptives developed
1985 to 1990:	Asthma controlled Bacterial and viral illnesses fall to new drugs
1988:	Anxiety and tension control achieved
1990:	Allergy relief perfected Autoimmune illnesses conquered Cancer cure available Depression relief reliable Hypertension therapy effective Mental illness successfully treatable

1990 to 2000:   Artificial womb in use
                 Contraceptives now safe, convenient,
                   and inexpensive
                 Permanent stimulator of intelligence
                   found
                 Safe, short-acting intoxicant available
                   to replace alcohol
                 Synthetic blood in use
                 Vaccine ends tooth decay

2000 or sooner: Aggression control achieved
                 Drugs available that safely heighten
                   perceptions, alter emotional
                   experience, and generate
                   unique hallucinations
                 Extension of childhood to delay
                   adolescence
                 Guilt provoked or relieved by drugs
                 Maternal behavior turned on and off
                   at will
                 Memory increased or shortened

Best Hopes for an End to Aging

Scattered around the world, particularly in the United States and Soviet Union, a hardy band of poorly funded researchers is chasing their version of the White Whale. The Moby Dick in this pursuit: aging itself. When they defeat it, they will change the world more than any scientists in history.

So far, gerontologists, specialists in aging research, have confirmed what most of us would have suspected: part of aging is simple erosion. Over decades of life, mechanical wear abrades our bones, toxins poison our cells, and light itself turns once-supple skin to leather. But they have also found that we carry within us at least two built-in clocks, one working at the cellular level, the other governing the body as a whole. As these timers run out, we age and die. It is by finding ways to control this process that scientists will give us the true elixir of life.

It will happen far sooner than we expect. The research areas below offer several ways to prevent or cure aging and age-related illness. All have produced significant results already. Almost surely, one or more will markedly extend the human life span before the century ends. If gerontology gets the support it deserves, today's young should keep their vigor into their eighties. People now in their fifties or sixties could soon find themselves growing younger. Who knows? Perhaps some day, even death will be defeated.

ANTI-AGING DRUGS NOW AVAILABLE

Compound	Effects
Bacillus cereus protease	Molecular cross-link dissolver
BHA (butylated hydroxyanisole)	Antioxidant (slows chemical reactions)
BHT (butylated hydroxytoluene)	Antioxidant
Centrophenoxine	Age pigment blocker
DMAE (dimethylaminoethanol)	Age pigment blocker
Selenium	Antioxidant
Vitamin C	Antioxidant
Vitamin E	Antioxidant
DHEA (dehydroepiandrosterone) (see ''Medicine for the Millenium'')	Hormone
Thymosin (see ''Medicine for the Millenium'')	Immune booster

Death Hormone

Yes, Virginia, there is a death hormone. From the time you were twenty or so, your own body has been trying to do you in. Sooner or later, it will succeed.

That is, it will if not for Dr. W. Donner Denckla of the National Institute of Alcoholism and Alcohol Abuse. For the last dozen years, Denckla has been single-mindedly tracking down the body's Benedict Arnold, a hormone that interferes with metabolism. He calls his discovery DECO, for "decreasing consumption of oxygen," which is its most obvious effect on cellular processes. After years of work, he has the hormone almost purified. Soon he can begin to search for an antidote.

DECO comes from the pituitary gland, a grape-sized knot of cells lodged inside the brain. It ages us by blocking the thyroid hormones, crippling a whole variety of functions. People with a defective thyroid may sleep fourteen hours a day, and they can put on ten pounds in a day almost without eating. Eventually, the muscles weaken and lose their coordination.

Most of us produce plenty of thyroid hormones well into old age. DECO prevents us from using them. The pituitary secretes a little DECO at first, raises its output slowly for several decades, then pours it out toward the end of life. DECO itself may not kill, but sooner or later it weakens us so that almost any stress can.

Nearly all the effects of aging can be traced to DECO. Denckla has proved this by removing the pituitary from rats and giving the animals thyroid, cortisone, and growth hormones, which are secreted only under its influence. With the source of DECO gone, most bodily functions quickly return to juvenile levels. Old rats' hearts and lungs become as strong as those of youthful rodents. Their immune systems regain nearly all their power to ward off infection. And more than one rat in five survives in glowing health to the age of thirty-four months, roughly equivalent to a human age of ninety-five! Currently, only one person in one hundred survives as long.

One obvious way to get rid of DECO is to create antibodies against it, just as the body uses antibodies to destroy bacteria and other foreign materials. Denckla is not sure that this will work, however. DECO may resemble some other pituitary products; antibodies against it might also destroy hormones we need.

Instead, he plans to search out a "releasing factor," a peptide from the hypothalamus that initiates DECO production. Then he will create an antidote to that. A blocker of the DECO production process, he says, would be chemically simple and so easy to produce that it could be cheaper than aspirin. Timetable for development: five or ten years—if his government funding holds out.

Cellular Timers

In 1912, the year he won the Nobel Prize, the Rockefeller Institute's renowned Alexis Carrel put gerontologists on a detour almost fifty years long. Dr. Carrel teased a bit of embryonic heart tissue from a hen's egg and put it in a flask of culture medium to grow. Thirty-five years later, carefully transferred to new flasks as they outgrew old ones, the cells were still multiplying. One of the great scientists of his time, Carrel had proved what had long been suspected: though a single cell may not be immortal, cell lines go on forever. So when animals age and die, it is not because their supply of viable cells gives out. There must be some other reason.

Unfortunately, Carrel was wrong. Careful as he and his assistants were, they had managed to add fresh cells to the culture each time they replaced the medium. When the last flasks were finally discarded in 1946, two years after Carrel's death, the oldest cell lines in them had multiplied through no more than roughly fifty generations.

That limit of fifty generations, plus or minus ten, is now known as the Hayflick limit after Dr. Leonard Hayflick, who discovered Carrel's error. Working at Stanford University in the late 1950s and early 1960s, Dr. Hayflick tried to repeat Carrel's work, fully expecting to establish an immortal line of cells from the lung of a human embryo. He couldn't do it. No matter how careful he was, the cell line always died out after roughly fifty generations. In a series of elegant experiments, he finally found out why: a timer somewhere in the cell's nucleus puts a limit on the number of times a cell can divide. Contrary to Carrel's theory, our supply of cells may indeed eventually become exhausted.

More recently, this idea has evolved into what's known as the commitment theory. According to Dr. Robin Holliday and his colleagues at London's National Institute for Medical Research, Mill Hill, cells start out as potentially immortal. As the generations go by, the cells change and become committed to a mortal form. The metamorphosis is random but inevitable. So far, no one has any idea why it occurs. When all other causes of aging and death have been defeated, the Hayflick limit may be the last barrier to immortality.

Cross-link Breakers

Almost forty years ago, Ditto, Inc., assigned a young scientist to figure out why duplicating film turned leathery and useless with time. The problem did not take long to solve. But as Johan Bjorksten worked, he noticed a strange similarity between the film's deterioration and the aging of human skin. This insight led Dr. Bjorksten to develop the first modern theory of aging. Now director of the Bjorksten Research Foundation in Madison, Wisconsin, he has been pursuing that theory ever since.

Duplicating film "ages" when the long, flexible molecules that form it become cross-linked—joined together into a rigid ladder. Many of the body's most important chemicals occur as long, easily cross-linked molecules similar to those in the film. Proteins can be cross-linked; so can DNA. And when they are, they no longer carry out their normal roles in the body. Skin, for example, sags and wrinkles because a protein called collagen, which supports the cells of young skin, becomes cross-linked and brittle.

Clearly, Bjorksten reasoned, the thing to do was separate the improperly joined molecules. In 1971, after almost thirty years of work, Bjorksten set out to find a bacterial enzyme to do the job. After all, if bacteria could not dissolve cross-linked molecules, the earth would already be buried under the laddered proteins of animals long dead.

It took another four years to single out a microbe known as *Bacillus cereus*. Painstakingly, the chemist purified the enzyme he needed. Then he injected it into aging mice. He found that after continued injections, the mice were "leaner and more youthful-looking" than their untreated peers. A way to slow and, perhaps, reverse aging was at hand.

But that was years ago. When will we get the anti-aging enzyme? Probably not very soon, it turns out. Bacterial enzymes, after all, are a kind of foreign protein; the body could reject them as it does a transplanted heart. A practical drug to fight cross-linking will take years of work to develop.

Despite Bjorksten's promising results, most gerontologists find his cross-link theory too simple to explain the complex phenomenon of aging. At best, they think a drug to fight cross-linking will slow only such symptoms as sagging skin, not aging itself. Even that limited success seems worth pursuing, but without the backing of other scientists, Dr. Bjorksten has won scant funding for his work. Chronically short of cash, he has been unable to follow up his crucial experiments.

Free Radical Inhibitors

Working at the University of Nebraska School of Medicine, Dr. Denham Harman thinks he has found Bjorksten's cross-linking agent in a species of chemical known as free radicals. If he is correct, simple home remedies for some effects of aging are already available.

In stable chemicals, electrons almost always occur in pairs. In a free radical, one electron of a pair has been stripped away, leaving the second desperate to find a mate. Free radicals attack proteins, DNA, and other long molecules, combining with them and sometimes setting off a chain of cross-linking reactions. It is free radicals that harm the cells in radiation sickness. They may even begin the transformation of normal cells to cancers. The mitochondrion, which supplies the cell's energy, seems particularly prone to free radical damage. And free radicals are easily generated from food, water, and air; tobacco smoke is filled with them.

Dr. Harman and others have dramatically increased the life expectancy of mice by supplementing their food with chemicals that destroy free radicals before the body is damaged. Common free radical inhibitors include vitamins A and C, the trace element selenium, and such food additives as BHA, BHT, and 2-mercaptoethylamine. In one experiment, ethoxyquin, an additive used in livestock feed, increased the mean life span of mice by nearly 75 percent. Astonishingly, Harman has also discovered that the offspring of treated mice live longer than others even though they themselves never receive free radical inhibitors.

These antioxidants increase only the average length of mouse lives, not their longest span. But they postpone the diseases of aging. In cancer-prone mice, the tumors appear later in life. The immune system remains strong months longer than normal. And treated animals can run a maze with fewer mistakes than others—a strong hint that free radical inhibitors may delay mental decline. For human beings, these benefits alone would justify the use of free radical inhibitors. Some gerontologists have already added massive doses of vitamin E to their diets. Most physicians advise against massive vitamin doses, as some vitamins—notably A and D—can cause dangerous side effects when taken in large quantities. Vitamin E, however, is not known to be harmful.

Lipofuscin Blockers

No one likes age spots; they're ugly reminders that we were born much too long ago. Some gerontologists suspect that they are far more than that. Lipofuscin, the material that forms the spots, may be not just a sign of aging, but a cause of further damage.

Lipofuscin is a granular, yellowish brown pigment full of fat and protein. Researchers suspect that lipofuscin, because of its composition, is formed from degenerating cell membranes. The pigment builds up in the cells—especially in muscles and nerves—until it occupies up to 40 percent of their volume. It concentrates in the lysosomes, the cell's garbage dumps, but large quantities also appear in the mitochondria, where it could affect metabolism like grit in a fine chronometer.

Drugs that block lipofuscin formation or help remove it from the cell extend lifespans markedly. A natural compound known as DMAE (for dimethylaminoethanol) is one such material, according to Dr. Richard

Hochschild of the University of California at Irvine. He suspects that DMAE also stabilizes the membrane that surrounds lysosomes, preventing toxic substances from escaping into the cell.

Another drug, centrophenoxine, both prevents lipofuscin formation and rids the cell of pigment deposits. Dr. Kalidas Nandy, of the Bedford, Massachusetts Veterans Administration Hospital, reports that old mice treated with centrophenoxine learn to run a maze almost as quickly as young ones. He and Dr. Hochschild have both found that treated mice live an average of 27 percent longer than untreated controls and have a maximum life span almost 40 percent longer—the equivalent of a 130-year human life.

DNA-Repair Stimulators

Ever since biochemists discovered that life is coded in our DNA, scientists have probed our genes for clues to the aging process. One theory holds that our DNA slowly deteriorates, causing the production of abnormal cell components. Simple mistakes in reproducing the genes during cell division cause some of the damage. Free radicals, viruses, cosmic rays, and many chemicals attack the DNA, producing further flaws in the genetic material. As defective gene products build up in the cell, they interfere with metabolism. Life slowly grinds to a halt.

There is at least some truth to this idea. Mice able to mend their DNA efficiently live longer than nearly identical rodents with poorer repair mechanisms. And stimulating DNA repair in the single-celled *Paramecium* lengthens the animal's life span.

At the National Institute on Aging, Dr. Richard Cutler thinks we could use these findings to create an anti-aging drug. His candidate: a piece of artificial DNA, with everything imaginable wrong with it. Called out to work on the defective DNA, the repair enzymes would fix the cell's own genetic material as well.

Immunomodulators

As we age, the immune system loses its ability to ward off disease. At the same time, for reasons that are not yet clear, it begins to attack our own tissues. Such disorders as rheumatoid arthritis, pernicious anemia, late-onset diabetes, and multiple sclerosis result, at least in part, from the immune system's mistaken assault. So may senescence and eventual death.

Any drug that could help the immune system to ward off illness or prevent it from attacking our own bodies should lengthen our lives. Both strategies have proven successful. UCLA immunologist Roy Walford has used high doses of drugs that block the immune system to prevent autoimmune disease in mice; it lengthened their lifespan significantly. Other researchers working with mice have tripled the animals' life expectancy with injections of infection-fighting white blood cells. Work in this field is only beginning.

Supergenes

While most researchers have been looking for the cause of aging, some are beginning to go at it the other way around. The trouble is not that something causes aging, they reason, but that the mechanisms ensuring our health give out.

Recently, scientists have begun to trace these mechanisms back to the genes that govern them. They have located several of the most important health promoters clustered on a single chromosome—the sixth—in an area known as the Major Histocompatibility Complex (MHC).

The MHC is already well known. It is this knot of genes that governs the so-called HL-A antigens, the biochemical identity cards that distinguish our own tissues from foreign invaders. Now, it turns out that the MHC is even more intimately tied into the workings of the cell. Coded within the complex are the genes for the DNA-repair enzymes, superoxide dismutase (an enzyme that protects against damage by some free radicals) and the mechanisms that control cellular levels of cAMP, the "second messenger" that carries hormonal instructions into the cell.

It seems that the MHC genes are carried together on the chromosome, are inherited together, and work together. So why can't they be controlled together to delay aging? Chances are they can, eventually. It could be many years before we learn to manipulate the DNA throughout the body, but the prospect is one of the most exciting in gerontology.

Sexual Medicine

Sex Stimulants

Forget oysters and "Spanish fly." Medicine is finally tracing the biochemical roots of desire. Even today, a willing physician might be able to write prescriptions for pleasure. Before 2000, success is assured.

Doctors picked up the track of this age-old fantasy when they noticed that some elderly patients receiving the drug L-dopa for Parkinson's disease began to make bold sexual advances toward their nurses. The drug, it turns out, heightens sexual interest in half the men who take it and in about one woman in five. L-dopa is a chemical forerunner of dopamine, which carries signals from cell to cell in parts of the nervous system.

Animal studies have shown the other half of the secret: reducing the brain's supply of serotonin, another neurotransmitter, also promotes sexual behavior. One of the best serotonin reducers is PCPA (parachlorophenylalanine), and rats given the drug show a dramatic increase in sexual activity. PCPA, however, is not ideal for human use. Its side effects include vertigo, headaches, and mental dullness—but there are many other possibilities. Clearly, the development of an ideal chemical aphrodisiac is on the way.

New Contraceptives

Demand for better birth control remains high. One tribute to this interest is the sale in the United States of a hormone with the jaw-breaking name of medroxyprogesterone acetate. To bar pregnancy, it is given to women as an injection every ninety days. Among the side effects are nausea, weight gain, and irregular bleeding. Despite its long use in Europe, the hormone is approved in the United States only as a treatment for uterine cancer. Yet, the manufacturer estimates that some ten thousand American women have adopted it for birth control anyway.

New contraceptive methods abound, despite tightening research budgets in the field. Among the most promising:

• Most likely to reach women in the U.S. soon is the subdermal implant, a small capsule of silicone plastic impregnated with a steroid called levonorgestrel. Inserted six at a time under the skin of the forearm, the implants prevent pregnancy for up to six years at a time, replacing the equivalent of 2,500 birth control pills.

• A whiff a day will keep the babies away if work on LHRH nasal spray is successful. LHRH is a pituitary hormone that usually promotes fertility. Given continuously in large doses, however, it shuts down both ovulation and sperm production. The hormone seems to work just as well for men as for women, but for men, it has an unfortunate side effect. Falling testosterone output caused by the hormone often destroys both men's libido and their secondary sexual characteristics.

• Then again, the most useful vapor may be the woman's breath itself. James G. Kostelc, of Philadelphia's Monell Chemical Senses Center, has found that certain "volatile sulfur compounds" in feminine exhalations vary as much as fifteen fold during the menstrual cycle. Kostelc traces the change to oral bacteria, whose population varies as estrogen levels do. If so, women may soon predict their ovulations, and thus avoid pregnancy, by a simple litmus-style test of chemicals in the mouth.

• A cottonseed derivative known as gossypol may prove effective as a male contraceptive. The extract is highly toxic in large doses, but scientists in China say that more than ten thousand men there have used the drug without harm. Sperm counts drop well below levels usually considered infertile, and the remaining sperm are nearly immobile and unable to reach the ovum. For those who use the gossypol pill and then decide they want a child, fertility returns about three months after usage is stopped.

Test-Tube Tots

As this is written, at least eleven clinics are producing or trying to produce test-tube babies: five in the United States, two in Germany, and one each in Britain, Australia, France, and India. The number grows yearly. Once scientists perfect a reliable method allowing women to carry a Petri-dish pregnancy to term, up to half a million sterile women could benefit in the United States alone. Yet, with hundreds of ova already fertilized and with thousands of women on the waiting lists, fewer than twenty test-tube babies have been born. Perhaps one woman in ten receiving a test-tube embryo has become pregnant, and many of those who did aborted spontaneously within six months. In all, test-tube babies have not been the breakthrough that news writers expected when England's Louise Brown was born on July 25, 1980.

But now it seems that the revolution is at hand. Obstetricians at the Royal Women's Hospital in Melbourne, Australia, have developed improvements in baby-making that may solve the problems of the Pyrex womb. Look for a test-tube population explosion within a few years.

Some other possible developments:

• Physicians working under Dr. Andrew Lopata have revived superovulation, an old egg collection technique. A drug called clomiphene is used to trigger egg production, allowing doctors to collect ova on schedule instead of waiting for the woman's natural cycle to provide them. Used with the hormone chorionic gonadotropin, clomiphene yields two or three eggs per cycle instead of only one. Drs. Patrick Steptoe and Robert Edwards, the British physicians whose work gave life to Louise Brown, tested this technique early on; they abandoned it because the resulting pregnancies aborted spontaneously. But the Melbourne clinic has had no serious problems with it, says Dr. Lopata.

• Starting on the ninth or tenth day of the woman's cycle, just at the end of the clomiphene treatments, the doctors use an ultrasonic scanner to search for a "preovulatory follicle," the puff of spongy tissue in which the egg is buried. The scanner uses high-frequency sound and a small computer to picture the follicle on a TV screen, revealing just when it will be ready for collection. An hour or two before the ovum is collected, doctors scan it again to make sure it is still in good condition.

• After implantation, doctors bathe the embryo with the culture medium in which it was fertilized. So far, it seems that the bath reduces the danger of abortion. Just why, no one knows.

Ice-Cube Babies

A couple may soon be able to put off raising a family for a few years without worrying that the delay will increase the risk of Down's syndrome and other birth defects. Researchers are working on a conceive-now-have-it-later plan that could solve such problems. Within a few years, prospective parents will be able to store their embryo in a clinic or hospital for temporary freezing. When they become financially or emotionally ready to proceed with having the child, the embryo will be removed from storage for thawing, and the pregnancy will proceed at a normal pace. Admittedly, the process may not win the approval of some religious groups, but the procedure is being mastered by scientists at this time.

For years, veterinarians have been freezing animal sperm in liquid nitrogen at -196 degrees Celsius (-320 degrees Fahrenheit), then using them as many as twenty-five years later. More recently, they have frozen whole embryos and have been able to revive more than half of them. At University College, London, Dr. David Whittingham raises perfectly normal mice from embryos frozen for seven years. Several American zoos are trying the technique as a way to save endangered species, and commercial cattle breeders now fly frozen calf embryos to overseas customers instead of paying to ship half-ton cows. It is this technique that doctors are now adapting for human use.

Human embryos have already been frozen and revived. At Queen Victoria Medical Center in Sydney, Australian scientists thawed two of the dozen tiny embryos they had put on ice; both resumed normal growth. And in Dr. Ian Craft's laboratory at Royal Free Hospital in London, England, two-celled human embryos are marking time in cold storage until the researcher is sure he can safely transfer a defrosted fetus into a would-be mother. Dr. Craft already has forty-five women standing in line to receive a baby. Their wait should end no later than 1983.

Select-a-Sex

By then, too, it should be possible to choose your baby's gender—at least, if you want a boy. Dr. Ronald Ericsson, a Sausalito, California physiologist, has already developed one simple way to skew nature's 50-50 odds of having a male child. Ericsson noticed that male-producing sperm swim faster than those destined to yield a girl child, so he forces them to race down a glass column full of human serum albumin. Of the sperm arriving first at the bottom, about 80 percent carry the male Y chromosome. These cells are used to fertilize the mother artificially. As a side effect, the method filters out misshapen sperm and those with eccentric swimming patterns, possible signs of a cell likely to carry a genetic defect. In early tests at Chicago's Michael Reese Hospital, the technique has given couples a 75 percent chance of having a boy. Still needed, says Dr. Ericsson, is a method for improving hopes of having a girl. It is, he reports, "all worked out in my head."

Body Scans

Remember when the CAT scanner became widely adopted in hospitals in the 1970s? Computerized axial tomography takes an entire series of X-rays from different angles through a thin slice of the body and uses a computer to recreate the inner organs. For neurologists, the device meant a revolution. Suddenly, they could see on a TV screen brain tumors, blood clots, and other life-threatening conditions that until then could be found only by surgery. Other physicians have found the scanner nearly as crucial. Despite price tags that range up to $1 million, more than 4,000 CAT scanners are now in use, one-third of them in the United States.

Today, a variety of new scanners is entering hospitals and research labs, giving wondrous views of the body. In the decades to come, they will make many of today's diagnostic methods obsolete.

DSR

A super-CAT scan, the Dynamic Spatial Reconstructor, does not just picture a blurred cross-section of moving inner organs. It offers clear, three-dimensional images and performs tricks that rival Hollywood's best special effects. It can pluck the heart from the chest, move it around, and cut it open. The muscle can be stripped away, leaving a clear view of the arteries. And it can all be done electronically, without ever touching the patient.

The secret is an elaborate array of X-ray tubes and matched sensors that rotate around the patient fifteen times per minute. With each pass, the machine generates 60,000 images of the body, scanning up to 240 slices at a time. Developed at the Mayo Clinic, the DSR probably will not replace CAT scanners. Instead, it will become the model for a new generation of CAT machines enormously more capable than today's models.

PET

Positron emission tomography unites the electronic magic of the CAT scan with the metabolic probes of nuclear chemistry. The combination can picture such invisible bodily functions as blood flow, drug uptake, metabolism, and protein synthesis.

A PET scanner looks much like a CAT scanner: a table ringed by sensitive detectors. But, instead of using X-rays, the detectors respond to positrons, atomic particles emitted by carbon-11, oxygen-15, and other radioactive isotopes. To take a PET scan, the patient lies on the table, his head inside the ring of detectors. He is given an injection of a positron-emitting chemical—often glucose—that flows through the blood to the brain. The number of positrons emitted from each part of the brain depends on how much of the chemical is being used. The scanner translates the positrons into an image of the brain.

Glucose, the brain's energy source, gives a clear picture of what part of the brain is in use. In a bright room, with the eyes open, a patient's visual cortex glows brightly. In a dark room or with the eyes closed, a normal person's visual centers are dim. But during hallucinations, the schizophrenic's visual cortex remains bright. In senile dementia, the patient's entire brain is dim, showing a low level of activity.

These new insights are only a beginning, say PET-scan researchers. Watch for wide-ranging revelations from the procedure about such illnesses as cancer, heart disease, stroke, and epilepsy. They should be coming along almost daily for the next ten years.

BEAM

Unlike other devices that picture the brain, BEAM relies on the body's own energy, rather than on X-rays or radioactive particles. BEAM stands for brain electrical activity mapping, and it produces a sort of super-electroencephalogram (EEG). Invented by Harvard neurologist Frank Duffy, BEAM uses a computer to convert the squiggly lines of an ordinary EEG into dramatic color maps of the brain's electricity.

BEAM is at its best when combined with a technique known as evoked potentials. The researcher gives the patient a sudden stimulus—a handclap, a spoken word, a flash of light—and BEAM displays the waves of electricity that flow back and forth across the brain in response. Watching evoked potentials, BEAM can pick out changes in the brain waves that reveal tumors, schizophrenia, epilepsy, and even reading disabilities.

Only a few BEAM-like devices have been built to date. But a Japanese company called Nihon Kohden plans to market one in the United States next year, and New Jersey's Braintach, Inc., is about to produce a machine patterned on Dr. Duffy's. As the use of BEAM machines grows, so will our understanding of the mysterious human brain.

NMR

In a strong magnetic field, some atoms whip themselves into line like tiny electromagnets. Nudged by a varying magnetic field, they send out weak radio signals. This phenomenon is known as nuclear magnetic resonance, and chemists have used it for years to track fleeting chemical reactions. Today, it is being exploited by some of the most promising new body scanners. The technique, pioneered by Dr. Raymond V. Damadian at New York's Downstate Medical Center, can be used to sense accumulations of hydrogen, phosphorous, and other elements in the body, mapping the distribution like a PET scan.

NMR scanning remains a research technique, but its clinical promise is vast. The U.S. Food and Drug Administration has rated it as the second most promising medical technology now under development (number one is hybridoma technology, which allows the production of pure antibodies to combat cancers and infectious diseases). Already, some researchers have reported that NMR can locate cancers of the breast, colon, and lung. Other likely candidates for NMR diagnosis include pneumonia and congestive heart failure. By 1985, according to the Health Care Financing Administration, some 1,500 NMR scanners, each costing $750,000, should be in use. On the far horizon, researchers say, NMR's magnetic fields may pump healing energies into diseased cells to repair their faulty metabolism.

Genetic Medicine

During the next twenty years, the genetic revolution will change medicine more than any discovery since we learned that microbes cause disease. From it will spring a host of new drugs, the ability to foretell illness from our individual genetic make-up, an enormous variety of new diagnostic tests, and perhaps cancer diagnoses and cures that work almost without fail. Someday, probably within this century, we will be able to cure inherited diseases by supplying missing or defective genes. At least one attempt has already been made in which a California researcher tried to cure two women affected with a potentially fatal blood disease.

Here are a few predictions.

1983: The first drugs from genetically engineered bacteria reach the market.

Human insulin will come first, growth hormone and interferon a year or so later. All three were at the top of the genetic engineers' lists when they discovered that chemicals from the human body could be mass-produced by inserting our DNA into microbes. Other early products of this pharmaceutical revolution include somatostatin, itself a hormone regulator, and thymosin alpha-1, an immune stimulator that could help ward off or cure cancer, infectious diseases, and aging itself.

TIMETABLE FOR GENE-SPLICED DRUGS

DRUG	EFFECT	IN USE
Human insulin	Antidiabetic agent	1983
Growth hormone	Growth stimulator	1984
Interferon	Anticancer, antiviral	1984
Urokinase	Blood-clot dissolver	1985
Leuteinizing hormone releasing hormone	Contraceptive	1985
Thymosin	Immune booster	1985
Factor VIII	Clotting agent	1986
Somatostatin	Possible use in high blood pressure and hypoglycemia	1986
Beta endorphin	Analgesic	1987
Dynorphin	Analgesic	1987
MSH/ACTH	Memory enhancer	1987
Bombesin	Appetite suppressant	1988
Cholecystokinin	Appetite suppressant	1988
Factor S	Sleep promoter	1988

A vast array of new drugs will follow. During the 1980s, the gene industry will bring us large quantities of urokinase, an enzyme that can dissolve blood clots leading to heart attack or stroke, serum albumin to treat shock, and clotting factors that will save the lives of hemophiliacs. But even these are only a tiny beginning. Of the 500 or so proteins in our cells that scientists have identified to date—less than 2 percent of the total to be found there—only a few have been examined as possible drugs. The rest have been far too rare and costly to test.

Already, the Congressional Office of Technology Assessment has identified forty-eight different hormones as likely targets of genetic engineers. Among the most intriguing compounds on this list are many peptides (small protein molecules) found in the brain. Included are:

• LHRH (luteinizing hormone releasing hormone)—possible aphrodisiac that has helped to overcome impotence and a good candidate for a nasal-spray contraceptive effective in both men and women.

• MSH/ACTH (melanocyte stimulating hormone/adrenocorticotropic hormone)—a learning and memory enhancer that may also be available as a nasal spray.

• Cholecystokinin and bombesin—appetite suppressants that may become tomorrow's dieting aids.

• Factor S—a sleep-promoting peptide.

• Dynorphin—an opiate-like pain killer 200 times more powerful than morphine.

1984: Monoclonal antibodies widely used for medical diagnosis.

It isn't difficult to produce monoclonal antibodies, substances derived from a single cell that scientists can use to attack disease or purify the body's chemicals. Just inject a mouse with the material for which you want the antibody, such as a virus or a protein from the surface of a cancer cell. Then, remove the animal's spleen, separate its antibody-producing cells, and fuse them with cells from a cancer. Culture each of the fused cells separately, and screen for the right antibody. Keep culturing the one you want. The antibodies produced by the cell line will react only to the specific protein you injected, in contrast to natural antibodies, which occur as mixtures that react to many different proteins.

The genetic engineering companies have been churning out monoclonal antibodies as quickly as they can develop new ones, and for good reason. One-fifth of the diagnostic tests now used—some $250 million worth each year—rely on antibodies to identify illness, pregnancy, or whatever. Today, relatively few of the immunodiagnostic tests that are theoretically possible have actually been developed, and those in use rely on mixtures of antibodies. Tests using monoclonals will be far more reliable, and probably cheaper. Two are already on the market: a pregnancy test used in Europe since 1981, and a new allergy test aimed at the consumer market.

In organ transplants, monoclonals will be invaluable. A transplant's success or failure depends on the so-called HLA antigens that mark our tissue as being our own. The more antigens that the organ donor and recipient have in common, the more likely a transplant is to succeed. Several hundred million combinations of antigens are possible, and identifying which are present has been a long and difficult process. Monoclonal antibodies will make it so quick and easy that Dr. Ivor Royston, of the Veterans Administration Medical Center in La Jolla, California, expects tissue typing to be done routinely. Tissue types could then be fed into a central data bank so that potential organ donors are matched with recipients minutes after a transplant is ordered.

Monoclonals will also be used to aid in the transplants themselves. In experiments with monkeys, Dr. A. Benedict Cosimi has already used pure mouse antibodies against a form of white blood cell to prevent rejection of donated kidneys. Working at Boston's Massachusetts General Hospital, Dr. Cosimi injected transplant recipients with antibodies to the "T" lymphocytes, one of the body's main defenses against foreign tissue. The injections cleared the lymphocytes from the bloodstream within minutes, blocking any sign of rejection. An antibody to the so-called "helper" T lymphocytes was even more effective. In monkeys, transplanted kidneys usually last about eleven days after the operation, then die under the attack of the recipient's immune system. After injections of the anti-helper antibodies, they survived seven to eight weeks.

Tagged with a radioactive element or one that blocks X-rays, monoclonals can also be used to locate tumors and damage caused by a heart attck. The antibodies are injected into the bloodstream and circulate freely until they reach the tumor or heart tissue. They then bind to the appropriate antigen, outlining its location for the X-ray or radio-scan.

As early as 1980, at least five companies were selling monoclonal antibodies for research. Products then included antibodies that could identify heart attacks, pregnancy, three forms of hepatitis, cancer of the colon and prostate, allergies, and immune deficiencies. One company alone, Bethesda Research Laboratories, reportedly had thirty different monoclonal antibodies under development. When the Food and Drug Administration gives its approval, perhaps as early as 1982, monoclonal-based diagnostic tests will begin to enter the market. By 1984, the trickle should be a flood.

1985: The Food and Drug Administration endorses antibody-guided drugs for use in terminal illness.

If monoclonal antibodies can carry a radioisotope or X-ray dye to outline a cancerous tumor, they should be able to carry a more powerful isotope or a poison to kill it. This idea has already shown considerable promise in the treatment of cancer. (See "Future Cures for Cancer," page 93.) Monoclonals have less obvious uses as well. Two such are the desensitization of allergy sufferers and the treatment of drug overdoses. In both cases, the antibodies would be used to block the receptors where the allergen or drug acts on the body. This principle is already used to create such drug antagonists as naloxone and methadone, which block the effects of heroin. In the near future, many more such treatments may be expected.

1986: California, known for its progressive health legislation, enacts a comprehensive prenatal screening law.

Prenatal screening will soon be available to all expectant mothers, not just those known to be prone to the risk of bearing a child with a congenital defect. At Stanford University, Dr. Leonard Hertzberg and his research team are developing a blood test for pregnant women that could replace today's amniocentesis. Rather than impaling the womb with a hypodermic needle to withdraw cells shed from the developing fetus, as is now done, doctors will use antibodies to capture fetal cells that enter the mother's bloodstream. Once perfected, this method will provide a simple, safe, and inexpensive way to detect birth defects soon after conception.

Gene-splicing techniques will further improve prenatal diagnosis. After a fetal cell has been retrieved from the mother's blood sample, its DNA will be broken down into small segments for direct analysis. Blood disorders cannot be identified through amniocentesis; they will be readily detected through gene-splicing techniques. A prenatal test for hemophilia has just been developed.

A similar test developed at St. Mary's Hospital Medical School in London can detect congenital defects as early as the ninth week. Dr. Robert Williamson and his co-workers collect cells from the chorionic villi, finger-like bits of tissue that form on the outer layers of the embryo and eventually form the placenta. These cells are not actually part of the developing fetus, but they have the same genetic coding. Their DNA can be analyzed for the presence of abnormal genes causing sickle-cell anemia and thalassemia—conditions that show up clearly in this test, though they cannot be found by amniocentesis.

By examining the DNA, doctors will eventually be able to screen fetuses for the diseases that will afflict them throughout their lives. Even now, it is possible to predict the illnesses to which we are prone by studying our HLA antigens, the cellular markers that identify our tissue as being our own. There are five sets of HLA antigens—A through D and DR—with a total of nearly 100 specific antigens between them. Each antigen is known by a letter and a number; A1, for example, or B8. All of us are born with a unique selection of antigens, five from each of our parents. Hundreds of millions of combinations are possible.

For reasons no one yet understands, many illnesses are far more common in people with certain HLA markers than in others. For example, psoriasis is five times as common in people with an HLA antigen known as Cw6 as it is in others. And ankylosing spondylitis, a kind of arthritis in which the spinal vertebrae fuse together, is 175 times as frequent in people with the B27 antigen as in the general population. Only 0.4 percent of all people develop ankylosing spondylitis; among young men with the B27 antigen, the rate is one in four. About 100 of these correlations are now known, and a dozen or so more are discovered each year. In the late 1980s and early 1990s, they will become a mainstay in the fight against disease.

FORTUNE-TELLERS IN YOUR GENES

ILLNESS	HLA MARKER
Alcoholic liver disease	B8
Ankylosing spondylitis	B27
Appendicitis	B12
Arthritis, post-infection	B27
Asthma	A1-B8, Bw6
Bladder cancer	B5, Cw4
Cervical cancer	B15
Coronary artery disease	Bw21
Cystic fibrosis	B5-B18
Diabetes, juvenile onset	B8, B15
Glaucoma	B7, B12
Gonorrheal urethritis	A29
Hay fever	A1-B8, A2-B12
Hepatitis	B8
Herpes infection	A1
Hodgkin's disease	A1
Hypertension	B18
Infectious mononucleosis	A10
Manic depression	A28, B17
Multiple sclerosis	B7, Dw2
Myasthenia gravis	B8
Preeclampsia	A1
Psoriasis	B13, B17, B37, Bw16, Cw6
Schizophrenia	A28, B17
Systemic lupus erythematosus	B8
Testicular cancer	Dw7

1987: First success in repairing a human genetic defect.

When the idea that biologists could tamper with DNA broke upon the world, the reaction was swift and frightened. Pickets stormed the laboratories, city governments met to consider banning the practice, and biologists themselves called for a moratorium on their work until its menace could be weighed. What they all feared was that science would make it possible to change the genes not only of bacteria but of human beings. That day may come sooner than even most scientists expect. As early as 1979, a team led by Dr. V. French Anderson at the National Heart, Lung, and Blood Institute managed to splice a gene into a defective mammalian cell, curing its inability to produce an essential enzyme.

It will be a long time before we can insert DNA into all the cells of an adult. There are simply too many of them, too hard to get at. The first successes will come from less ambitious efforts—very possibly work such as that attempted by Dr. Martin Cline of the University of California at Los Angeles Medical Center.

Dr. Cline attempted in 1980 to cure two young women of beta zero thalassemia, an often fatal illness caused by a defective hemoglobin gene. Almost unknown in the United States, the disease is common in Italy and Israel, where the patients were born. Cline tried to cure the women by removing some of their bone marrow, where the blood cells form, inserting functional genes for hemoglobin into the cells, and injecting them back into the patients. The experiment did not cure the thalassemia, but it did show that the procedure can be carried out safely. The next step is to find some way of making sure the hemoglobin genes are incorporated into the proper position on the chromosomes of the recipient cells. Until that is accomplished, there is little chance that such hemoglobin will be produced. It is a difficult problem to solve, but with so many scientists working on it, the task should not take long.

Soon, it may be possible to correct genetic defects in a developing fetus. Yale University biologist Frank Ruddle has already implanted two genes into fertilized mouse eggs, returned the eggs to their mother's womb, and reared baby mice with foreign DNA engineered into every cell of their bodies. In Dr. Ruddle's initial experiments, the procedure worked in only 2 of 230 attempts, but that score is sure to rise. There is no scientific reason why this could not be done in human beings today.

1989: A resuscitated federal Occupational Safety and Health Administration bans the assignment of certain workers to jobs that are potentially hazardous to people of their genetic makeup.

On-the-job hazards have been one of the most controversial subjects in modern labor relations. The recognition that many jobs abound with cancer-causing chemicals, irritating dust, and other possible health risks have spawned an encyclopedia full of regulations designed to protect workers from their effects. But it is not environmental chemicals alone that subject people to the risk of cancer and other illnesses. Many people can associate for years with toxic chemicals and remain unharmed, while others succumb almost immediately. At least half the risk is carried in our own genes.

This is a relatively new discovery. The trend was noticed among dye and rubber workers using a group of chemicals known as arylamines. That arylamines cause cancer was first suspected in 1895 and finally proved in the early 1960s. But it turns out that arylamines themselves are harmless; the body converts them to carcinogens with an enzyme called n-acetyltransferase. Our chances of developing cancer from arylamines depend on how much of this enzyme we possess, and levels vary widely. Nine out of ten Orientals have large amounts of it, and therefore have a high risk of cancer. Among Israelis, the rate is about three in ten. In North American Caucasians, it is about one in two. These people should avoid jobs that expose them to arylamines.

Another illness with both environmental and genetic components is chronic obstructive pulmonary disease (COPD). Almost any severe irritant can cause COPD, including tobacco smoke, dust, and air pollution. Whether it will cause disease in any individual seems to depend on the level of a protein called alpha-1-antitrypsin, and that depends on our genes. Most of us produce enough of this protein to protect against COPD. Those who carry one abnormal gene, known as the Z gene, have a greater risk of COPD than others. Among those with two Z genes, roughly 70 percent will develop COPD. They should shun high levels of dust, hay, cotton lint, sawdust, molds, and other lung irritants.

Diseases caused or aggravated by job conditions in genetically susceptible workers include sickle-cell trait, hemolytic anemia, and congenital defects in the children of working women. Many more will surely be found.

To date, there have been few coherent attempts to protect these vulnerable workers. When American Cyanamid moved to restrict women of child-bearing age from jobs that exposed them to lead (which could prove toxic to the fetus of any woman who became pregnant while working with the material), four employees brought suit to halt the practice. They had been forced to undergo sterilization in order to keep their jobs, they charged, while men faced no such restriction. The trial court agreed that their civil rights had been violated.

Such cases could slow attempts to protect susceptible workers from job hazards. However, other major companies have also adopted job restrictions to protect the fetuses of pregnant employees, and it seems likely that the principle will be extended to cover other uniquely susceptible workers.

2000: Most human genes mapped.

It takes roughly 100,000 genes to build a human being. Almost every cell in our body contains one copy of each gene somewhere on one of forty-six DNA strands, our chromosomes. By early 1980, roughly 350 genes had been located, and the number was rising by 2 or 3 per week. At that rate, only 1 percent of our genes would be traced to their chromosomes by the end of this century. However, the gene-splicing technology, which has brought a revolution to drug manufacturing and the diagnosis of disease, is also speeding the search many times over.

For practical medicine, gene-mapping may reveal the cause of disorders that have long remained obscure. Two such illnesses are cystic fibrosis and Huntington's chorea, a fatal nervous disorder. In other cases, the genetic map will explain mysterious features of known diseases. Beta thalassemia has been perplexing because it kills some patients yet leaves others only mildly anemic. The reason: at least three forms of the disease exist, each caused by a different kind of damage to the same gene. Soon, practical tests for these defects will let doctors predict the course of their patients' illness and perhaps tailor treatments to meet their special needs.

By 2000, the task of mapping the human gene should be nearly completed. Many of medicine's mysteries will have been solved by then.

New Drugs for the Millennium

In the next five years, a host of superdrugs will bring advances in health care not seen since the birth of penicillin. Heart disease, high blood pressure, arthritis, and perhaps cancer may fall to new pharmaceuticals. Not even obesity is safe from the new medications. They will be potent, relatively free of side effects—and often expensive. Among the most interesting:

ICR (Instant Cold Relief)

Interferon (IF) may not be the panacea physicians once imagined. Then again, it may. Once too rare for human testing, dozens of different types are now being produced by the pound from genetically engineered bacteria. This ready supply has let researchers test a wide

MEDICINE CHEST 1990

Item	Active Ingredient	Effect
ICR (Instant cold relief)	interferon nasal spray	prevents cold
MigrainEx	prostaglandin inhibitor	ends headache
Ultrimmune	thymosin	blocks infection, lowers high blood pressure, slows aging
Memorine	choline/physostigmine	memory booster
Lysessin	vasopressin derivative	memory booster
Sobrane	catecholamine stimulants	instant sobriety
Agex	dehydroepiandrosterone	slows aging, prevents cancer & obesity
DMSO	dimethyl sulfoxide	universal tonic

variety of possible new uses for the fabled cancer cure. Among its successes to date:

• When volunteers at England's Harrow Hospital had human cold virus injected into the nose, nearly all got massive head colds. Eleven lucky patients, however, were given interferon nasal spray first. Three showed minor symptoms, according to Dr. David A.J. Tyrrell, but not one got a full-fledged cold. Interferon injections often produce a headache and fever, but the spray's only side effect was mild irritation.

• Interferon causes the disappearance of benign juvenile papilloma, a non-cancerous tumor that swells within the throat, sometimes strangling the victim.

• After trying to get rid of them for eight years, a patient at the University of Pittsburgh was so covered with warts that even surgery was useless. Five months of generalized IF therapy failed. But then Dr. Monto Ho and his colleagues tried injecting the wonder potion straight into the warts. At the highest doses, up to a staggering 2 million units, the warts vanished. Six months later, they had not returned.

• Cholesterol levels fell markedly among older women receiving IF for breast cancer. According to doctors at the University of Wisconsin, part of the decline was in high density lipoprotein, which helps the body get rid of extra cholesterol. But total cholesterol levels fell even further. And at Houston's M.D. Anderson Hospital and Tumor Institute, six women showed a marked decrease in total cholesterol, but none at all in beneficial HDL. Could IF prevent heart disease? Maybe.

• In one of the largest tests to date, Cuban doctors gave IF to 400 children suffering from dengue fever, a tropical illness characterized by liver failure and hemorrhaging. After only three days of shots, the children's liver functions improved. Hemorrhaging, usually seen in 10 percent of untreated children, never appeared.

• Victims of multiple sclerosis seem to do better when IF is injected straight into their spinal column. Physicians at Millard Fillmore Hospital in Buffalo, New York, report that "exacerbations," periods of markedly worsening symptoms, were half as common in MS patients given interferon as in those who received only standard treatments.

Not all the reports about IF are so promising. Working with rats, Dr. Charles Pfau and colleagues at the National Institute of Health tried the drug against relatively mild strains of a virus causing lymphocytic choriomeningitis, a destructive inflammation of the tissue surrounding the brain. It turned out that the weak virus was driven into the brain itself, causing far more damage than usual. For some human illnesses, the researchers conclude, IF may not be such a good idea.

MigrainEx

Doctors have been eyeing prostaglandins (PG) for years, and with good reason. These hormone-like substances display extraordinary powers. They open blood vessels and lung passages, trigger birth or abortion, prevent peptic ulcer, and both promote and inhibit blood clotting.

Some twenty-five or thirty major illnesses can be traced at least in part to prostaglandin disorders. In diabetes, PG may stop the pancreas from recognizing glucose in the blood, causing it to ignore the need for insulin. In Hodgkin's disease and other cancers, PG may prevent the immune system from destroying the tumor. And PG may set off a migraine headache. Aspirin calms aches, lowers fever, and reduces inflammation because it is a potent PG inhibitor.

To date, prostaglandins may have few medical uses other than inducing labor. However, a prostaglandin known as PGE_1 is now saving "blue babies," born with heart defects that draw blood away from the lungs. PGE_1 holds open the ductus arteriosus, a fetal blood vessel usually sealed off a few days after birth. The treatment gives the infants a better oxygen supply and allows them to gain strength before surgery. (Ironically, an excess of natural PG may keep the ductus open after birth, a condition that also requires surgery. Doctors are now testing PG inhibitors to close the vessel when it is no longer needed.)

In the next few years, prostaglandins and their inhibitors should come into their own. Among the conditions they will aid:

Headaches. No one knows what causes a migraine headache, but there are a couple of likely theories. Both depend on PG. Dr. Morton Sandler of Queen Charlotte's Maternity Hospital in London thinks that migraine occurs when a PG, perhaps thromboxane A_2, causes cranial blood vessels to spasm. Injections of thromboxane A_2, he notes, cause throbbing headaches. At Baylor College of Medicine, Dr. John S. Meyer traces it to prostacyclin, a PG that dilates the vessels. In either case, PG inhibitors could cure the problem. A few doctors have reported good results in preliminary studies.

Menstrual pain, bleeding, and infertility. Uterine PG seem to cause the monthly cramps that afflict a third of young women. Unfortunately, it takes a far more potent PG inhibitor than aspirin to ease the condition, says Cornell pharmacologist Wah Yip Chan, who has been experimenting with ibuprofen, one such drug. At the University of Edinburgh, physicians have tested women with excessive menstrual bleeding and found high levels of a PG called prostacyclin, which reduces blood clotting. And according to Dr. Terrance S. Drake of the National Naval Medical Center, PG that inhibit pregnancy in rabbits flood the womb of women suffering from mild endometriosis, a leading cause of infertility.

Heart disease. Patients with chest pain due to heart ailments have large amounts of thromboxane A_2, which squeezes blood vessels shut and promotes blood clotting. Prostacyclin and PGE_1 block thromboxane's effects, and both have proved useful in treating heart disease.

Prostacyclin ended chest pain for ten out of thirteen heart patients given the drug, says Dr. Andrew Szczeklik of the Copernicus Academy of Medicine in Krakow, Poland. None of the patients had a recurrence for at least two weeks, and two remained free of angina at rest for six months.

PGE_1 eliminated angina for five of Dr. William E. Shell's patients, he reports. The sixth was markedly improved. Dr. Shell of Cedars-Sinai Medical Center in Los Angeles suspects that either PGE_1 or prostacyclin might also prevent heart attack and sudden death in coronary artery disease.

Peptic ulcers. Many PG derivatives block secretion of stomach acid, just as cimetidine does. Unlike cimetidine, they don't spread through the body, so few side effects are expected. One altered version of PGE_2 known as arbaprostil is being tested at twenty hospitals. In the first study reported, the compound healed ulcers in nearly two-thirds of the patients who used it.

Rheumatoid arthritis. Several prostaglandin inhibitors, including aspirin, are already used to block arthritic joint inflammation, but far stronger ones are on the way. One promising group resembles amino acids with a boron atom substituted for one of the carbons. Originally designed to fight cancer, the drugs proved only weakly effective. Then scientists at the University of North Carolina School of Pharmacy at

Chapel Hill tested them against a form of rheumatoid arthritis in rats. Arthritic flare-ups vanished for months, according to Dr. Iris Hall. Better yet, she adds, the drugs had no visible side effects.

Ultrimmune

A small gland just behind the breast bone, the thymus, is responsible for much of our immune response. Around the age of fourteen, it begins to shrivel. As it shrinks, so does our ability to deal with infection. Its most important hormone may soon become one of our most valuable drugs.

Thymosin, discovered by Drs. Allen L. Goldstein and Abraham White in 1965, contributes to the maturation of T cells, a form of white blood cell critical in warding off disease. Children born without T cells can survive only when imprisoned in germ-free isolation chambers, and doctors have seized upon the hormone to free them.

Thymosin could also mean freedom from a host of diseases that plague the aging, ranging from simple colds to cancer, which many researchers believe occurs only when the immune system fails to guard against aberrant cells. It may even slow aging itself. Now working at George Washington University, Dr. Goldstein has begun to test the effects of thymosin in aging mice. Will it extend their life spans and ours? Results should appear in 1983.

Even before it's used against aging, however, thymosin may put an end to hypertension, the so-called silent killer. Dr. Helen Strausser of Rutgers University Medical School noted that patients with hypertension often have compounds in their blood that attack the kidneys and other pressure regulating organs. They also have antibodies against these compounds. Anything that promotes this immune response should help control hypertension, Dr. Strausser reasoned, so she tried injecting thymosin into hypertensive rats. The result: pressure reading dropped almost instantly to near-normal levels. Human trials are due soon.

Memorine

Quickly, now, what is your Social Security number? What did you have for lunch last Tuesday?

If your mind is feeling a little foggy these days, the next five years will hold good news for you. After decades of trying, medical researchers are finally beginning to understand the chemistry of the human mind. Their work now promises to give us a whole series of drugs that can strengthen the memory and sharpen the intellect.

Much of the new information comes from studies of senile memory loss. Researchers have long suspected that senility is caused by a deficiency of acetylcholine (AC), which carries signals between many of the brain's nerves. Now, apparent proof has been found. According to Dr. Joseph T. Coyle and co-workers at the Johns Hopkins Medical Institutions in Baltimore, Maryland, nerves deep within the brain supply the cerebral cortex, where memories are stored, with a key enzyme needed to produce AC. These nerves often degenerate with age, depriving the cortex of the neurotransmitter. Memory fades with them. Dr. Coyle and others are now searching for ways either to prevent this damage or to restore the AC supply.

Two likely candidates are choline and lecithin, chemicals found in some foods. The body converts them to AC, and both have built stronger memories in many experiments. Another drug, physostigmine, promotes the action of AC within the brain. It, too, improves memory. And Drs. Bruce S. Peters and Harvey S. Levin of the University of Texas Medical Branch at Galveston say a combination of lecithin and physostigmine works while neither drug will on its own. They all work best in patients with only mild memory losses, and several studies have found that they improve recall in those with normal memories. Some researchers have suggested that AC promoters may even head off memory loss before it sets in.

Another memory drug, known only as PRL-8-53, was discovered by chemists searching for a tranquilizer that would not dull the mind. What they produced doesn't tranquilize very well, but it does seem to boost mental performance. In a test by Nikolaus R. Hansl, a neuropharmacologist at Omaha's Creighton University, more than 100 student volunteers took both the drug and a standard test of memory and mental sharpness. Their ability to recall nonsense syllables and to draw sets of geometric figures from memory were dramatically improved.

But the most impressive memory promoter is vasopressin, a natural hormone the body uses to help maintain blood pressure. No one knows how it works, but some people using vasopressin have had to give it up after finding themselves so flooded with memories that they could not focus on their daily activities.

The effect has been confirmed in many studies. Researchers at the National Institute of Mental Health tried dosing twelve volunteers with a vasopressin derivative known as 1-desamino-8-D-arginine vasopressin. Six were healthy college students, four were depressed women, and two were undergoing electroshock therapy for severe depression, which often induces partial amnesia. All but one of the depressed women found their memories markedly improved. Dr. J.J. Legros of the University of Liege, Belgium reports that vasopressin restores failing memory in the aged. And Dr. J.C. Oliveros of the Hospital Clinico de San Carlos in Madrid tells of using it to restore memory to a fifty-five-year-old man suffering amnesia from head injuries sustained in an auto accident. Lysine-8-vasopressin, sold under the brand name Diapid, reportedly is equally effective.

Save for PRL-8-53, all these memory boosters can be had today.

Sobrane

Take two of these, and you'll be sober faster than a traffic cop can reach for his ticket book. It's not just an idle fantasy. Researchers have found two possible routes to a so-called "amethystic" that will almost instantly dry out the besotted.

Alcohol depletes or blocks the catecholamine system, the nerve pathways that depend on adrenalin and related compounds. So, stimulating adrenalin production should clear the fuddled mind. Many drugs promote adrenalin, and many have already been proved impractical. But two look promising: ephedrine, found in some asthma drugs, and l-dopa, used to treat Parkinson's disease.

The other path to an amethystic starts at the cell membrane. Dr. Yedi Israel at the University of Toronto has found that alcohol blocks the electrical currents that ordinarily flow through the nerve's cell membrane. And Dr. Dora Goldstein of Stanford University reports that alcohol makes these membranes unstable; the molecules in them move randomly and may be unable to perform their normal functions. A drug that stiffens these membranes may also block intoxication, but it is likely to take longer to operate than the catecholamine stimulators.

How long will it be before one of these routes gives us some form of instant sobriety? Dr. Ernest Noble, a leader in this research from the University of California at Irvine, estimates no more than ten to fifteen years

Agex

It's a glutton's dream. Eat what you will, as much as you want; you won't get fat.

It's also a universal cancer preventive.

And it slows aging dramatically.

It is dehydroepiandrosterone (DHEA), a natural hormone produced by the adrenal gland. In the young, the body produces more DHEA than any other hormone. Later, though, it falls off drastically. For decades, no one could figure out what use it is. It is a male sex hormone, but too weak for that to be its major function. DHEA also inhibits an enzyme called glucose-6-phosphate dehydrogenase (G6PDH). But what good is that?

Then Dr. Arthur Schwartz of Temple University's Fels Institute noticed an old report that women who secrete subnormal levels of DHEA metabolites tend to develop breast cancer. DHEA, he knew, prevents obesity in a strain of mice that characteristically grow fat, yet does not change their appetites. Then Dr. Schwartz recalled some forty-year-old studies in which mice had survived to nearly double their normal span when given plenty of vitamins and minerals but fed at near-starvation calorie levels. The treatment had kept the mice thin, of course, and it had markedly lowered their cancer rates. Could DHEA operate in the same way?

In theory, it was possible. The cells use G6PDH to make NaDPH, a chemical required for many metabolic processes. Two of the most important processes that require NaDPH are DNA replication—a key step in cancer formation—and the synthesis of fat.

Schwartz tested DHEA in mice with a genetic tendency to develop both obesity and cancer, in mice that develop cancer but not obesity, and in cell cultures. The cell cultures confirmed that DHEA slowed DNA synthesis, confirming his ideas about the anti-cancer effect. In the mice, the hormone blocked obesity and cut the cancer rate. After a year, the treated mice were glossier of coat than their peers and markedly less grey. Will they actually live longer? We will know soon.

DMSO

Will the 1980s be the decade when dimethyl sulfoxide finally wins organized medicine's approval? Not if the Food and Drug Administration has its way. The agency steadfastly refuses to certify the solvent for use against any illness other than a rare bladder disorder called interstitial cystitis. In 1981, it went so far as to seize not only the DMSO at a Buffalo, New York outlet, but also books describing the compound's use. Until the New York Civil Liberties Union stepped into the case, the FDA threatened to have the volumes burned—a move forbidden even to crusaders against pornography.

Despite this less-than-objective campaign, DMSO is sold across the country. One measure of its popularity is its price in drug stores—up to twenty times its industrial cost. Sold as a solvent, it can be used as the customers please. They please to use it for an astonishing variety of ailments. Most popular as a linament for sprains and muscle aches, DMSO soothes burns, calms gouty and arthritic joints, and is said to relieve even the maddening itch of herpes infections.

With the FDA's reluctant permission, some thirty research teams have been testing DMSO's powers in a number of diseases and traumatic disorders. The results have often been promising. In myasthenia gravis, a fatal disorder in which the patient's own antibodies block communications between the muscles and the nerves, DMSO cuts antibody levels by more than two-thirds. It protects the brain from damage during surgery and after head injuries, says Dr. Maurice Albin of the University of Texas Health Science Center in San Antonio. And Dr. John Gelderd, Texas A & M College of Medicine, reports that it helps to heal otherwise paralyzing spinal injuries. Sooner or later, such discoveries are almost sure to change the FDA's stand against DMSO.

In the long run, though, it probably doesn't matter. Encouraged by the wide-ranging reports of DMSO's healing properties—and by the absence of proof that it is in any way harmful—the states of Florida, Louisiana, Oklahoma, Oregon, Texas, and Washington have already given their doctors the right to prescribe it for a variety of disorders. More are sure to follow. If DMSO is not already in your medicine cabinet, it will be by 1990, with or without the FDA's approval.

Vaccines

You won't find them in your medicine chest, but they will be among the biggest medical news of the next decades. The first hint of things to come appeared in mid-1981, when scientists at San Francisco's Genentech, Inc., developed the first gene-spliced vaccine—against foot-and-mouth disease. The announcement attracted headlines this sleepy field of vaccines hadn't seen since Salk and Sabin conquered polio more than twenty years earlier. Genetic engineering and other sophisticated technologies are about to deliver many more such innovations. Likely candidates for future production include an all-purpose flu vaccine and vaccines against cholera, sleeping sickness, and hookworm. Here are some examples:

• A vaccine to prevent gonorrhea appears imminent. Microbiologist Charles Brinton and his coworkers at the University of Pittsburgh have been testing a vaccine made from gonorrhea pili, hairlike strands with which the bacteria cling to the linings of the urinary and reproductive tract. The vaccine, Dr. Brinton notes, seems to block infection by any of the fifty-odd gonorrhea strains, not just the one used to prepare it.

• Strep infections kill 5,000 or more newborn babies each year and leave at least 6,000 with epilepsy, hearing loss, blindness, or mental retardation. Now immunologists at Temple University in Philadelphia and at Baylor University in Houston have produced two different strep vaccines. To protect infants, infected mothers would be vaccinated during pregnancy if they were expected to have an early or difficult labor—risk factors in the illness. One or both of the vaccines should be in use soon.

• Like a butterfly, the malaria parasite rotates between three separate forms during its complex life cycle. It has been difficult to create a vaccine against any of these forms, and no vaccine can attack more than one of them.

Now researchers at the New York University School of Medicine have the beginnings of a breakthrough. According to Drs. Ruth S. and Victor Nussenzweig, a malaria parasite that infects mice becomes harmless when treated with X-rays. Yet, it still provokes the immune system, protecting mice, monkeys, and even people against future infection. The Nussenzweigs have also produced pure antibodies against a protein called Pb-44 that occurs only in the infective form of malaria. These antibodies also protect mice against infection. Neither treatment can destroy the parasite for more than a few hours after infection, but a separate project at England's Wellcome Research Laboratories reports production of an antibody against a later stage.

How long will it be before malaria vaccinations reduce an age-old scourge to a minor health problem? Expect it well before 2000.

• Some 200 Americans die of hepatitis B annually, and up to a quarter-million others suffer nausea, fatigue, and often serious liver damage. It may even promote liver cancer. Worldwide, it affects more than half a billion people. New vaccines may do away with it. One called Heptavax-B should soon be generally available, but it is not likely to be widely used. Three doses protect against hepatitis for five years, but the shots will cost up to forty dollars each.

To make a cheaper vaccine, gene-splicer William Rutter of the University of California at San Francisco has taken the DNA for a hepatitis-virus protein and transplanted it into yeast. Unlike genetically engineered bacteria, which produce only the protein, the yeast seems to add sugar and fat found in the natural infectious particles. The combination should yield an economical vaccine as potent as Heptavax-B, and stronger than today's gene-spliced versions.

• An untreatable form of sleeping sickness, Chagas disease, attacks the heart and nerves of some ten million South Americans. Rats try to fight off the infection with a class of antibodies known as IgG. This reaction gave Drs. Allen B. Clarkson, Jr., and George H. Mellow an idea. Many arthritis patients, they knew, produce so-called rheumatoid factors, a kind of antibody that reacts with IgG. Could rheumatoid factors help IgG do away with Chagas disease? In early tests carried out at the Albert Einstein College of Medicine, it seems that they can. Next steps: confirm that it works in people, and find some way to stimulate rheumatoid factors in Chagas victims.

• It's not often that science finds a 100 percent effective vaccine. For people in the Third World, where pure water is rare, a typhoid vaccine that potent seems like a miracle. Swiss researcher Rene Germanier has managed to find a mutant strain of self-destructive typhoid bacteria. When swallowed, the living bacteria provoke an immune reaction that blocks future infection, then vanish before they can cause any harm. Dr. Germanier of the Serum and Vaccine Institute in Bern tested the vaccine in more than 16,000 six-year-olds in Egypt. Two years later, not one had contracted typhoid, which is prevalent in that country.

Bionic
Organs

Dedicated physicians and engineers have worked for decades to develop artificial organs. It will be a long time before we can replace our own body parts as easily as those of a 1973 Buick, but the attempt is beginning to pay off. Computers and new materials that can be implanted harmlessly in the body are bringing about a revolution in healing as important to those with bodily impairments as antibiotics are to pneumonia victims. A few early successes are described below.

Artificial Pancreas

Insulin may save a diabetic's life, but it's far from perfect. Our natural supply of insulin jumps dramatically when we eat, then drops as we digest the food. A shot of insulin, in contrast, sends our supply skyward whether we've eaten or not. Then blood levels of insulin fall continuously, even if we eat again. This difference may cause such diabetic complications as progressive blindness and kidney damage. Many research projects have been seeking ways to deliver insulin as it's needed. Among the top contenders:

• A titanium pump used by University of Minnesota surgeon Henry Buchwald. Implanted over the chest muscle, the pump was stitched into its first human patient at the end of 1980. It delivers a steady flow of insulin into the blood, eliminating destructive ebbs and surges. Though it doesn't vary insulin dosages in response to meals, a disadvantage for some patients, the Minnesota pancreas is considered useful for up to 80 percent of diabetics. A controlled-dosage model is already being tested.

• A variable insulin delivery pack devised by Sandia National Laboratories in Albuquerque and the University of New Mexico. According to Drs. R. Philip Eaton and David S. Schade, the device nestles behind the rib cage and drips insulin into the body cavity where it is absorbed into the bloodstream. A hand-held controller sets the dosage magnetically from a one-microliter droplet (about three one-hundred-thousandths of an ounce) every four to sixteen minutes to a droplet every eight seconds at mealtime. A commercial model, not due for several years, could hold a month's insulin and, refilled by injection, last most of a decade.

• Like the New Mexico pump, the PIMS (programmable implantable medication system) is governed with a hand-held controller. In addition, doctors will be able to regulate the device over the telephone. Human tests are scheduled for 1982, says Dr. Christopher D. Saudek of Johns Hopkins University, Baltimore, who will head the trials.

• Sugar sensors. The perfect artificial pancreas won't be just controllable; it will respond on its own to blood sugar levels, adjusting the flow of insulin automatically, just as a natural pancreas does. Until recently, glucose sensors have been too complex, short-lived, and easily damaged by body chemicals to be used in an artificial organ. One possible breakthrough in this field comes from Ebtisam Wilkins and C. Odayle of the University of New Mexico at Albuquerque. The pair has developed what they call the coated wire glucose sensor. Two fine electrodes would be implanted in a small vein and used to regulate an insulin pump like those already being tested. It will be another year before the New Mexican scientists know whether their sensor is sturdy enough for use in an implant.

• Human pancreas cells. Often attempted in the past, pancreas transplants have such a high failure rate that they have never caught on. Recently, doctors have tried separating islet cells—the insulin producers—from the pancreas, shielding them inside tiny capsules and implanting them in diabetes victims. Pores in the capsule wall are large enough to let nutrients and insulin pass, yet small enough to block antibodies and leucocytes that would destroy the islet cells. In theory, encapsulated islet cells could give diabetics a normal insulin supply that varies according to need. Trials are under way at several medical centers, including Boston's Joslin Clinic, the University of Minnesota, the Mayo Clinic, and the Medical College of Virginia. They look promising, so far, but the final verdict is still far off.

Electro-Ears

If something's gone wrong with the ear, why not build an electronic substitute? After all, every telephone converts sound to electricity, which is what the nervous system operates on.

Such a procedure is not as simple as it sounds. Biomedical engineers have been working on ear replacements for over a decade with marginal success. Portable microcircuits have not been up to the task of converting sounds as complex as speech into recognizable nerve signals. Hisses, whistles, and odd clangs were about the best the microcircuits could manage. And no ear implant can work unless the patient has an intact acoustic nerve, which many deaf people do not have.

No one has managed to replace lost acoustic nerves, but doctors have finally built electric ears that can begin to help other deaf patients. At the House Ear Institute in Los Angeles, Dr. William F. House and his colleagues have tested a device that translates sound into electrical impulses and feeds them to a wire implanted in the cochlea—the nerve center where the normal ear converts sound to nerve signals. Patients using the implant can understand at least some speech, Dr. House says, somewhat like listening to a mistuned radio.

Another system, being tested at the University of California, San Francisco, allows patients to understand up to half of common words— not enough to hold a conversation without lip-reading, but still a big help. The difference between the UCSF device and the House ear is that this one supplies eight different nerve signals to the cochlea. In theory, such implants should offer far better sound discrimination than single-channel ones. Some doctors hold that it would take 100 implanted electrodes to provide full speech recognition.

At the University of Utah, Dr. Donald Eddington seems to have cut that down a bit. Using a six-electrode implant, he reports, volunteers recognize word combinations and sentences with about 75 percent accuracy. The device is still too large to be practical, but Dr. Eddington hopes to shrink it soon to pocket size.

Artificial Eyes

The artificial eye has been in the works for more than fifteen years. Progress has been slow. The breakthrough that could turn this fantasy into reality has never appeared. Now, it may finally be at hand. It comes not from medicine, but from computer science.

Work on the artificial eye began as early as 1965 when surgeons at the University of Utah inserted an array of sixty-four tiny electrodes into the brain of a man who had been blinded in a hunting accident. Hooked to a TV camera, the panel stimulates his visual centers, producing tiny dots of light known as phosphenes. In the laboratory, the device lets him "see" the difference between large horizontal and vertical lines. He can even read Braille letters five times faster than with his fingertips. But the equipment is so cumbersome that it's useless in his daily life.

Dr. William H. Dobelle, who now heads the artificial-organ project at New York City's Columbia Presbyterian Medical Center, hopes eventually to raise the number of electrodes in the brain to 512—enough to provide primitive, but useful, sight. The electronics will then be miniaturized so that a tiny TV camera can be mounted in the eye socket, the electronics on a pair of eyeglasses. Just how long this will take, Dr. Dobelle is unwilling to guess.

However, before his work is complete, an even more spectacular accomplishment may render it obsolete. At tiny EMV Associates, Inc., a Maryland research firm, computer scientists are trying to make an electrode panel that will grow into the brain. Etched on a chip of protein, its wires will be small enough to link with a single brain cell. Embryonic nerves will be glued to the panel, each stimulated by a wire, and the cells will grow down into the brain's visual cortex to make the connection. The combination, says James McAlear, EMV's technical genius, should provide vision roughly as clear as a static-filled black-and-white TV. Target date: 1991.

Bionic Lungs

They'll come, though probably not soon. Dr. Pierre M. Galletti of Rhode Island's Brown University has been testing artificial lungs in sheep for several years now, the latest development in a research program that stretches back to 1957. In the newest model, blood flows through a coiled bundle of braided plastic tubes riddled with tiny pores through which oxygen enters and carbon dioxide leaves. It functions in sheep for several hours, but only as an assist. The animals still have one lung working normally.

Physicians are not yet looking to the research for a permanent lung replacement. For now, they would be happy with a device that could give injured lungs a rest, preventing further damage. The best hope so far is a technique called $ECCO_2R$—extracorporeal carbon dioxide removal—using a primitive artificial lung that circulates blood through a thin membrane instead of Dr. Galletti's microporous tubes. Combined with mechanically assisted breathing, the procedure reversed acute respiratory failure in seven of eleven patients, says Dr. Luciano Gattinoni of the University of Milan. Patients treated with the procedure improve visibly within half an hour, according to Dr. Theodor Kolobow of the National Heart, Lung, and Blood Institute. Some have remained on the machine for nearly a week.

Liver

It carries out an astonishing number of vital chemical reactions, including many that rid the body of accumulating poisons. The liver may be one of our most complex organs. It also has tremendous recuperative powers; given a machine to take over for it temporarily, the liver could restore itself even after a now-fatal illness. To date, nothing has even come close to duplicating its many functions.

One minor success comes from the Cleveland Clinic. Doctors there have used activated charcoal and an ion-exchange resin, often used to purify water, to cleanse the blood of its toxins. Four patients comatose from acute liver failure have been treated with the device; three regained consciousness, but only one survived. Five others with less severe liver ailments have also been helped by detoxification.

Another technique that may offer a partial substitute for the liver is being tested in patients with phenylketonuria. PKU victims are born without an enzyme that breaks down phenylalanine, an amino acid found in food. Unless they are recognized early and placed on phenylalanine-free diets, the compound builds up in their bodies, causing irreparable brain damage.

The only way really to "cure" PKU would be to supply the missing enzyme. Unfortunately, injections of it are destroyed rapidly by other enzymes in the blood. It may also set off an allergic reaction. At Yale University and at Roswell Park Memorial Institute in Buffalo, New York, doctors have avoided that by fixing the enzyme to the walls of porous tubes. As blood flows past a bundle of the tubes, phenylalanine from the plasma enters the pores and is broken down by the enzyme inside. The technique removes most of the phenylalanine, yet protects the enzyme from destruction and averts an allergy. Eventually, bundles of tubes containing a variety of enzymes could replace many functions of a failing liver.

Perhaps even more promising is a hybrid organ made of living cells locked in plastic. Pathologist Carl F.W. Wolf of Cornell Medical College has been experimenting with a device containing cells from a rat hepatoma—a liver cancer. Like any cancer, the cells grow continuously, ensuring a steady supply for the artificial organ. And because they come from the rodent's liver, they carry on most normal hepatic functions as well. There's a lot of engineering to be done before the unit can be tested even in animals, Dr. Wolf reports. But for the long run it may be the best hope for an aid to the ailing liver.

Skin

It's our largest organ, probably fifty pounds worth on an average-sized man, and it's our primary defense against bacteria. When a severe burn strips away large portions of skin, death from an overwhelming infection is an ever-present threat. In the United States, 130,000 people are hospitalized with severe burns each year—with 10,000 cases fatal.

For Mark Walsh, death seemed almost inevitable. An electrician, the twenty-five-year-old Walsh was working in an aerosol-can factory outside Boston when an explosion seared the skin off 80 percent of his body, a full forty pounds of flesh gone in an instant. Surgeons at Massachusetts General Hospital used as much of the unharmed skin as they could to begin covering his wounds. When they ran out, they turned to a new development from the Massachusetts Institute of Technology: artificial skin.

The skin comes in three forms, all invented by teams based at MIT. The version Walsh received is the product of Ioannis Yannis, a polymer engineer, and Harvard surgeon John F. Burke. Like natural skin, it is made up of two layers: an outer surface of silicone plastic, and a base of collagen and a natural polymer called glycosaminoglycan. Collagen, a protein that Drs. Yannis and Burke extract from cow hide, holds the cells of natural skin in place. Glycosaminoglycan is a supporting material extracted from shark cartilage. Placed over a wound, the plastic film remains in position until natural skin replaces it from beneath.

The other skin substitutes use the patient's own cells. One, devised by Dr. Howard Green, covers the wound with a single layer grown from the epidermis, the outer layer of skin. The other, invented by Dr. Eugene Bell, uses fibroblasts—cells that produce connective tissue—trapped in a layer of collagen as its base. The fibroblasts grow into a flat sheet, then are seeded with epidermal cells that cover the inner layer.

So far, neither of the natural-cell techniques has been used for human patients. But the all-synthetic skin used by Yannis and Burke has already shown just how important such advances will be. For Mark Walsh, and a few other lucky burn victims, it has meant life itself.

Future Cures
for Cancer

Universal Vaccine

The breakthrough may already have happened. Scientists have discovered that all cancer cells, no matter where they form, produce a substance known as chorionic gonadotropin (CG). This protein is also manufactured by the fetus to prevent the mother's immune system from rejecting fetal cells as foreign. It may perform the same function for a tumor. If this work pans out, it may be possible to make a universal vaccine against cancer. The right inoculation could trigger the body to produce antibodies against all CG-producing cells, automatically destroying any future cancer and perhaps wiping out existing tumors. The major drawback would be that women who took the vaccine could never bear children, since the antibodies would cause a miscarriage. A universal cancer vaccine could be in wide use by 1990.

A few vaccines against specific cancers are already in the works. A scientist at George Washington University, Dr. Ariel Hollinshead, has already developed a vaccine against four types of lung cancer by purifying the antigens found on the surface of the tumor cells. In her experiments, only 17 percent of the immunized patients died of the cancer, compared with more than half of those who did not receive the vaccine.

Monoclonal Antibodies

Closely related to the vaccines, monoclonal antibodies against cancers are already proving their worth. In an early experiment with leukemic mice, they proved more effective than anyone could have hoped. The six untreated mice used as controls died within three weeks. Of the mice that received monoclonal antibody injections, two had prolonged lifespans and four were totally disease-free forty-five days later.

Buoyed by these results, researchers have gone looking for antibodies against human cancers. The National Cancer Institute spends some $90 million a year on immunological research. In 1981, some 70 percent of the investigators receiving those funds were working to find monoclonal antibodies against cancer cells. Antibodies have already been developed against cancer of the pancreas and colon and against several forms of leukemia. Rumors of cancer cures by these antibodies are echoing through the research community, to be confirmed or refuted very shortly.

Interferon

The body's famous anti-viral agent has not proved to be a panacea against cancer, but it does have its uses.

• Dr. Frank Rauscher, research director of the American Cancer Society, reports that interferon now has a success rate of up to 15 percent in melanoma, a rapidly fatal skin cancer, and 25 to 40 percent in advanced breast cancer, non-Hodgkins lymphoma, and myeloma—cancer of the bone marrow.

• Dr. Norwood O. Hill of the Wadley Institute of Molecular Medicine in Dallas reports that interferon clears all leukemia cells from the blood and most or all from the bone marrow. But it takes enormous doses—20 to 160 times larger than normal. The treatment produced remissions in six out of seven patients with acute lymphocytic leukemia and in two out of three with acute myelogenous leukemia.

• From Rotterdam's Erasmus University, Dr. William Weimar has announced that mesothelioma, a tumor derived from the membrane that lines the body cavity, vanished for at least eighteen months after interferon treatment. The cancer, rare and hard to treat, is not directly fatal, but patients usually die of complications within six months after diagnosis.

Once available only in quantities that could have vanished with a sneeze, several forms of interferon are now being produced in kilogram batches. Thus, clinical trials are expanding rapidly, and we can expect a flurry of stories about it for several years. Assuming no severe problems show up in current safety tests, interferon should win approval from the Food and Drug Administration by 1984 and reach the market later that year.

Medical Frontiers

Many developments in medical science are so new that we have not yet had time to reap their benefits. Some are treatment methods with extraordinary benefits that have yet to reach general practice. Others open the way to new research. A few are so vast that no one can see more than the outlines of their promise. These are the frontiers of medicine. Science has begun to probe many of them in the last decade. Before 2000, their practical value will begin to appear. Here are just a few.

Cloning

Carbon-copied people, a science fiction fantasy of the 1970s, could become a reality as early as the 1990s. At least one prominent investigator of human reproduction asserts that it could be done today.

In theory, cloning should be easy. All it takes is to replace the nucleus of an egg cell with one from the creature you want to duplicate. With a little luck, the cell starts to divide, just as a normally fertilized egg would. After eight or nine divisions, the tiny artificial embryo is ready to implant in the womb of a host mother. Dr. John Gurdon of Oxford University managed to clone frogs as early as the 1960s.

Successes might be rare in mammals as complex and easily damaged as man; a would-be clone doctor might produce only one healthy baby per hundred tries. But all it would take is patience.

Dr. Landrum B. Shettles of the Oasis Clinic in Las Vegas reports having used a tiny glass pipette to remove the nucleus from human cells that ordinarily give rise to sperm (it could as easily have been the nucleus of cells from a woman). Dr. Shettles implanted these cells in ova from which he had removed the nucleus. It was the most difficult way to make a clone yet devised. Yet, in three cases, the "fertilized" egg grew normally until it was large enough to implant in a host mother. Less than nine months later, the first human clone, a genetic duplicate of the man who donated the nucleus, might have been born. Lacking official permission to proceed, Shettles never took that final step.

In 1978, science writer David Rorvik published *In His Image*, a book that purported to be the story of a New Jersey millionaire who secretly had himself cloned. The story touched off a public debate over the ethics of human cloning that took months to die down. We could conceivably witness another such controversy—this time fueled by an actual living duplicate of its single "parent"—at any moment.

Protein Index

The human body, scientists tell us, contains probably 50,000 different kinds of protein, fewer than 2 percent of which have been identified. Within ten years, it should be close to 100 percent, because of the work by Drs. Norman G. Anderson and Leigh Anderson, Argonne National Laboratories in Argonne, Illinois. This development will usher in a new era in medicine.

The researchers are using a technique known as two-dimensional electrophoresis (2-DE) to compile a catalog they call the Human Protein Index. 2-DE separates cell constituents by subjecting them to an electric field. Supported on a glass plate coated with gel, the materials move across the plate, propelled by the force of the electricity. How quickly each molecule moves depends on its weight and electric charge. Small, highly charged molecules travel quickly; larger and less heavily charged ones lag behind.

Applied to a human cell, 2-DE can separate several thousand different proteins into dots scattered across the gel. Each shows up clearly, even if the cell contains only a few billionths of a gram. To identify each protein requires far more complex methods, but it need be done only once. Once a protein is analyzed, the scientists can recognize it by comparing its position in a 2-DE pattern with those of the known proteins in the Index.

For doctors trying to diagnose a patient's illness, the change will mean a revolution. Certain diseases, especially some forms of cancer, produce special proteins not normally found in the body. Others pour proteins into the blood or urine. Working with Chinese hamsters at the Upjohn Company, Drs. David Sammons and Lonnie Adams have found a liver protein that changes position on a 2-DE "scan" in animals likely to get diabetes. Many more such markers will be discovered as the Protein Index is compiled.

Is the patient excreting a viral protein that reveals an infection? Has a heart attack spilled characteristic enzymes into the blood? It won't take long to find out. Within ten years, doctors should be able to diagnose nearly any illness in a few hours simply by looking at the patient's 2-DE patterns.

Leprosy

It doesn't take a glamorous breakthrough or brilliant insight to make a frontier. Sometimes a small, homey development will do it. Such is the achievement of J. Kazda of the Institute for Experimental Biology and Medicine in Borstel, West Germany.

Scientists have spent decades searching for a way to grow leprosy bacteria in the laboratory, hoping eventually to produce a vaccine to prevent this age-old scourge. But *Mycobacterium leprae* are choosy about their environment, growing only in man and between the toes of the nine-banded armadillo. It's made them an inconvenient bug to work with. (Another form afflicts the water buffalo, but that doesn't help the search for a human leprosy cure.) Now, at last, Dr. Kazda has it, a home in which leprosy bacteria can live and multiply in comfort, making their long-sought contributions to medicine.

The development comes none too soon. The U.S. Center for Disease Control estimates that there are 11 million lepers in the world. That number is about to leap, the agency believes, because the bacteria are growing drug-resistant.

Dr. Kazda's discovery? Leprosy grows in peat moss.

Plasmapheresis

Also known as blood washing, it can rid us of toxins, antibodies, and other noxious substances. It may be one of the most promising therapeutic techniques of the 1980s.

In plasmapheresis (PPH), the patient's veins are connected to a machine rather like an artificial kidney. It separates the blood cells from the plasma, taking three or four hours to complete the job. The cells are diluted with an artificial plasma substitute and returned to the patient's body. The plasma and whatever toxins it contains are discarded. Variants of PPH are used to separate white blood cells, platelets, and other blood fractions.

ILLS AIDED BY PPH

Acquired factor-VIII inhibitor	Insulin-resistant diabetes
Asthma	Kidney-transplant rejection
Blood-group sensitization (Kell)	Lupus
Crohn's disease	Macroglobulinemias
Cryoglobulinemia	Meningococcemia
Cutaneous vaculitis	Methyl parathion poisoning
Dermatomyositis	Multiple myeloma
Exophthalmic goiter	Mushroom poisoning
Familial hypercholesterolemia	Myasthenia gravis
Glomerulonephritis	Polyarteritis nodosa
Goodpasture's syndrome	Post-transfusion purpurea
Guillain-Barre syndrome	Primary biliary cirrhosis
Hemolytic disease of newborn	Raynaud's disease
Hereditary angioneurotic edema	Rheumatoid arthritis
Hypertriglyceridemia	Subacute bacterial endocarditis
Hyperviscosity syndromes	Thrombotic thrombocytopenia
Idiopathic thrombocytopenia	Thyrotoxicosis

It seems a little strange to label PPH a "frontier." U.S. physicians ordered something like 100,000 treatments in 1980 alone. Yet, doctors are finding uses for this technique almost as fast as they can think of new ones to try. Done before a kidney transplant, PPH protects the donated organ against rejection. In myasthenia gravis, it seems to ease the patient's weakness temporarily. And in some cancers and Waldenstrom's macroglobulinemia, where overproduction of plasma proteins makes the blood too sludgy to flow properly, PPH cuts symptoms dramatically.

But it is the technique's promise in treating more common disorders that excites many physicians. Its best-proved use is in rheumatoid arthritis (RA), where most doctors remove both plasma proteins and some white blood cells. Twenty treatments or more may be needed. Dr. Daniel J. Wallace of Cedars-Sinai Medical Center in Los Angeles has used the technique in several dozen people with severe RA. Many showed significant improvements in such clinical criteria as morning stiffness and grip strength.

In another series of tests, rheumatologist Max I. Hamburger, State University of New York at Stony Brook, found a 50 percent reduction in morning stiffness after treatment. For some patients, the improvement lasted three to six months. Similar successes have been reported, with less certainty, in diabetes, systemic lupus erythematosus, and asthma.

For the moment, it looks as though PPH will continue to find new uses. The flaw is its price. At up to $850 a treatment, PPH can cost nearly $20,000 per patient. Despite this, many doctors expect to see 1 million treatments per year performed in the U.S. alone by 1985.

From a New York dermatologist named Norman Orentreich comes a more speculative, and perhaps even more promising, use for PPH. Dr. Orentreich invented the hair transplant and pioneered dermabrasion, now widely used for the removal of skin imperfections. He reportedly has one of the largest dermatological practices in the world, but his real love is research into the aging process. In PPH, he suspects, he may have found a way to slow aging itself.

Dr. Orentreich was led into his research by the work of Alexis Carrel during World War I. Carrel had studied wound healing in an attempt to improve military medical care and noticed that the older the animal he studied, the slower its wounds healed. Later he discovered that cell cultures grew slower in blood plasma from old donors than in plasma from young ones. If something in old plasma interferes with growth, could it be the cause of aging? And could getting rid of it slow our deterioration with age? Orentreich decided to find out.

For nearly twenty years now, he has been plasmapheresing rats, dogs, and human beings. In one study of beagles, Orentreich spent over $1 million to keep forty dogs, giving them PPH regularly throughout their lives. The patients in his human studies are treated weekly. At least one has been in the study for more than a decade. In all the experiments, the results have been the same: plasmapheresis reduces blood cholesterol levels, triglycerides, and lipoproteins. By several objective measures, the patients seem healthier. People who have received PPH report that they feel better. And there have been no signs of harm. But do the people really age more slowly? Dr. Orentreich says it will take him several more years to be sure.

Foodless Feeding

Surgeon Stanley Dudrick has developed the first new way to eat since evolution created the mouth. Thanks to his work, hundreds who once would have starved are now leading normal lives. In the near future, it could be thousands.

Some twenty years ago, Dr. Dudrick lost three patients in a single weekend—after operations that had gone without a hitch. The trouble was that his patients couldn't eat in the normal fashion. They required intravenous feeding. A normal IV provides only a third of the calories needed during recovery. A stonger glucose solution destroys the blood's chemical balance. Eventually, the vein collapses, if infection does not set in first. And IV feeding supplies only sugar, not the fat, protein, vitamins, and minerals the body demands. Like thousands of others each year, Dudrick's patients died of malnutrition. The young surgeon, then an intern at the University of Pennsylvania Hospital, set out to spare other patients the same fate.

Try as Dudrick might, there was no way to get a strong enough nutrient solution through his patients' veins. It took him six years fo find the answer now known as Total Parenteral Nutrition (TPN). In desperation, he finally fed a powerful nutrient solution into the superior vena cava, the large vein that drains blood from the upper trunk and leads straight into the heart. Doctors at that time feared that a tube there might cause a heart attack, infection, or some other fatal complication. But Dudrick's first human patient, a baby with a nonfunctional intestinal tract, thrived—until the hospital committee overseeing her treatment decided to try weaning her back onto a normal diet. She died soon after.

A few patients on long-term TPN succumbed to obscure nutritional deficiencies while the physicians learned precisely what had to be in the solution. That problem has been largely solved. Other doctors lost patients when they tried TPN, but Dudrick was sure that sloppy technique was to blame, not the procedure itself. Dudrick has since been proven correct. The procedure is now safe when performed by experienced surgeons.

In the relatively few years since Dudrick developed it, TPN has proved so valuable that some doctors rank it with antibiotics and transplants as one of the most important medical advances of the century. A growing body of surgeons is learning to use it, and the number of patients saved each year is rising rapidly. TPN will soon cease to remain at medicine's frontier.

Electrohealing

In some of medicine's most promising research, scientists are talking to our cells in the cells' own language. When they tell an injury to heal, it doesn't ask questions. It heals. The language the cells speak is electricity. Given a message they can understand, broken bones mend, severed nerves unite, lost limbs regrow. It seems that even cancer cells obey the order to become normal again.

This bodily communications system was discovered by Dr. Robert O. Becker. Working at the Veterans Administration Hospital in Syracuse, New York, he was trying to solve an old mystery. Why is it that an injured salamander can grow back up to one-third of its body mass, while its close relative the frog cannot? Dr. Becker's search led him to the so-called injury current, a flow of electricity that occurs at the site of a wound. These currents were much stronger and more enduring in the salamander than in the frog. And when Becker lopped off a rat's leg and treated the wound with a current like the salamander's, the limb started to regenerate.

Becker spent the next five years trying to explain his discovery. He found that the current draws cells from the bone marrow toward the injury. On route, they lose their normal form, changing to something that resembles an embryonic cell. From this condition, they can evolve again into the specialized cells needed to rebuild lost tissue. This process builds a new limb in salamanders because their legs contain the large quantities of nerve tissue needed to produce a strong electrical current. It fails in frogs and men because our limbs do not. And this current flows constantly, Becker found, not in the momentary spikes of normal nerve signals. For these discoveries, he has reportedly been nominated for the Nobel Prize.

Another likely Nobel Prize recipient is Dr. Andrew Bassett of New York City's Columbia-Presbyterian Medical Center. An orthopedic surgeon, he uses electric currents to knit broken bones that standard treatments cannot heal. Instead of inserting electrodes into the break—as Becker has done with great success—Dr. Bassett positions electrical coils around the bone. The coils carry not steady current, but carefully sculpted pulses whose messages to the bone depend on their strength, shape, and timing. The currents they generate in the bone are incredibly weak, only a few billionths of an ampere. (A 100-watt light bulb uses just under one ampere of current.) Yet the cells act on them almost without fail. Some 85 percent of Bassett's patients heal under the coils' influence when all the conventional therapies have failed. Similar treatments have successfully healed cuts, burns, and bedsores.

Early in his career, Bassett experimented with cats, trying to heal a severed spinal cord by wrapping it in a sleeve of filter material. Hundreds of thousands of nerve fibers would grow across the gap in the cord. But by the time they got to the other side, the nerves there had already formed abnormal connections with neighboring cells, leaving no room for the arriving fibers. Tiny electric currents such as those that Bassett's coils induce can prevent the abnormal connections, giving the nerve a chance to reunite properly. In early studies, it looks as though a way has been found to heal paralysis caused by spinal injury.

The pulses used in Bassett's device were designed by Dr. Arthur Pilla, an electrochemist who worked for a battery manufacturer. He heard of the research at Columbia-Presbyterian and immediately joined the staff. Dr. Pilla also works with researchers around the country, helping them to design their experiments. In some of these studies, the results have been just as spectacular as those of Becker and Bassett.

At the University of Kentucky Medical School, Dr. Steven Smith has been working with healing coils designed by Pilla. In one study, they managed to get frogs to regrow lost limbs. In another, they speeded regeneration in salamanders by a factor of four—or stopped it completely depending on the kind of pulses they used. But in their most important studies, they found a pulse that kills cells from a lymphoma, a variety of cancer. Other pulses turned the lymphoma cells into fibroblasts, a cell found in connective tissue throughout the body.

The cancer-killing pulses seem to work in animals as well as in cell cultures. Working with Dr. William Riegelson of the Medical College of Virginia and Drs. Lary Norton and Laurie Tansman of New York's Mount Sinai School of Medicine, Pilla injected mice with deadly melanoma cells. The animals survived an average of only twenty-seven days when untreated and thirty-six days given standard drug therapy. But mice given the same drugs and treated with the coils lived an average of forty-three days. Pilla is cautious about his results. The pulses, he says, will probably have to be tailored for each patient and each type of tumor. But his work could be the start of a cancer cure.

There's more. Pilla suspects that his electromagnetic fields could change—sometimes improve—the workings of the brain. At the Los Angeles Veterans Administration Hospital, Dr. Ross Adey is proving it. Dr. Adey has used a radio to focus pulses on the heads of cats and monkeys while the animals were being trained. The pulses strengthened their memories and speeded learning markedly.

Just where this work will lead, it is still too early to guess. Bone healing is already in daily use. For burns and bedsores, electromagnetic pulses seem almost ready for the doctor's office. To be certain that pulses can cure cancer, heal damaged nerves, and hurry learning, more work is needed. So far, it seems as though the entire body can at last be healed of almost any injury. Not a single area of medicine will remain unchanged by this research.

Brain Mending

Even without pulsed instructions, some parts of the body can repair themselves. Bones usually regenerate when broken, the liver can heal all but the severest damage. One organ that could never restore itself is the brain—or so scientists have thought. Recently, they have discovered that the nerves of a damaged brain begin to grow, sending fine sprouts toward nearby cells to restore broken connections. Eventually, in some cases, the nerves can resume many of their normal functions.

Now physicians are learning to take advantage of this ability. In experiments that could someday repair damaged brain tissue, they are using foreign cells to replace lost functions. Such illnesses as Parkinson's disease, Huntington's chorea, senility, and the effects of stroke may someday be cured by the procedure.

At the National Institute of Mental Health, Dr. Richard Wyatt and his colleagues have been working with rats damaged in a part of the brain known as the substantia nigra. The injury deprives the rats of dopamine, a neurotransmitter, causing tremors like those of human Parkinson's disease. Dr. Wyatt found he could ease the palsy by planting the damaged area of the brain with nerve cells from the substantia nigra of fetal rats. Examined a year later, the cells had grown into the brain, linking with the nerves around them. And because the membranes around the brain hide it from the immune system, there was no sign of rejection.

In similar work, a team at the University of Rochester (New York) School of Medicine and Dentistry has managed to better the condition of rats with diabetes insipidus, a defect in which nerves of the hypothalamus fail to secrete the hormone vasopressin. Dr. Don Gash and his coworkers took hypothalamic nerves from fetal rats and installed them in diabetic adult rats. Again, the fetal brain cells grew into the adult organ and took over for the missing nerves. The success offers few direct benefits to human health. Diabetes insipidus is rare in human beings, occurring only after head injuries, and it can be treated with artificial vasopressin. But the work did confirm that brain grafts can help in human illnesses.

The trouble with these experiments is that they rely on cells from a fetus, and using cells from an aborted or miscarried human fetus brings up ethical questions that few would care to face. And some physicians believe that nerves from an aborted fetus would not do. They contend that the cells must come from a living embryo. Unless this problem can be resolved, there is little hope that human brain grafting will ever be adopted, no matter how promising it seems.

Fortunately, Dr. Barry Hoffer of the University of Colorado may already have found a way around it, at least for patients with Parkinson's disease. Certain cells in the adrenal gland grow from the same embryonic tissue as the brain's nerves, and they still produce the dopamine these patients need. Dr. Hoffer and Richard Wyatt have implanted these cells into the brains of rats and found that they grow into the recipient's brain and restore lost functions just as substantia nigra cells do. So it seems that human Parkinson's patients, though perhaps not others, may eventually supply their own brain implants.

In fact, the first step in this direction has already been taken. At Karolinska Hospital in Stockholm, Sweden, surgeons have already experimentally planted adrenal cells in the brain of a Parkinsons' victim. The implanted cells took hold and survived in the brain, but they did not render the patient symptom-free. Still, the operation shows that this kind of operation is possible.

3 EARTH: A CHANGING ECOLOGY

3 EARTH: A CHANGING ECOLOGY

Since our emergence as a species, the only home mankind has known is earth. We have transformed this abode from a place in which we were mere participants to one that we now overrun, abuse, and, to some extent, control. We live everywhere. We distort geographic features, change weather patterns, and leave our mark across the entire planet.

In the past, this dominance has been a sign of strength, a symbol of expanding human capability. Now, however, it has become a curse. We must finally begin to restrain ourselves or else face the consequences of an uninhabitable planet, one doomed through man's relentless exploitation of nature's most valuable resources. Over the next few decades, we will have to confront the damage we have wrought over several centuries. The question remains whether or not we can correct our past mistakes, or at least slow the pace of destruction.

Most Polluted Areas in the Twenty-first Century

As industry emerges in the Third World and the environmentally profligate ways of the developed nations persist, earth's ambience will continue to decline. The areas cited below hold certain dubious distinctions in the realm of environmental degradation.

The Most Polluted City

Mexico City may hold two distinctions by 2000. It will be the world's largest city and also its most polluted. Greater Mexico City's 1980 population of 15 million will reach 32 million in 2000, assuming that it grows at the current rate of 5 percent annually. At the same time, increased Mexican oil and natural gas production will contine to boost manufacturing, 80 percent of which will be centered in the Mexico City area. Although unemployment will still be severe, enough people will be able to afford automobiles so that there will be 6 million pollution-spewing cars in the metropolitan region.

Then, as now, Mexico City's air pollution will be aggravated by the city's high altitude and its location in the bowl of a mountain range. By 2000, the city will have to imitate today's Tokyo by dispersing oxygen supplies throughout the city to aid people overcome by persistent clouds of toxic gases. An oxygen-replenishing greenbelt of trees and grass, most likely planted around the city in the 1990s, could come too late to relieve the pollution problems.

Fleeing rural poverty, some 800,000 people will crowd into the city each year. They will find themselves packed into thousands of expanding slum pockets. The lack of running water and proper sanitation could create sewage problems that would make parts of twenty-first century Mexico City look like one of the festering cities of medieval Europe.

The World's Unhealthiest Environment

Within the next few years, the city with the most intense pollution problems, however, may well be Cubatao, located in Brazil's coastal lowlands. Since 1980, the city has been called "the valley of death," because the mayor refuses to reside there, and a contingent of state workers abandoned the city when the government refused to supply them with gas masks.

One of the world's largest petrochemical centers, Cubatao lies on a coastal lowland crossed by four stagnant rivers. The toxic gases produced by the chemical plants are trapped in the moist air by a range of hills, and these fumes hover over the city, generating an incredible, deadly pool of pollution.

Will the city ever be cleaned up? It seems unlikely. Brazil has fueled its growth by relentless exploitation of natural resources. Foreign manufacturers have invested in Brazil precisely because they are able to avoid the troublesome safety and health measures required in more developed countries. Saddled with an immense debt, Brazil is desperate for foreign money and expertise.

The individual statistics of such a scenario are frightfully alarming. Tens of thousands of residents could suffer lung and other pollution-caused ailments. Of every thousand babies born, eighty could be dead at birth, while another eighty could die within a week after birth. Most of these infant victims will probably be deformed. A conservative estimate is that pollution in Cubatao will be twice as bad in 2000 as it is today.

The Most Deteriorated Environment

The Caribbean Sea will suffer the worst environmental devastation of the next century. It will be transformed from a seemingly pristine paradise into an ecological sewer within a few decades. The U.N. Environmental Programme has already described the Caribbean as one of the most polluted and endangered areas in the world. The Sea is a natural trap for pollutants that are swept in from as far away as Venezuela and Brazil, contained by ridges and deep basins that prevent natural flow to the open sea. Runoff from Mexican and American croplands combine with untreated sewage from Havana and other island cities to compound the problem and choke the marine environment.

As the more economically sound islands, such as Jamaica and Cuba, begin to develop large-scale industry, they could well increase the pollution. Even the less stable island nations may damage the environment through an increase in tourism that will bring added auto emissions and construction.

Haiti faces a unique fate. By 1980, the lack of affordable fuel resources on the poverty-wracked island had forced inhabitants to chop down most of the island's trees for fuel. Many experts estimate that by the late 1980s, Haiti will be virtually barren of trees, with a devastating erosion certain to follow.

The World's Worst Noise Pollution

The city with the world's worst noise pollution by 2000 will be Cairo. Some 16,300,000 people will then live in this Egyptian city, and due to government industrialization programs, many of the people will own cars.

Cairo drivers have long been infamous for their predisposition toward horn honking. They seem to honk at anything that moves, including people on the sidewalks or other objects that appear in no imminent danger of being struck. If this habit continues as traffic increases, the din of the traffic, added to the city's industrial clamor and the perennial sound of construction, could make Cairo by far the noisiest city on earth.

Other Polluted Cities in the Developed World

Los Angeles, for all its reputation as the city of endless sunshine, stands to become another of the most polluted cities by the century's close. Years of fighting smog have helped little. In fact, by 1978, Los Angeles's smog had actually increased despite a decade of anti-pollution measures. By 2000, nearly 16 million people will live in the Los Angeles metropolitan area, and experts maintain that most of them will still be dependent upon their automobiles.

The unique environmental danger in Los Angeles derives from auto pollutants that react with the area's high temperatures and abundant sunlight. The smog that results could make the Los Angeles environment unhealthy for more than 200 days a year throughout the 1980s. By 2000, the environment may be a health hazard virtually every day. The relaxation of environmental safeguards in the early 1980s will undoubtedly contribute to this development.

With 26 million residents by the turn of the century, Tokyo will not lag far behind. Pollution in Tokyo will be so severe by the next century that many citizens will need to wear gauze masks in public. Tokyo's problem stems from the reluctance of local officials to crack down on auto pollution in Japan's highly industrialized society.

The Coming
Quakes

The earth never ceases its inexorable shifting. At a stately, ageless pace, continents move, islands appear, and mountains vanish.

The pace of earth's change is too slow for us to see or feel. We only realize it through cataclysmic disaster. Earthquakes, volcanoes, and floods are all part of the constant process of transformation. Such natural disasters reveal only a fraction of the forces involved, yet that fraction is powerful enough to terrify and awe us all. The most feared catastrophes are earthquakes. Here are the most likely earthquake sites for the next fifty years.

California

It is inevitable that California eventually will be rocked by a massive earthquake, but the state will not slide into the ocean. So much attention has been devoted to this impending quake, that sometimes such predictions are taken as jokes. Anyone who lives through such a quake will not laugh, even if the aftermath may not be as dire as some have predicted.

In January of 1979, scientists detected an ominous shift in the San Andreas Fault—the biggest of several faults running the length of California. Previously, scientists had believed that the fault, with Los Angeles on one side and the Mojave Desert on the other, was being compressed. This impression reassured them, because earthquakes occur when two formations of rock slip up and down against each other along a fault. It seemed to scientists that with the earth's strata jamming against one another, like two pieces of wood held tightly in a vise, there appeared little chance of an earthquake.

Then, two different teams of scientists discovered that the fault had widened by almost eight inches. Slight as this seemed, it indicated that the vise was loosening and could allow the strata to slip, causing a catastrophe. Californians have had enough warning so that any resulting damage should be contained. Predictions about when the California quake will come vary widely, but many geologists believe it will strike within the next twenty years.

The Missouri Valley

The residents of the area where Missouri, Arkansas, Kentucky, and Tennessee meet along the Mississippi River may not be so fortunate. New Madrid may catch them more unaware.

Named after a small town in Missouri, the New Madrid Earthquake that rocked the Mississippi Valley in the 1830s was one of the most violent quakes to strike North America in the last several centuries. But because the area was still sparsely settled, the quake left no great impression on history. Only geologists made note. However, seismologist Otto Nuttli recently observed a series of small earthquakes in the area, and said, "Everything points to something big happening in New Madrid." The big tremor may indeed return.

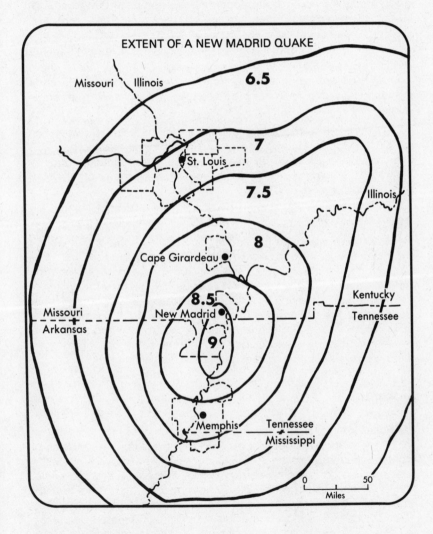

EXTENT OF A NEW MADRID QUAKE

But residents remain unconcerned. The mayor of New Madrid, Jimmy Cravens, told a reporter, "All of us who grew up around here have felt earthquakes. It makes good coffee-shop conversation. That's about all."

Still, the Midwest Research Institute in Kansas City has estimated that an earthquake the size of the first New Madrid quake, if it hit at night, would kill nearly 300 people, injure perhaps 27,000 more, and cause $3.2 billion in damages.

That earthquake, geologists believe, is inevitable and could prove more destructive than the Great California Earthquake of 1906, because most of the people in the Missouri Valley area remain totally unprepared. In an area that stretches from northern Mississippi to St. Louis, only the city of Memphis has made contingency plans for an eventual quake.

The effects of a major quake in this region may linger longer than those in California. Much of the area is economically stagnant or in a state of decline. St. Louis, for example, suffers from industrial atrophy and high unemployment. The same holds true for many other towns and cities in the area.

Iran

The oil-rich deserts of the Persian Gulf sit along one of the world's most active faults. Iran has been jolted by severe quakes several times since World War II. Early in the 1980s, if such a pattern holds, Iran may be shaken by its most severe earthquake yet. While the physical toll of the quake will be high, its political ramifications could be far more devastating. The earthquake may even shatter the autocratic Islamic government of the Ayatollahs, bringing chaos to Iran and possibly to the entire region. This earthquake could prove to be one of the most internationally significant natural disasters of the century.

Krakatoa

Nature never forgets. The most startling quake of the years ahead will be the global shudder that accompanies the sudden re-eruption of Krakatoa, an island off the coast of Indonesia. On August 27, 1883, the huge volcano on Krakatoa destroyed itself in the largest single explosion ever seen on earth. The planet was banded by dust for months afterward, bringing on one of the coldest winters in modern times. The mountain itself disappeared and now rests some 300 meters below the sea. However, geologists fear that even this tiny remnant of the island will be obliterated when the submerged volcano erupts once again at about the turn of the century, and we may face frigid years once again.

The Spreading Deserts

As the twenty-first century approaches, deserts will continue their accelerating spread across the face of earth, claiming up to one-third of the world's present agricultural land by 2000. Human greed and ignorance have contributed to the growth of deserts at an alarming pace. Largely through erosion and destructive farming methods, twenty-three square miles of arable land are engulfed by deserts every day. Each year, an area equal in size to Massachusetts becomes wasteland.

Desertification is a process as old as Western civilization. Some 8,000 years ago, the land around the Tigris and Euphrates rivers—the Fertile Crescent—was rich in grassland and forest. As shepherds built the first great cities, however, they cut down trees and built irrigation canals. With the remaining grass devoured by growing herds, the soil gradually eroded. Silt clogged the irrigation canals. Wars and upheavals wrecked the complex society needed to keep the land green. Today, the Fertile Crescent, covering much of Iraq, is barren.

Similar changes have happened almost everywhere man has been careless with the soil. When Carthage, for example, was a great empire, North Africa was a breadbasket of the world. That land is now the Sahara Desert. Such deterioration continues into modern times. Even in the United States, careless farming, soil erosion, and drought created the Dust Bowl of the 1930s.

Unless major changes are finally made in the way we treat our land, desert will eventually consume most of the arable land in twenty-four nations in Africa and Asia, many of them already poverty-stricken. Desert could claim significant land masses in at least twenty-three other countries, including Spain, South Africa, the Soviet Union, India, Australia, Chile, and Bolivia.

The major battlegrounds in the struggle between mankind and the encroaching wasteland will be:

Sahel in North Africa

The worst desertification is taking place in the Sahel, a great dry plain stretching 2,000 miles from Senegal to Chad. In the 1950s, French colonial authorities sank wells, inoculated livestock, built irrigation systems and mechanized farming. Their efforts back-fired. Free from disease, the herds grew and devoured the grass that protected the soil. The irrigation and mechanization also helped destroy the topsoil. A five-year drought that began in 1969 brought a famine that killed 100,000 people and greatly sped the Sahara's march to the south.

In 1950, Nouakchott, a city in Mauritania, was many days by foot from the Sahara. In 1980, it was *in* the Sahara. In 1955, acacia trees, which need only a few inches of rain a year, were common around Khartoum, the capital of the Sudan. By 1981, the nearest acacia tree was forty miles south of the city.

By 2000, the Sahara will march another forty miles south into Mauritania, Mali, Niger, Chad, and the Sudan. Most of western Africa will suffer from the drought and the withering of grassland and farmland that precede the Sahel.

Nile Basin in Egypt

The technological marvel of the Aswan Dam, completed in 1971 to block the Nile in southern Egypt and create power, has upset the river's age-old pattern of annual flooding. In recent years, the Nile's flood has been induced by man, and has been far less effective than nature's method. The annual silting of the Nile Valley during the floods was all that prevented this area from joining the surrounding desert. Now, some ecologists fear, the Nile may prove unable to hold off the encroaching sand. If the Nile Valley falls, desert will claim an unbroken stretch from the western tip of Africa, through the Sinai, and up the curve of the Mediterranean.

Dust Bowl in the Central United States

Even the United States will lose land to the desert. A recent Bureau of Land Management survey reported that 50 million acres of American drylands were in "poor" or "bad" condition. States like Kansas, Oklahoma, and Colorado are most likely to suffer. With American topsoil eroding at an average rate of nine to twelve tons per acre a year, some of this land will certainly be claimed by the desert.

Southwest Plains in the United States

The desert will reclaim lands once made fertile by irrigation. As predicted by Huey D. Johnson, head of California's resources agency, parts of the San Joaquin Valley may follow the same fate as the Fertile Crescent. Parts of Arizona, New Mexico, and Texas will also turn to desert when over-grazing, over-planting, and over-irrigation erode the topsoil and leave the land white with residues from fertilizers and the muck of dried up rivers.

Amazon Valley in Brazil

In 1980, in the Amazon River Basin, at least 1 million trees were felled by man each day. Every year, 62,000 square miles of forest will disappear. Giant tractors, with hundred-yard chains stretched between them, will create wide swaths of land through the jungle. To clear land, fires are sometimes set so large they can be seen in satellite photos. At this rate, the Amazon forests may be disappearing by 2000 at a frightful pace.

With the jungle cover gone, the thin layer of soil will quickly wash away. Most of the soil will turn into laterite, a hard-packed crust useless for farming. Laterite will not even absorb rainfall, so the sporadic deluges of water will run off and carry away surrounding soil. Since half of Amazonia's rain was generated by water evaporating from the jungle, the jungle itself will disappear. The Amazon river basin will one day be a drought-ridden, barren wasteland.

The Greenhouse Disaster

Many scientists believe that a disastrous warming of earth's atmosphere that could transform the planet is already occurring. This predicted "greenhouse disaster" would change the world into a murky place where swamps and rain forests alternate with sullen deserts. Land mass would diminish, seasons would be altered, and a vastly different climate would emerge.

The causes are to be found in one simple chemical formula: carbon dioxide, CO_2. Every year about 12 million pounds of man-made carbon particles are poured into the air by factories and cars, where they combine with oxygen into carbon dioxide. The ocean and the air can absorb some of the particles without harm, but apparently not all. Since the Industrial Revolution in the nineteenth century, the amount of carbon dioxide in the air has increased by about 10 percent; increases have been noted even in remote areas of Hawaii. Many scientists believe that the amount of carbon dioxide in the air will double in the next fifty to seventy years.

Consequences of a Greenhouse Disaster

As carbon dioxide builds up, the atmosphere, like the glass roof of a greenhouse, holds in an increasing amount of heat. This raises the temperature gradually and flattens out the natural variations in earth's climate. Some scientists estimate that the greenhouse effect could raise earth temperatures by as much as 3.3 degrees Celsius, far more than the shifts that began or ended the Ice Age. The consequences of such a change include:

• More rain in some regions. One research team states that a temperature shift of less than one degree would vastly increase rain in the arid Middle East, Canada, the coastal United States, India, and China.

• Less rain in others. At the same time, a one degree temperature shift would decrease rainfall in Europe, most of the Soviet Union, North Africa, and midwestern America. The reason is that an altered temperature would shift wind patterns, changing the locations where sufficient moisture for rainfall would most often build up. World desertification would now slow, but its impact would shift to new regions.

• Polar ice cap melting. An increase in global mean temperature of two to three degrees Celsius could melt parts of the polar ice, raising ocean levels by fifteen to twenty-five feet. Shorelines and the banks of inland waterways would be flooded. Most of the world's great cities, which lie near water, would be flooded. Manhattan, built on an island, would be especially vulnerable.

• Economic chaos. Increased rain could spur Canadian wheat production and expand grazing lands in Mongolia. On the other hand, it might create more severe monsoons in India and devastating erosion in the Middle East. Decreased rainfall would bring crop failures to Russia and vastly decrease food production in America's breadbasket. In short, the climatic changes would cause economic confusion and political turmoil.

The Florida Scenario

Can it happen? In 1971, Stacey Hicks of the National Oceanographic Survey found that the rise in world ocean levels had jumped from a rate of one foot to three feet per century. That may not sound like much, but experts warn that the greenhouse effect might intensify the increase still more over the next decades.

As noted by Stephen Schneider of the National Center for Atmospheric Research, the flooding of the world's shorelines is literally too vast and too incredible a disaster for human beings to grasp easily. Yet, the center has prepared a scenario that predicts what would happen to Florida if the greenhouse effect did melt the polar ice. The Center predicts that the flood will occur gradually. Schneider will not attach specific years to his predictions, but over the next twenty-five to fifty years, here is what could happen to Florida as the waters rise.

• Beaches become steadily smaller. Within a decade of the disaster's emergence, beaches become thin strips of virtually unusable, wave-battered sand.

• Vacation homes are engulfed by floods. Banner headlines tell the story of the destruction of posh retreats along the shore. Tourism revenues evaporate. Insurance becomes impossible to obtain for shore residences.

• Counter-measures, such as erosion-resistant landscaping and sea wall construction are undertaken, but the environmental shift is inexorable. Slowly, the barrier islands along Florida's coast shrink. Within twenty years, Key West is uninhabitable and Miami Beach is facing severe ecological damage.

APPROXIMATE AREAS IN FLORIDA FLOODED
BY A 15—25 FOOT (4.6—7.6 METERS) RISE IN MEAN SEA LEVEL

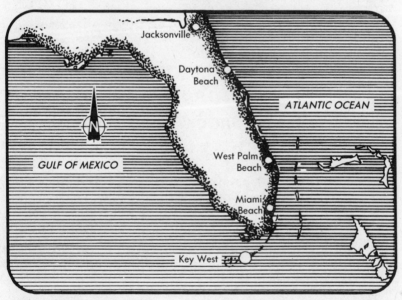

Map prepared by S.H. Schneider and R. Chen at the National Center for Atmospheric Research. It shows the approximate areas in Florida that would be flooded by a 15—25 foot rise in mean sea level. Such a flooding is possible, perhaps as soon as several decades from now. If the predicted carbon dioxide-induced climatic warming occurs, it could warm the polar regions enough to cause the West Antarctic ice sheet to break up. In that event, about half the state's population and some $70 billion in real property would be displaced.

• After about thirty years, the entire southern tip of the state, including all of the Miami/Ft. Lauderdale metroplex, lies underwater. Every city along the coast—Ft. Myers, Tampa, Daytona Beach—will be deluged.

• As the oceans crest, one-third of the state lies beneath the sea; more than half the population has been displaced. Property worth $72 billion (in 1972 dollars) has vanished. From the air, only the tips of the "white refrigerator" beachfront motels of Miami Beach now mark its location in the triumphant water.

• Florida's devastation won't stand alone, of course. With Boston, New York, Philadelphia, Washington, Houston, Los Angeles, San Francisco, and Seattle flooded, there will be little outside aid for the devastated citrus state. Many countries will be likewise affected.

This is only a scenario, of course. No one knows if the greenhouse effect will cause such a catastrophe. But as Schneider says, the potential damage is so immense that it might be well worth the effort to cleanse the atmosphere of carbon dioxide before such a disaster befalls us.

Places That May
Be Underwater
by 2100

One of the most powerful forces for change on earth is water, but few of us think of the oceans and rivers as engines for reshaping the world. Yet, all the continents are merely islands dotting the vast waters that cover most of the earth. Over the next century, water will change the shapes of many land surfaces. In 2100, we may have to swim or sail to many places to which we can drive today.

Barrier Islands

America's eastern and Gulf coasts are protected by an uneven picket chain of thin, sandy islands. From Fire Island, New York to Padre Island, Texas, these slivers of land buffer the shoreline from the effects of winds and water, slowing erosion and providing a nursery for helpful plant life. However, barrier islands are never permanent. They shift several feet per year and can vanish entirely during a violent storm. The map of America's coast today looks far different from one drawn in colonial times.

These changes would not be a problem were it not for the fact that many barrier islands have become tourist playgrounds. Atlantic City, Cape Cod, Miami Beach, Key West, and Hilton Head in South Carolina are all such examples.

Within the next fifty years, a massive hurricane will inevitably blast across at least one of these places, creating an incredible disaster. The land will shift radically, buildings will topple, people will be trapped, and hundreds—even thousands—of lives will be lost.

We always think that land is solid and eternal. But the forces of nature ultimately dictate what will remain, and what will disappear.

Southeastern Texas

Houston and Galveston lie at or near sea level. Both are industrial cities that use immense quantities of water. These two factors will combine to put large parts of both cities underwater within fifty years if civil leaders are not careful. Simply stated, southeastern Texas is sinking because it is pulling too much water out of the deep underground. The cavities created by depleted water supplies pull surface land masses downward. Over the past fifty years, some 1,300 square miles of coastal land have subsided by more than a foot. Houston suburbs already sustain major flooding damage with every severe storm. We may have to view Galveston someday through glass-bottom boats.

Venice

Venice is one of the world's likeliest places to sink. The historic Italian city has struggled in the past few years to reverse this trend and remove the pollution that now plagues this once-beautiful resort. Technologically sophisticated methods, such as the pumping of inert gases into crucial supports to create pressure, have been used to keep the city afloat. But a worldwide rise in ocean levels, estimated at one to three feet per century, may finally doom Venice by the middle of the next century. As global water levels rise, Venetians may find it impossible to keep their city afloat. At the least, storm damage and the erosion of the city's base will vastly increase in the future.

Bangkok

Bangkok parallels Venice in many respects. Once a city of canals, it is no longer. The waterways have been filled in for roads and construction sites, destroying the natural drainage of Bangkok's marshy land. The problem has been compounded by the unrestrained pumping of drinking water. The capital of Thailand has sunk by as much as eight to ten centimeters a year in some places. Scientists warn that to halt the process the residents of Bangkok must learn to rely on surface water. But so far, the city has not heeded the warnings. As Cambodia's Angkor was lost to the jungle centuries ago, parts of Bangkok may be lost to the ocean by 2000.

Winners and Losers in the Animal World

As industry and spreading population change the environment of earth, animals struggle to survive. Over the next 50 to 100 years, hundreds of common species will vanish forever, while others will flourish in the harsher world of the future. And, over the long course of time, evolution will run its inevitable course, creating new beasts to conquer a world millions of years hence, when mankind may be as much a memory as dinosaurs are today.

Animals Likely to Vanish Within Fifty Years

Pollution, poaching, man's encroachment on wildlife habitats, and ecological shifts will destroy five animal species that have played important roles in the human imagination.

Grizzly Bear. Grizzlies will vanish partly because they have become a threat to the stream of vacationers who have inundated the American wilderness. Since the 1970s, grizzly bears have made a number of unprovoked attacks on campers in Glacier National Park. Previously, the bears stayed out of people's way, but scientists have speculated that with more and more campers and hikers invading the wilderness, the grizzly bear may have lost its fear of humans. Campers will continue to flock to state and national parks in record numbers, while public sympathy for man-attacking grizzlies will diminish. A thousand or so remain today, but under continued human assault, the grizzly bear may well join the ranks of other animals unable to adapt to man's presence.

African Elephant. Poaching may make efforts to save the African elephant futile. Outside of game preserves, these intelligent animals are often slaughtered casually by farmers who fear that their crops will be trampled. Even in the game parks, high prices for ivory have lured poachers. The worst danger, however, may be over-grazing, especially in the Tsavo game park in Kenya. If elephants continue to deplete the grass that is their food supply, a famine could devastate the herds. A resulting decline in reproduction would ensure that the African elephant would become extinct.

Sperm Whale. The sperm whale may also vanish. The whale population as a whole will decrease by 30,000 in each year of the 1980s. Half of these will be sperm whales, most of whom are threatened because of demand for sperm oil as a specialized industrial lubricant. Even the discovery that oil processed from the jojoba plant can replace sperm oil may not be enough to save the sperm whale from extinction.

Gorilla. The gorilla is another species that may be unable to survive in a land changed to suit man. The destruction of its native habitat by African industry and agriculture has diminished the number of gorillas. Worse, the gorilla, an intelligent creature, seems unable to adapt to the urbanization of Africa, much less to captivity. The last gorilla may well die in a zoo during the twenty-first century.

Whooping Crane. The survival of the whooping crane seems unlikely. The bird can survive only in a special environment of shallow water and grassy marsh. While the crane flourished in prehistoric days, little more than 1,500 were left by the time the Pilgrims landed in the seventeenth century. The draining of marshes and the predatory ways of hunters have since depleted the species. By 1937, no more than 18 wild birds remained. Due to strong preservation efforts, 115 of those wild birds were alive in 1979.

It won't take much, however, to make them succumb. Past attempts to encroach upon the birds' sanctuaries in Arkansas and Saskatchewan by opening the land to private development have narrowly been averted, and those efforts continue today. The birds are exposed to various dangers all along their migratory route, and many of the crucial landing spots on the route are threatened. In 1975, for instance, a flock of whooping cranes nearly landed in a marsh plagued by an outbreak of fowl cholera. Only the desperate attempts of the U.S. Fish and Wildlife Service succeeded in scaring off the birds before they could land. But such an outbreak in the future is always possible.

Animals Likely to Prosper Over the Next Fifty Years

While some animals disappear in the cloud of human pollution, others thrive on adversity. Those creatures who survive by scavenging and those fortunate enough to live in the few places humans still avoid, may flourish in the decades ahead.

Coyote. The coyote is an example of an animal so adaptable and plentiful that its kind will flourish in the twenty-first century. Once found only on the Great Plains, the coyote had spread by 1925 from Alaska to Central America, and from Hudson Bay to the East Coast and the Gulf Coast. News reports in 1981 even told of frequent sightings of the animal in outlying suburbs in California and the Southwest. The coyote will prosper by producing many offspring, by staying out of man's way, and by eluding man's efforts to destroy it. The animal will roam over such a wide area that sporadic anti-coyote efforts will not threaten the species.

Baboon. Millions of years ago, baboons made the transition from forest to grassland, just like their human cousins. In the next century, the baboon will adapt once again, this time to the urbanization of Africa. Smart and aggressive, baboons will be able to modify their habits and social structure to find food in settled areas—often by raiding farms—and will cannily defy attempts by man to exterminate them.

Black Bear. The black bear, in contrast to the grizzly, will make a quiet comeback. When marginal, unproductive farmland in New England and Appalachia is abandoned, forests will return, providing new food and shelter for the black bear. Relatively unaggressive and willing to eat anything, the black bear will flourish in the Smokies, the White Mountains, and all along the fringe wilderness of the East Coast.

Penguin. Some animals may even benefit from the slaughter of other species. The penguin, for instance, will flourish because of the killing of the whales, which compete with it for food supplies. As the whale population declines, penguins—whose habitats are far from the human path—will take advantage of the abundant Arctic Ocean environment to become the dominant species on the poles.

Seagull. Wherever you find garbage, you find seagulls. They feast on the flotsam of coasts and ocean vessels. In a perverse form of symbiosis, pollution benefits seagulls. The dirtier the ocean and the more crowded the coastal areas, the more these birds will have to eat. Seagulls will be so successful in the decades ahead they could become an even more serious nuisance on beaches and around coastal airports.

Cockroach. The ultimate survivor, it hides superbly under the nose of man and lives on the detritus of other species. The cockroach is a masterpiece of natural engineering, an unmatched surviving machine—tough on the exterior, simple and hardy on the inside, and infinitely adaptable. Some scientists even believe cockroaches may thrive in the radioactive environment following nuclear war. Whatever the future brings, it will be good news for the already innumerable cockroaches. One rule of thumb says that for every urban human there are 100 cockroaches; that number can only go up.

Fanciful Animals of the Future

Evolution is a constant, but very slow process. Over the next 50 or 100 years, many animal species will become extinct, while others may be altered by the work of genetic engineers. The natural evolutionary course of animals is much harder to observe, as many changes will not take hold for millions of years.

British writer and paleontology expert, Dougal Dixon, has predicted the kinds of creatures that may inhabit the earth 50 million years from now. He foresees a demise of carnivorous creatures, including the eventual extinction of man. Those animals who have become primarily dependent upon man, like the horse and cow, also face similar extinction. But other species will evolve, mutate, and continue to roam the planet. Based on Dixon's research in biology, botany, and zoology in his book *After Man*, here is a sampling of his new animal species.

Lutie (*Microlagus mussops*). The lutie is a direct descendant of the rabbit species, but has adapted many of the characteristics of small rodents, such as voles and mice, in order to survive. Its large, cylindrical ears and bushy tail suggest the rabbit ancestry, but its thin, rodentlike body and finely shaped claws are similar to those of a rat. These new features enable the lutie to hide in crevices, tree roots, or underground holes during the day. It feeds almost always at night and hunts in the woodlands, where conditions are most favorable for its survival.

Purrip Bat (*Caecopterus*). The bat appears more resistant to evolutionary pressure than virtually any other species. The bat retains its basic shape and nocturnal lifestyle, despite millions of years of evolutionary change. The purrip bat's only added feature is a set of elongated, almost Mickey Mouse-like ears, which extend vertically from the front of the face. The ears, almost five times the actual length of the entire face, are equipped with a broader hearing frequency, unlike those of its ancient ancestors which could only respond to higher-pitched cues. This enhanced auditory system enables the purrip bat to pick up sounds at many frequencies from its terrain, making the bat both a more effective predator and defender. The purrip bat is named for the unusual noises that it emits.

Oakleaf Toad (*Grima frondiforme*). The oakleaf toad presents an example of evolution related to dietary habits. Its ancestors relied exclusively on insects for food, but having developed over the eons a highly maneuverable tongue and camouflaged body, the toad has become an eater of meat. It derives its name from the external covering on its back, a body growth which creates the appearance of a fallen fern or oak leaf. The oakleaf toad positions itself in wooded areas and waits for small animals to come by. It uses its wormlike tongue and powerful jaws to ensnare and swallow the hapless animal.

In winter, the toad's back turns emerald green, making it highly visible to its chief predator, the rat. The balance of nature therefore works to insure that the population of the oakleaf toad will not grow out of control.

Vortex (*Balenornis vivipera*). The vortex is the largest animal that survives on the planet, and it flourishes in large numbers in the oceans. Its massive fins, powerful tail, long body, and neckless head suggest the extinct whale species, but the vortex is a descendant of the ancient penguin family.

While most penguin breeds were dying out, one species managed to survive by incubating its eggs in the mother's body and hatching its young in the ocean itself. This prevented the eggs of newborn penguins from being killed by landbound predators. Not only has the vortex become completely aquatic, but its evolutionary success has been duplicated by other birds.

The vortex does not possess mammary glands, so that its young are forced to fend for themselves at birth. Unlike a reptile, however, the vortex is warm-blooded. The vortex's overdeveloped beak is used to draw in plankton.

4 SPACE: THE NEW FRONTIER

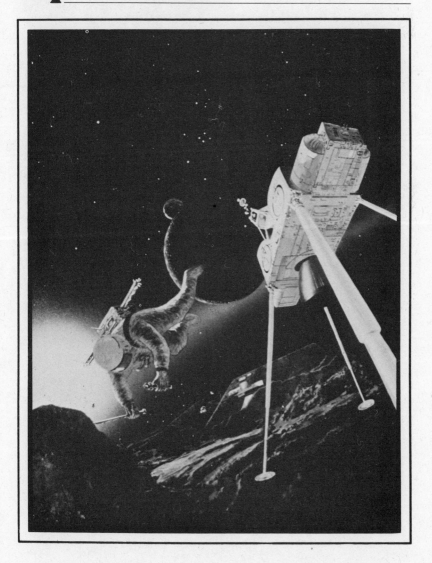

4 SPACE: THE NEW FRONTIER

As we try to patch up our traditional earthly home, a new potential home will be appearing in the future—in space. The next fifty years present challenging strides for space development. Man will, with certainty, begin to manufacture, build, defend and live in space. Our capabilities to enter and conquer strange and alien environments will once again become a virtue. We may one day find it more productive to develop space rather than preserve earth.

If so, our space-dwelling grandchildren may know earth only as the big, blue marble that floats in the darkness—somewhere out there.

Space Missions through 2000

The 1960s were space travel's decade of infancy. The 1970s were its adolescence. The 1980s and 1990s will be the years of its emerging maturity and broadening impact on life. The number of space missions from around the world will increase dramatically over the next twenty years as the use of satellites expands enormously. Many more nations will join the Space Age.

At the center of space development over the next two decades will surely be the U.S. space shuttle. However, the development of other projects will also flourish. Here is a country by country review of space missions, other than those of the shuttle, planned for the next decade and beyond.

Australia

In 1985 or 1986, the Australians plan to launch their own domestic satellite communications system, using multi-purpose satellites and 1.5 meter diameter television relay stations. Australia can cover its vast terrain more efficiently from space than through any ground-based system.

Austria

This tiny nation is currently studying the possibility of joining the Swiss in a project to place its national broadcasting system in space. Target date: 1986.

Brazil

This active South American country has undertaken the "Complete Brazilian Space Mission," a $1 billion program with 1,000 scientists and technicians working to launch four Brazilian satellites by 1993. In 1983, Brazil hopes to launch its Probe 4 rocket, which will rise 600 miles above earth's surface. A satellite planned for 1988 will help with Brazil's weather-forecasting. The nation's first communications satellite, *Brazilsat*, will also head spaceward during the 1980s. For Brazil, space is an important component in the quest for world recognition as a major power.

Canada

Part of Canada's domestic satellite communications system, the *Anik B*, is already in place. *Anik C*, the second stage of a system designed to bring modern communications to the most remote corners of this vast commonwealth, should head spaceward soon. Space development will be a mark of Canadian social and economic independence, as well as a method for tying together communications in a far-flung country with recurrent weather problems.

European Space Agency

In 1983, the European Space Agency, with American help, launched *IRAS*, the Infrared Astronomical Satellite. This $21 million project is designed to study infrared wavelengths without interference from earth's atmosphere. The Europeans will also join the Americans in the giant space telescope project (see United States, page 130).

When Halley's comet first appears in late 1985, ESA plans to send *Giotto*, a Halley's comet intercept-satellite aloft on its Ariane rocket. *Giotto* will measure the comet's composition and attempt to record images of its solid core.

Finally, in 1987, ESA will launch *Hipparcos*, the High-Precision Parallax-Correcting Satellite, which will measure the positions and motions of some 10,000 stars with greater accuracy than ever before. It will make possible the most complete and accurate star map in history and should help scientists understand quasars and other phenomena of the universe.

France

On its own, France intends to launch the *TDF-1* television satellite during 1985. At about the same time, the French will join the Soviets for a second round of Venera missions to study the surface and atmosphere of Venus.

One of the Venera ships will leave Venus to intercept Halley's comet in 1986, where it will film this celestial visitor using a French camera.

Germany

Using a design virtually the same as France's, Germany's *TV-Sat* will be launched in late 1984 or early 1985.

India

The Indians hope to launch *Insat 1*, a pair of domestic communications and information satellites by mid-decade.

Italy

Italy will take its television stations into space during 1985 when it launches *L-Sat*, its domestic video satellite.

Japan

Somewhere in the first half of the 1980s, probably in 1984, the Japanese will launch *BS-2*, a pair of spacecraft that will provide broadcasting direct from space into individual homes.

Luxembourg

Even tiny Luxembourg is considering heading into space, contemplating a 1985 launch date for its *Luxsat*, a direct-to-home space broadcasting satellite.

Scandinavia

A troubled project but still possible, *Nordsat* is a joint venture of the Scandinavian countries and should head spaceward in 1986. It will provide direct satellite-to-home communications for Scandinavian countries, assuming that socialist politics and lack of funds do not handicap the mission.

Sweden

On their own, the Swedes are considering sending up a satellite for testing communications via space as a first step toward establishing a full satellite communications network.

Switzerland

On its own, or with Austria, the mountain nation plans to launch a direct-to-home broadcasting satellite in the mid-1980s. Such a system could enable the Swiss to communicate more effectively across obtrusive mountains.

United Kingdom

In Britain, an officially sponsored government program for developing direct-to-home satellite broadcasting is competing with a similar private plan. SBC, or Satellite Broadcasting, is a government plan that aims to get a direct broadcast satellite aloft by 1986 or 1987. STV, or Satellite Television, is the private program, which also has a target date of 1986.

United States

A number of companies are vying to become involved in America's direct satellite-to-home broadcasting program.

Comsat/STC has already applied to develop pay television for American satellite broadcasting by 1985. DBS Corporation has proposed to the Federal Communications Commission a plan for leasing access to the world's most powerful direct-satellite broadcasting system, while Hubbard Broadcasting has suggested a DBS network for TV stations. RCA as well has offered itself as a potential operator of a direct satellite broadcast system. Such satellite operations should be underway by 1986.

In addition to its communications work, America's space effort will emphasize international cooperation and the study of distant objects. NASA is cooperating with Europe on *IRAS* (see European Space Agency, page 128).

In 1984, NASA hopes to use the shuttle as a launching pad for *Galileo*, a probe designed to fly deep into Jupiter's atmosphere. The craft will penetrate to a layer where pressure is ten times that of earth and will circle the giant planet for some twenty months.

Later in the decade, about 1985, the shuttle will carry aloft a giant space telescope that will be monitored jointly by the Americans and Europeans.

Next will come a United States solo effort, the *VOIR*, or the Venus Orbiting Imaging Radar spacecraft. Here, too, the shuttle will serve as a launchpad for the probe, which will penetrate Venus's thick cloud cover and send back pictures of its shrouded surface. The photographs should be able to define details as small as 150 meters in diameter.

In mid-1986, with some luck the United States will again become involved in an old mission, the *Voyager II*. At that time, the solar system probe will come into range of Uranus. If all systems are still functioning, the spacecraft will beam back the most detailed pictures ever recorded of the distant planet.

The United States military space program will also be active over the next decade. *DCS III*, currently being built, is a military communications satellite to be used in the late 1980s. The satellite will be shielded from nuclear radiation and will be electronically guarded against jamming. *P80-1*, an Air Force satellite, will communicate with earth using lasers instead of electromagnetic waves. In 1984, when the U.S. Air Force launches P80-1, it will also activate project Teal Ruby, a mission designed to send some 150,000 no-blink, infrared detectors into space to protect the United States from sneak missile launchings. If this operation succeeds, another satellite, the *HALO* (High Altitude Large Optics) will then carry 10 million detectors into orbit.

Military position control will be enhanced when the Global Positioning System goes spaceward during the mid-1980s. This project will use eighteen NavStar satellites orbiting in a belt at 16,000 kilometers. Each satellite will carry an extraordinarily accurate atomic clock. Receivers on ships will measure the gap between the time signals that are received from the different satellites. These differences will precisely measure the ship's location. Even squads of soldiers on foot patrols will be able to use the satellites to find out where they are located, whether in dense jungle or mountainous terrain, within sixteen meters.

American space missions of the next two decades will reflect the financially hamstrung position of NASA. Many projects will be joint endeavors with other countries. The course of U.S. space flights over the coming years will also demonstrate the incredible breadth of the Shuttle's capabilities and the enhanced central role of the military in orbit.

USSR

The Soviets have always been intrigued by Venus, and they plan another round of Venera missions to learn still more about this cloudy inner planet. *Venera 15* and *Venera 16* will be launched in 1984 and will reach Venus in 1985, with the French cooperating on the project. In 1986, one of the Venera ships will veer off to intercept and record Halley's comet. Other specific missions in the Soviet's guarded space program are not known. It is safe to assume that the U.S.A.-USSR space rivalry will continue apace.

Space Vehicles and Equipment

For the first two decades of space exploration, space vehicles and equipment remained remarkably constant. The look, the scientific processes, the engineering, and the planning of these missions remained more or less the same from Mercury through Apollo. The coming decade, however, will witness enormous changes in how we travel in space and what we can do while we are there.

The key to these transitions, of course, is the U.S. space shuttle, the world's first fully reusable spacecraft. In fact, the shuttle isn't merely a

SBR SPACECRAFT FLIGHT SEQUENCE

● FLIGHT NO. 1

● FLIGHT NO. 2

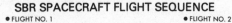

● 460km/28.5 i Orbit
● SPACECRAFT ELEVATED AND SPRING SEPARATED
● TRANSFER TO 830 km/28.5 i WITH AUXILLARY CHEMICAL PROPULSION SYSTEM
● STORE IN ORBIT
  ● LAUNCH CONFIGURATION
  ● MINIMUM DRAG ATTITUDE STABILIZED
  ● ACTIVE TT&C SYSTEM

● RENDEVOUS WITH SPACECRAFT (830 km, 28.5 i)
● COOPERATIVE DOCKING MANEUVER
● STABILIZE IN SPACECRAFT DEPLOYMENT ATTITUDE
  ● SPACECRAFT ARRAY IN PLANE OF ORBIT

SBR SPACECRAFT ASSEMBLY SEQUENCE

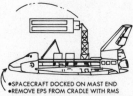

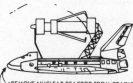

● SPACECRAFT DOCKED ON MAST END
● REMOVE EPS FROM CRADLE WITH RMS

● REMOVE NUCLEAR REACTOR FROM CRADLE WITH RMS
● POSITION AND ATTACH TO S/C MAST

● PARTIALLY OPEN S/C RADIAL ARM ASSY
● POSITION AND ATTACH EPS TO END OF ARRY CORE STRUCTURE
● RELEASE S/C FROM DOCKING MAST (RMS ATTACHED)
● ROTATE S/C 180 (x, y plane) AND DOCK WITH EPS END TO DOCKING MAST

● ROTATE ASSEMBLED S/C TO DEPLOYMENT ORIENTATION
● PREPARE ASE INTERFACES FOR DEPLOYMENT

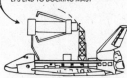

SBR SPACECRAFT LEO DEPLOYMENT SEQUENCE

● EXTEND NUCLEAR REACTOR RADIATOR
● CHARGE AND CHECKOUT COOLANT SYSTEM
● EXTEND S/C RADIAL ARM STRUCTURE
● DEPLOY RADAR ARRAY
● EXTEND S/C MAST
● PERFORM CAPTIVE SYSTEM TESTS
● SEPARATE AND PERFORM FREE FLIGHT TESTS
  ● POWER SYSTEM (FULL POWER)
  ● ATTITUDE CONTROL SYSTEM
  ● ELECTRIC PROPULSION SUBSYSTEM
  ● RADAR SYSTEM
● INITIATE TRANSFER MANEUVER TO GEO

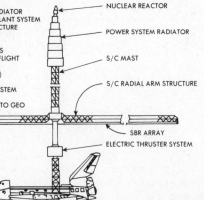

NUCLEAR REACTOR

POWER SYSTEM RADIATOR

S/C MAST

S/C RADIAL ARM STRUCTURE

SBR ARRAY

ELECTRIC THRUSTER SYSTEM

single vehicle; it is a family of ships, a generic shell that can be shaped into numerous specific spacecraft, allowing the shuttle to assume many diverse functions for the various needs of space travel.

Apart from the shuttle, both the Europeans and the Soviets will be hard at work on their own advances during the next decade. Here is a survey of some of the most important and interesting pieces of equipment that will ply the avenues of space in the immediate future.

Shuttle Vehicles

The space shuttle can change its configuration for every mission. Over the course of the 1980s, this so-called space truck could take many forms. Here are some of the more intriguing.

The Flying Nuclear Power Plant. Nuclear power plants will be placed in an orbit near earth during the 1990s, at a distance from which power is still retrievable, but where pollution waste remains at a considerable distance from earth. NASA and private scientists have designed a small nuclear power plant that fits inside the space shuttle. Once in orbit, the shuttle opens its cargo doors and unfolds the nuclear plant core. Then, using specially designed gantries and grabbers, the shuttle crew can construct the plant, called a Shuttle Based Reactor or SBR, without going near it.

When complete, the plant will look like a gigantic beehive. At its tip lies the reactor core. Beneath this is a ridged radiator, then balance and transmission arms, and a small thruster rocket at the base. Once the plant is constructed, the shuttle can come home and the nuclear plant will remain, generating power in space. Each plant will create considerably less power than an earth nuclear station, but the United States could safely operate whole phalanxes of nuclear generators in an orbit. The space nuclear generator will probably be a government project with backing from utilities and energy companies. Its first use will be to bring permanent electricity to space construction operations.

Space Generator. Another shuttle configuration, the space generator, will be a precursor to space factories. Any space manufacturing will require a constant rechargeable power source. NASA has devised a 25-kilowatt power plant that can head into space inside the shuttle, then can be unfolded and left at any space factory site. The plant uses solar electric cells arrayed in fanlike plates to create the power. This assembly is connected to a tiny rocket and control system. It can move about as required, keeping the sun in focus for maximum energy production, or attaching itself to various ports as needed. Sched-

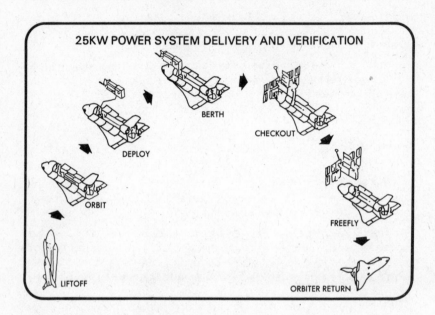

25KW POWER SYSTEM DELIVERY AND VERIFICATION

uled for testing in the late 1980s, the generator will be the first component of an orbiting industrial park.

   Solares Orbiting Space Mirror. Researchers at NASA's Ames
Research Center in California have proposed using the space shuttle to
construct and put in place gigantic orbiting space mirrors that can gather

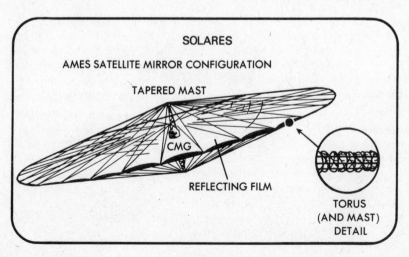

SOLARES

AMES SATELLITE MIRROR CONFIGURATION

TAPERED MAST

CMG

REFLECTING FILM

TORUS
(AND MAST)
DETAIL

sunlight and focus the beams on vast arrays of solar cells or solar collectors on the earth's surface. Ames' scientists estimate that the shuttle could carry four 1-square-kilometer mirrors per flight. These mirrors could be used to test the concept's feasibility. Later, large mirrors could be put in place, vastly reducing American foreign energy needs. The Ames team predicts that a system could be in place by 1990.

Shuttle Passenger Liner. The shuttle's early missions will be centered on science and commerce payloads. Plans have also been drawn up to use the ship as a passenger carrier. NASA is designing a shuttle so that it could ferry some 10,000 people into space annually at 74 passengers a trip. It could, stated a report to a 1980 NASA shuttle conference, "revitalize a sense of direction in America, and transform the nation which was the first to set foot on another world into a genuinely spacefaring community." Frederick Jackson Turner's "frontier thesis," suggesting a correlation between American land expansion and the "national character," which was originally propounded in the late 1880s, will be revived by a new generation of American pioneers.

European Spacecraft

The European Space Agency has always relied, with mixed success, on a family of rockets called Ariane. Over the next decade, the Europeans will continue to develop this program, attempting to enlarge and improve their standard craft. At the beginning of the 1980s, the Europeans were still using Ariane 1 rockets. By 1983, however, they will progress to Ariane 2 and Ariane 3 ships, which will increase the efficiency of liftoff power and payload weight.

The workhorse of Europe's space efforts in the 1980s, though, will be the Ariane 4. It will carry twice the payload of Ariane 1 at less cost per kilo. In some ways, it will be even simpler than its predecessors. And, importantly for the conservative Europeans, it will utilize well-tested and understood technology.

Late in the decade, the ESA may move on to Ariane 5, a much larger and more complex spacecraft, large enough to hoist a reusable mini-shuttle into orbit. Its booster stage should be recoverable as well.

Soviet Spacecraft

Attempts to predict future Soviet space projects are, at best, guesswork. The Russians shroud their space program in a veil of bureaucratic secrecy. Even the most informed space observers can only hope to

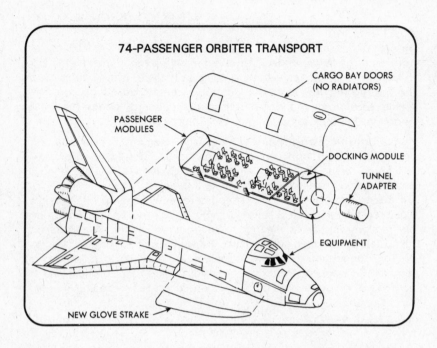

74-PASSENGER ORBITER TRANSPORT

CARGO BAY DOORS
(NO RADIATORS)

PASSENGER
MODULES

DOCKING MODULE

TUNNEL
ADAPTER

EQUIPMENT

NEW GLOVE STRAKE

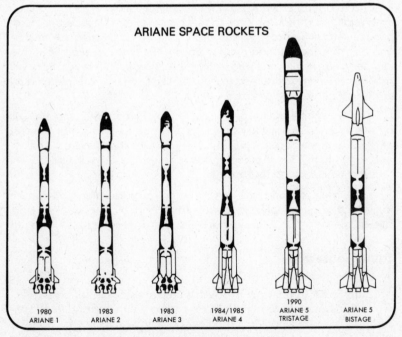

ARIANE SPACE ROCKETS

| 1980 ARIANE 1 | 1983 ARIANE 2 | 1983 ARIANE 3 | 1984/1985 ARIANE 4 | 1990 ARIANE 5 TRISTAGE | ARIANE 5 BISTAGE |

spot trends. Here are some speculations about Soviet space goods over the next decade.

Shuttle. Numerous reports have the Soviets readying their own shuttle. French sources report that the Russian plan is to use a traditional booster to launch the reusable craft, but that it will land like an airplane. Observers in the West are not sure when we might see this vehicle, but the general consensus is that the Russians are in a final stage of preparation.

Space Station. The Salyut-6 space station has been responsible for most of the Soviet space endurance records, but signs now indicate that the Russians plan to set up something larger and more permanent in space soon.

In June 1981, the Soviets launched a big, new spacecraft, the *Cosmos-1267*, to dock with Salyut. The linked craft have a mass of some fifteen tons, a huge object in space. The linking of large ships with a central orbiting pod probably represents a first step in the USSR's plan for a huge space station or military base. The Russians, however, lack boosters powerful enough to lift an entire space station into orbit, so the system will be launched in separate parts. While the U.S. focuses its plans on the shuttle, the Soviet emphasis will be on the space platform.

Super Booster. America's *Saturn V* booster could lift some 100 tons into orbit. None of the Russian spacecraft has ever come close to such a level of thrust. Now, though, rumors hold that they are trying once again to engineer their own super booster. In the late 1960s and early 1970s, Russian attempts to build one of these booster systems caused the destruction of three rockets. But the Russians have made great strides since then and may have better luck this time around. In general, space development by the USSR in the years ahead may still remain behind American efforts, but the number of flights will continue to surpass American efforts.

Space Support Systems

The advances in space hardware won't be confined to ships. A wide range of support and work systems will be initiated or improved over the next decade, too. Here are a couple of the most striking.

Manned Maneuvering Unit. If the space shuttle is going to be carrying factories and power plants into space, crew members will need something more sophisticated than plastic tethers to support them on extravehicular work details. Technicians are creating a resourceful space backpack for work in space that should be ready by 1985. It contains a personal propulsion unit and controls, so that the astronaut will have far more accurate control over his movements in space. The unit fits comfortably into the autonomous life support systems designed to allow the astronaut to range far from his ship without any tether.

Remote Manipulator. This gigantic robot arm, designed by the National Research Council of Canada, will be one of the most frequently used adjuncts to the shuttle. The robot arm is as massive as it is delicate. It has all the joints of a human arm over its fifteen meter length, can lift 30,000 kilograms, but is gentle enough to pluck sophisticated electronics gadgets from orbit without damaging them. In orbit, such a device can remove old satellites from their posts, put new ones in their place, serve as a crane for space construction, and handle many other tasks.

Space Tug. Some kind of small, highly maneuverable space vehicle will undoubtedly be designed for trips between installations in orbit. Building materials will have to be hauled, crews moved, messages sent. The space tug was part of the original proposal for the space shuttle program but was axed in budget cuts. By the mid-1990s, however, the tug will be back, probably as a vehicle that is shipped into space in pieces and assembled in orbit. It will probably look a little like the rockets Flash Gordon used to sputter about in.

Future Space Vehicles

Once man's presence in space is firmly established through the shuttle and space platforms, scientists will have to develop vehicles that can operate free from the constraints of escaping gravity and atmosphere. True interplanetary spaceships will be engineered in the early part of the next century. Already scientists are thinking about the best ways to design and power such ships. These are some of their ideas.

Pulsed Nuclear Engines. Project Orion at the General Atomic Corporation in California studied the use of small fission bomblets that can explode behind a massive push plate, propelling the spacecraft. Such a system avoids the thermal problems inherent in a continuous nuclear reaction without too significant a loss of power. Recently, scientists have suggested that laser-imploded fusion pellets might create the same propulsion effect with less heat and waste than fission.

Uranium Tamped Self-Focusing Magnetic Field. A variation on the fusion engine, this system uses a self-focusing magnetic field and a low-voltage electron beam to create a fusion reaction. If uranium has been tamped or wedged to a high density, and surrounds the fusion field, the free neutrons that flow outward from the fusion reaction should establish a secondary fission reaction in the uranium that adds significantly to the engine's power output.

Antihydrogen Fuel. Work at the Jet Propulsion Laboratory in California indicates that anti-matter—particles that are the exact opposites of normal nuclear particles and destroy these nuclear particles when they touch—might make an excellent advanced rocket fuel. One proposal suggests using small amounts of antihydrogen to serve as the initiating energy source for a fusion reaction. Lasers could be used to manufacture as much as a kilogram a day of antihydrogen, according to Jet Propulsion scientists, an amount which would be enough fuel to sustain space missions to the farthest corners of the solar system. By carefully mixing antihydrogen and hydrogen, the engine could create a sustained force drawn from energy released when the opposite forces destroy one another.

Design of a Solar System Space Ship

The solar system space ship in the next century will need to be large, able to carry a payload that will amount to 20 percent of gross weight capacity, and capable of sustaining high speeds for trips of long duration. Several possible designs could accomplish the needs. Jet Propulsion scientists cite two possibilities in particular:

Hypersonic Advanced Spaceship. This vehicle combines characteristics of a jet plane and an interplanetary craft. The plane is configured somewhat like the shuttle, using three different propulsion

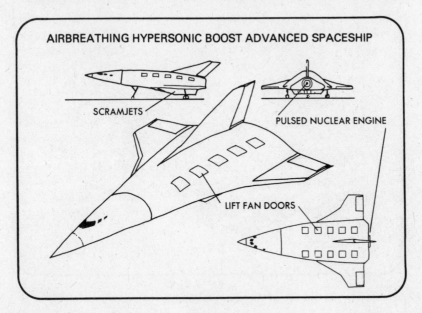

AIRBREATHING HYPERSONIC BOOST ADVANCED SPACESHIP

SCRAMJETS

PULSED NUCLEAR ENGINE

LIFT FAN DOORS

systems. Lift-off comes through fans that push the plane vertically to about 30,000 feet. There, the vehicle begins a controlled dive. At 1.2 times the speed of sound, scramjet engines are lit and propel the plane toward the edge of the atmosphere. At the edge of the atmosphere, parallel to the horizon, the ship fires its nuclear engine and takes off for space. Such a vessel could be feasible by 2050.

Boron-Fueled Spaceship. This ship's engine is so powerful that it can, in the words of a Jet Propulsion Laboratory report, "be nearly contemptuous of gravity." The boron-fueled ship can ascend from the surface of the earth to the surface of the moon at a constant acceleration of 1 g. The boron ship uses anti-matter energized reactions of boron, a solid element that absorbs particles and energy effectively. The ship would weigh 167,000 pounds with a storage capability of 25,000 pounds.

This spaceship will be a true cruiser—broad, flat, and controllable at any speed. The pulsed nuclear engine's small size and awesome power are the keys to its success. We may, however, only see this kind of ship by the end of the twenty-first century.

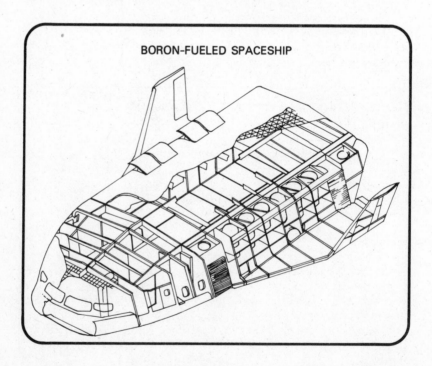

BORON-FUELED SPACESHIP

Space Industry

The prospect of financially profitable industries in space by 2000 or 2010 may sound like the far-fetched schemes of idle dreamers or the ideas of science fiction writers. But skeptics voiced similar doubts about the explorers and navigators of the fifteenth century who believed that a New World was waiting to be discovered. The new era of space will be no different. Only the most entrepreneurial businessmen, the most far-sighted investors, will recognize the potential riches that space will yield. They will become the Rockefellers and Carnegies of tomorrow.

Historically, it has most often been private industry—not the government—which has financed the exploration of new terrains. As the twentieth century draws to a close, we will see the private sector emerge as the leader in space development and thereby perpetuate the historical tradition begun by the gold prospectors who flocked to California in the 1850s or the European companies that carved out China in the nineteenth century.

For the entrepreneur of tomorrow, here are descriptions of likely space industrial projects of the next 100 years.

Telecommunications

Each month, the percentage of the world's television, radio, and telephone messages carried over satellites increases. Already most inter-city and international transmissions go through space, rather than across or below the ground. Ground communication will soon become the exception, and space transmission the norm.

Virtually every developed nation plans to use space for developing advanced telecommunications systems. Satellites will provide viewers with literally hundreds of television channels, electronic mail services, teletext computer information services, data processing hookups, and more. Huge profits will be reaped from the continuing development of such telecommunications systems.

Here are descriptions of several potentially lucrative business ventures.

• A large multi-channel, high-power data-transfer satellite in orbit could link all the printed books and magazines in the United States onto a central data bank. Using a one-meter antenna on a house roof attached to an inexpensive, low-power radio and data terminal inside the home, one could have access to all the volumes within the Library of Congress and the New York Public Library. By 2000, this equipment could be placed in any private dwelling at a very reasonable price.

A SPACE FACTORY

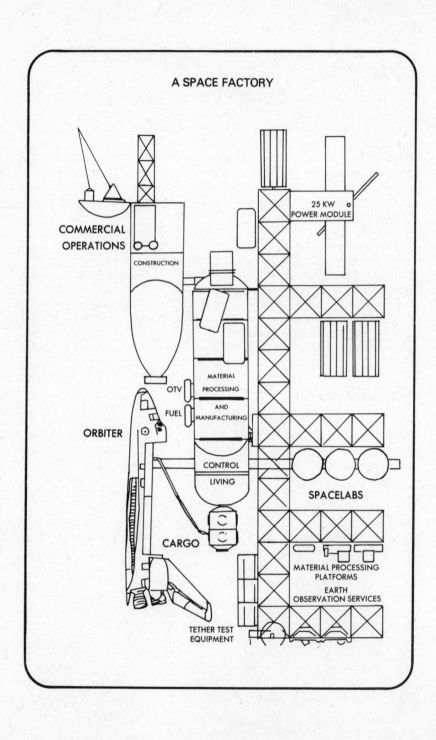

COMMERCIAL
OPERATIONS

CONSTRUCTION

25 KW
POWER MODULE

OTV

FUEL

MATERIAL
PROCESSING

AND

MANUFACTURING

ORBITER

CONTROL

LIVING

SPACELABS

CARGO

MATERIAL PROCESSING
PLATFORMS

EARTH
OBSERVATION SERVICES

TETHER TEST
EQUIPMENT

• The data satellite industry, even if only 10,000 public libraries used the service, could provide annual revenues of more than $100 million. After ten years in operation, with some 1.5 million businesses involved in the venture, annual revenues could range from $3 to $5 billion.

• Space-com wrist-radios are a fascinating product that could be derived from space networks. Besides telling time, a watch could enable you to talk to anyone in the world who had a similar device. Through a process known as complexity inversion, a satellite orbiting in space will make global communication as simple as telling time. The unit cost of the transmitting watch could be as high as $300 at first, but would drop to $30 within a ten-year period. Calls similarly will drop from an average of $3 to 30¢ per call within five years. Within two decades, the service could extend to 50 million global users and yield revenues of some $30 billion annually.

In the future, each home will become a terminal in a worldwide network of information producers, processors, and users. The world will be linked more tightly than ever before. And space will be at the heart of this vast social transformation.

Materials Processing

The European Space Agency's Spacelab will head into orbit on its 1984 shuttle flight. The first materials processing center to go into space, it will be a harbinger of many commercial experiments and enterprises to follow. The lack of vibration and gravity in the space environment allows for materials to be processed in a way not possible on earth. Furnaces, for example, can be controlled to generate heat far more precisely. Suspensions can sustain themselves indefinitely. Electrophoresis and other flow-related processes can be undertaken with far fewer problems than on earth.

NASA's timetable for the development of materials processing in space appears on page 144.

The industrial applications of space materials processing will have the most significant impact on crystal growth, solidification of liquids, biological separations, and fluid mechanics. The products that could come from these operations include: enhanced semiconductors, solar cells, new metal composites, synthetic superconductors, improved fiber optic glass, new pigments, better membranes, cell purification products, and better pharmaceuticals. Here are some examples of specific space materials likely to result.

Space Jewelry. The glamor and uniqueness of space jewelry, fashioned out of space alloys, could capture anywhere from 1 to 10 percent of the jewelry market by 2010. Like diamonds during the Renaissance, space jewels may become an exotic, highly desirable luxury for wealthy people in the next century.

NASA'S TIMETABLE FOR THE DEVELOPMENT
OF MATERIALS PROCESSING IN SPACE

1985	1990	1995	2000
Demonstrate technology and accumulate data using variable gravity capabilities on ground and in space.	Demonstrate new manufacturing concepts. Provide national facilities for independently funded users and opportunities for commercial partners.	Develop low cost automated space systems and provide flights for reimbursable commercial users.	Demonstrate extraterrestrial materials processing controlled from earth.

Perishable Cutting Tools. Perishable cutting tools (PCT) used in lathes and other machine-cutting operations are extremely expensive to manufacture on earth. A PCT made of a hard alloy manufactured in space, one with a longer tool life or a faster cutting speed, would find a market at a competitive price. Projected revenues, even by 2000, could exceed $250 million.

Crystalline Semiconductor Materials. Space-made semi-conductor materials will be used to manufacture maintenance chips for one's digital watch or pocket calculator, providing that the crystalline material can be obtained from space at a reasonable cost.

Monitoring

The earth, in these crowded, troubled times, desperately requires as much information about itself as can possibly be attained. Space provides the perfect vantage point for observation.

Weather. Weather satellites have already proven helpful in forecasting. Satellites launched in the years ahead will track more systems at once, will be able to make out smaller details so that storms can be detected sooner.

Geology. Sophisticated satellites that are linked electronically will be able to monitor geological trouble spots and earthquake faults all over the globe at the same moment, trading information and aiding enormously in the prediction of quakes and other natural disturbances.

Agriculture. Spacecraft will be able to ascertain where water supplies exist and where they will be needed. Agricultural planning will make tremendous strides, with satellites able to monitor crop growth patterns. Such satellites will prove invaluable in determining the agricultural productivity of other nations.

Transportation. Linked satellites can determine where every air vehicle on the planet is at any given instant. Transportation planning and routing will be enhanced, delays reduced, and collisions made even less likely than they are today. Such systems will also provide vital military information about enemy forces.

Military. Spy satellites will not only keep track of enemy aircraft and missiles, but may also knock them out from the sky, preventing offensive missiles from reaching their destinations.

Shipping. A satellite in geosynchronous orbit could be used to track every package and suitcase shipped in the United States. Items mailed from any post office or transportation terminal would have a low-power radio transmitter attached to them. The satellite tracking system could locate any stray item on the ground to a distance within 100 feet. The service would generate revenues in the first year of operation of about $8 million, but could top $300 million after twelve years. In the hands of a totalitarian regime, this satellite tracking system could also be used to follow the precise movements of all of its citizens.

Energy

Energy production facilities on earth are limited by size and by the dangers posed to humans by pollution. In space, these constraints disappear. A power station could cover hundreds of miles, and no individual would be bothered by heat, radiation, or any other pollutant. As a result, many scientists feel space is the perfect area for development of new energy supplies.

Energy Grids. A huge solar-powered grid could be placed in orbit between the earth and sun. If covered with solar cells or plastics that conduct electrical currents, such a grid could generate huge amounts of electricity. The resulting power could be beamed to earth in the form of electromagnetic waves or as energy-enhanced lasers.

Mirrors. Another energy possibility involves building giant mirrors in space that reflect sunlight to solar collection sites on our planet's surface. These huge power stations could be located in the center of deserts and other unpopulated areas.

Asteroid Factories. Not unlike the fictional *Star Trek* spaceship of the 1960s, real space factory ships, equipped with electronic gear and lasers, could collect millions of tons of valuable metals and process them on the way back to earth. Metal-rich asteroids, the remains of planets that once orbited between Mars and Jupiter but exploded long ago, contain gold, silver, platinum, iron, nickel, copper, manganese, carbon, potassium, and phosphorus in enormous quantities. At least forty of these asteroids are each larger than the entire length of Massachusetts.

For those prospectors not interested in asteroids, the moon itself will become a valuable source for metals. Iron, nickel, and gold lie beneath the lunar surface. Aluminum and titanium could be used to build structures on the moon or elsewhere, while existing quantities of carbon and silicon could be used for manufacturing electronic components. Better yet, rocket ships may one day not even be needed to bring these products back to earth, as the moon's light gravity could allow payloads of materials to be electronically catapulted back to earth.

Real Star
Wars

Though Hollywood's versions of war in outer space always take place in the distant future, real battles in orbit may be coming soon. There is at least some evidence that they may already be here.

Outer space is of critical strategic importance. Consider, for instance, communications. Most of the world's long-distance messages are forwarded to their destinations by satellite. Both the United States and the Soviet Union depend heavily on orbiting communications relays for their worldwide defense strategy. In an atomic war, blocking satellite-carried information for even a few minutes might mean the difference between surviving a bitterly destructive clash and complete annihilation.

Nor are these the only strategic targets in orbit. Obvious ones are spy satellites and the early warning network for nuclear missile attack. Navigation and weather satellites are also essential for modern military planning. All of these could be destroyed by military satellites with telling strategic effect.

Both the United States and the Soviet Union are developing specialized satellites for war in space. They come in two types: the antisatellite satellite (ASAT) and the antimissile satellite.

ASATs. The Soviet Union deployed the first hunter-killer satellites as long ago as 1968. They were primitive devices designed to maneuver near their target and explode, riddling it with shrapnel. This first generation of space weapons is already obsolete. In March, 1981, the Soviets launched two satellites almost simultaneously. One was a dummy satellite, a target. The other was a new-generation ASAT. The ASAT reached orbit, tracked down its target, and shot it out of the sky with a missile. It was not the first test of the system, but it was the first acknowledged success.

Military space-watchers think there may have been an earlier Soviet triumph in space, however. When RCA's communications satellite *Satcom III* was launched in 1979, something very odd happened. It disappeared. And since satellites do not usually vanish without warning of a malfunction, many military observers are convinced that *Satcom III* may have been the first victim of a Soviet hunter-killer ASAT.

After ignoring the Soviet ASAT program for years, the United States is now developing its own satellite killer. Unlike the Soviet satellites, the American space weapon is a small air-to-space missile carried under the wing of a fighter plane. Its first tests are expected some time in 1983.

Rockets, of course, are rather crude weapons for the high-tech world of space wars. Slow at best, they can be very inaccurate. Something better is needed.

Lasers. The super-concentrated light of an enormous laser can do damage in two ways. As a continuous beam, it can burn a hole through almost any material. Fired in a series of rapid pulses, the energy will also beat a hole in a target mechanically, like a hammer or a wave on a seashore. Very rarely would a target be hit in a fuel tank or some other place that would make it explode. Instead, the beam "kills" its target by penetrating the skin of a missile, then attacking the internal mechanisms to cause a malfunction.

One handicap of lasers as antimissile weapons is the enormous amount of energy needed to burn or break the hardened ceramic skin of an ICBM. To focus the beam on the same tiny area of skin from thousands of miles away for the seconds needed to do fatal damage requires astonishing marksmanship. And it is very difficult to know when a laser has done enough damage to put a missile out of commission. The laser might damage the missile's guidance mechanism while leaving the warhead untouched.

For these reasons, lasers will be used mainly as antisatellite weapons. A satellite's electronic eyes are designed to pick up even the dimmest light or infrared radiation. This very sensitivity makes them vulnerable. Even a relatively weak laser fired from earth's surface could temporarily blind a satellite, just as you can blind yourself by staring directly at the sun.

Putting a satellite-hunting laser into orbit would make it far more efficient. The targets, nearer and moving across the laser's field of view more slowly, would be far easier to hit. If necessary, the laser ASAT could fly along next to its target, concentrating its beam on the victim's sensors for as long as required to do the intended damage.

Particle Beams. Another sort of "directed energy" weapon, the particle beam, is more likely to be used against missiles. A particle beam is a vast spark of electrons or ions (atoms that have been stripped of at least one electron) that have been electromagnetically supercharged with energy. Striking a target, this artificial lightning can punch a fist-sized hole in microseconds.

Fired from a satellite 600 miles up, a particle beam would reach an ICBM at the top of the atmosphere in 3/1000 of a second. In that time, a missile traveling at 5,000 miles per hour would have traveled less than twenty-two feet. Given radar that could track several targets at once and a way to redirect the particle beam quickly, the satellite could knock out 100 ICBMs before the last one had moved 5 miles. Directed energy weapons, especially particle beams, stand to make both ICBMs and antiballistic missiles obsolete.

The First Battle in Space

The scene: Low earth orbit in the late 1990s. It is an ordinary day at *Astrolab*, the orbiting science laboratory funded by the United States Congress. On earth, the U.S. Tracking Board shows all in order—except eight small, red blips representing unidentified satellites. And eight Soviet ASATs are missing from their standard orbits.

The U.S. ASAT commander watches the screen for a few seconds, then feeds some information into a nearby computer terminal. Eight blue dots appear on the big board, representing eight Starfighters, the U.S. ASATs. It takes more than twenty minutes for the Soviet and U.S. ASATs to converge on *Astrolab* from their positions around the world. As the Soviet ASATs draw within firing range of *Astrolab*, the Starfighters are close behind. Following them is *Fort Apache*, the U.S. manned military station in orbit.

The combat is brief but intense. Particle beams and laser fire flash wildly; the older ASATs lob rockets that create brilliant, if silent, explosions outside *Astrolab*'s windows. Most of the "kills" by directed energy are marked only by small burns on the disabled craft.

As the last Soviet ASAT approaches and fires its lasers at *Astrolab*, *Fort Apache* blasts away at long range with particle beams. The Soviet weapon overloads the infrared sensor that is part of *Astrolab*'s weather station, destroying it. Then, the ASAT is pounded by particle beams. In half a second, it is scrap metal drifting in the void.

Total time for the first real star war? From first shot to last: thirteen minutes, thirty-two seconds. Casualties: eight Soviet ASATs destroyed or disabled, seven U.S. ASATs destroyed, one *Astrolab* sensor disabled. No humans killed, wounded, or captured. In satellite warfare, human beings will plan the grand strategies; aiming and firing the beam weapons will almost always be done more efficiently by computers on the satellites themselves.

Costs for Space Industry

While space may tempt the entrepreneurial corporation, such industrial endeavors will not come cheap. Using 1979 dollars, here are NASA's projected costs of some typical services in space.

COSTS FOR SPACE INDUSTRY

Services in Orbit: Cost (1979)	New Facility User Cost at low use rates
Space factory rent	$150,000/$200,000/yr
Communication platform construction	$628/lb
Materials processing platform rental	$30,000/day
Electrical power	$50/KWH
Satellite repair	$2.5 million/visit
Personnel billeting rate	$1,250/day
Cargo rates to geosynchronous earth orbit	$18,800/lb.

Space Careers

By 2050, it is estimated that thousands of people will be living in space. Here's a list of likely job opportunities.

Computer Programmers and Hardware Experts. These people will be essential to the success of any space industry. Their expertise will range from navigation to robotics.

Space Habitat Builders.

Industrial Engineers. People will be needed to run equipment, oversee mining operations, act as robot technicians, and perform countless other tasks.

Flight Crew Members for Shuttle Flights.

Support and Life-sustaining Industries. Job opportunities will include hotel management and restaurant or food service positions.

Manufacturing and Mining. The weightlessness of space may make steel production a reality in many space settings.

Living in Space

The urge to reach out and settle new regions has persisted in every age of human history. Wherever people have been able to conceive of viable habitations—from the frigid Arctic to wind-swept tropical islands—they have moved and often prospered.

Now the ultimate unexplored reaches of space lie open for pioneering settlements. Plans are already drawn for several types of space colonies, and the implementation of these ideas should follow swiftly on the heels of space manufacturing projects and military development. Orbital space may soon become like the old West—the preserve of rugged miners and builders, dreamers and soldiers.

We stand on the threshold of human habitation of space. Our grandchildren may come down to earth to visit us only on holidays. The path toward space colonization can be seen clearly in projects proposed over the next twenty years.

Space Stations

Skylab and Salyut are precursors of true space stations to come. The USSR (see page 135) is reportedly formulating plans for a jigsaw space platform of rockets with a central pod.

The Johnson Space Center in Houston, meanwhile, has plans for an American space station that would orbit some 300 kilometers above the planet. Eight to twelve people would inhabit the $9 billion facility, coordinating American activity in space. The Marshall Space Flight Center plan is less ambitious. It envisions a station somewhat like that of the Russians, consisting of a number of Spacelab modules docked together at a cost of just $1 billion. By the end of this decade such pioneering space stations will be launched.

Moon Station

Other space scientists propose the moon as a practical alternative to an orbiting space station. They point out that coordination of the facility could be handled from the moon with ease, while a moon base could double as a mining operation or factory.

The most striking moon plans come from Georg von Tiesenhausen and Wesley Darbro of the Marshall Space Flight Center. Their idea is to place a factory on the moon that would in turn manufacture parts for an identical factory that would make more parts.

Even as early as 1952, John von Neumann proposed an elaborate theory for a self-replicating factory. Employing his basic ideas, the Marshall team produced engineering plans for a moon factory that would use the lunar surface's raw materials to create new factories. The facility would have four parts: 1) a collection unit that would mine material; 2) a process unit that would manipulate these resources; 3) a production system that would fabricate them into sub-assemblies; and 4) a universal constructor, a maze of computers and robots that would arrange the pieces according to detailed instructions into a replica of the original facility. Each new plant, of course, would contain its own universal constructor, endowing the operation with a robotic immortality.

The first moon factory could manufacture its counterpart within one year. Within thirty years, such reproduction capabilities would increase the number of factories to 1,000.

The Marshall team points out, however, that engineers would stop the replication process before this point, and would retool the existing plants to make other products. Within one generation, a major manufacturing center on the moon could develop.

Military Bases

The new generation of high-tech military satellites will gradually create the need for supervisory and decision-making personnel in space. Both the United States and the Soviet Union have played with the idea of establishing a manned military presence in space. Both plans remain highly tentative, but if either nation proceeds the other will follow quickly.

Space Colonies

Author and scientist Gerard O'Neill's dream of a civilian space colony remains well off in the future, but it will be technically feasible by 2010. O'Neill proposes a city of 10,000 people that would be built for geosynchroneous orbit above the earth. The cylindrical city would spin slowly along its major axis, creating a semblance of gravity. Environmental engineering techniques already in use today could cover the surface of the cylinder city with a verdant setting of grass and trees. Fiber optic light would simulate the passing of the sun overhead, so that citizens would not suffer chronobiological shock.

The most serious drawback to this design would be the missing sky. If "up" in the cylinder is a view of its opposite side, people could suffer from the consequences of prolonged vertigo, for they would look up and see other people and buildings that would be standing upside down. One solution might be to generate a gentle haze along the cylinder's midline. This covering would preclude any sunny days in the colony but would give the impression of a cloudy sky overhead, rather than the looming presence of a suspended village.

More likely than full space colonies in the short term are transient construction camps. If factories and other commercial facilities are to be built and maintained in space, they will need quarters for the contruction and maintenance teams. At first, these jobs would be handled by shuttle crews, but eventually a permanent presence would be required. Some smaller version of O'Neill's cylinder may be used to give workers a suitable living habitat that would have both "inside" and "outside" areas. Such environmental amenities would make workers' stays in space physically and psychologically less trying. By 2050, there may be 7,500 people living and working in space.

Seeking Life
in Space

The search for interplanetary life will continue throughout the coming decades. Space satellites will penetrate deeper into the cosmos than ever before, and they may pick up signals with an enhanced clarity. Computer analyses of the mass of incoming data increase our chances of recognizing and interpreting any signal that we might receive.

Two basic concepts outlining future probes for interplanetary life are proposed by scientists today.

Terrestrial Chauvinism. This school, expounded by scientists like Jesco Von Puttkamer of NASA, holds that most civilizations in the universe either stabilize or perish at about the technological level that earth has now achieved. Therefore, the kinds of signals that man should search for are similar to those that we find on earth: electromagnetic pulses, laser vibrations, and monochromatic, digital signals from the areas of the universe closest to us.

Eternal Evolution. The other argument holds that our historical pattern on earth is largely parochial and irrelevant to the rest of the universe. Many civilizations, these scientists propose, may have already outstripped us eons ago or may have developed in totally different ways. Robert Jastrow, Carl Sagan, and other notable scientists belong to this school. They believe that we should scan the deep heavens, looking at subtle nuclear and magnetic variations, extraordinary power sources like quasars, and phenomena like black holes, and we should exhaustively investigate the edges of our capabilities—the highs and lows of energy systems and spectra. Findings from such studies would presumably give us the clues to extraterrestrial life.

Both methods will be used in the years ahead. Researchers are looking for any recurring pattern or occurrence that cannot be explained by natural phenomena. The likelihood of us hearing, "Hello out there," is, of course, extremely remote. Far more likely will be some utterly incomprehensible signal whose only significance to us may be a pattern some computer can recognize.

A growing group of scientists, however, not yet embraced by the mainstream but including such eminent names as Francis Crick, the decoder of DNA, and British astrophysicist Sir Fred Hoyle, holds that we may already have evidence of life in space. That evidence, they maintain, is our very existence. This school believes that life on earth resulted from organic particles rained down upon the planet from outer space.

Hoyle even believes that he has found such molecules within the viewable universe. This argument is new and controversial, and has shocked the scientific establishment. Eminent scientists like the late Dr. Rene Dubos dismissed such theories, claiming that they reflect the escapist tendencies too often at work in research science today. At the moment the jury is out on the validity of these claims because they seem so strange as to defy acceptance. But if such claims prove true over the next couple of years, the search for the first signs of life in the universe may have already ended. Then the question will become merely how the organic particles from space first landed and spawned, not if they exist at all.

Beyond this speculation lies the basic question of whether we would necessarily understand or recognize the sign of another civilization even if it were there. Man has always assumed that reality is the same throughout the universe; that intelligence in some form vaguely analogous to our own is a norm; that what we perceive as elements and waves are so perceived by others; and that zero remains zero everywhere.

Such theories may not hold true. New concepts in cosmology and quantum physics indicate that the fabric of reality is much more complex than we had ever imagined. In fact, one leading cosmologist and Nobel Prize winner, John Wheeler of the University of Texas, believes that reality may be a social construct as different for each civilization as its religion. The verifiable truth may differ from one form of life to another. He tells this story: Imagine that you and friends are playing the guessing game Botticelli. Your friends think up a name, and you will attempt to guess it by asking questions. When you leave the room, they decide to trick you. They will think of no single name. Whenever you ask a question, they will conjure up a new name that will fit all the past questions and answers.

Therefore, each time you ask a question there is a name that is true, but that truth changes with each turn. Eventually, you will guess the same name your friend has in mind on that turn. You will say, ''That is the name.'' And you will be right. But if you had asked different questions, the name—the reality—would have been different. In this way, Wheeler speculates, reality differs with the questions we ask. And what we find to be true may be a coincidence of what the truth really is and what we are looking for. An infinity of other possibilities might be equally true.

If this is the case, other civilizations may inhabit realities so different from our own that we could never communicate with them in any way, nor could we recognize their signals.

5 THE BUSINESS SECTOR

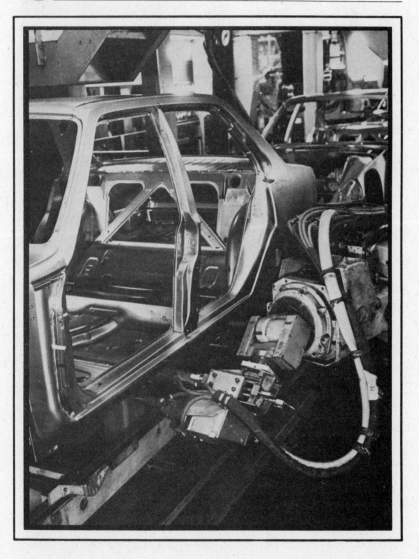

5 THE BUSINESS SECTOR

Business is one of the most volatile spheres of daily life. Corporations wax and wane, economies spurt and sputter, individuals prosper and go bankrupt. For all its image of solidity, the business world must remain flexible, adapting to new developments in science, political fluctuations, and ever-changing consumer demands.

Over the next fifty years, an incredible array of new technologies will move from the lab into the commercial sector. These will be the years when computers, robots, genetic engineering, space manufacturing, and thousands of other important processes will make their mark. This era may also be marked by economic difficulties in the developed world, brought about by pollution and resource shortages. The Third World, on the other hand, will charge into a new industrial age with the same fervor that characterized American industrial expansion in the days of Carnegie, Morgan, and Rockefeller.

How we make money, what we spend it on, what we buy, and who makes those products will change in the decades ahead. Many careers will vanish, while unexpected ones will arise. In short, the business sector of tomorrow will be as different from today's world as the horse and buggy economy of the 1800s was from our own times.

American Income and Essentials: 2000

By 2000, most Americans will be experiencing a new prosperity. The problems of shrinking energy supplies and spiraling costs will be offset by developments in computers, genetic engineering, and service industries that will bring about lifestyle changes that will in turn boost the economy. Basically, Americans will be able to simplify their lives and spend less money supporting themselves. Indeed, energy conservation will force Americans to become more resourceful fiscally and to spend less on many items.

Housing

The percentage of income the typical American family spends on housing will decline from 21.3 percent to 19.1 percent by 2000. As land gets more densely populated, housing plots and dwellings will grow smaller, with duplexes, townhouses, and condominiums becoming more common. Many old, larger homes will be broken into two or more living units. The prevalence of smaller families and larger energy bills will reinforce the trend to make compact housing units.

Food

Food costs will continue to increase over the next twenty years, although not as fast as wages, because genetic engineering, aquaculture, computers, and robot farm workers will make farms more productive. In addition, health-conscious Americans will eat less in the future, especially such meats as beef and pork. This trend means that the percentage of income the typical family spends on food will decline from 20.7 to 19.6 by 2000.

Clothes

Clothing expenses will decline too, as improved synthetic fibers make clothes cheaper and more durable. Still, the lure of fashion will continue to attract buyers to more expensive clothes, so that the savings will be slight, a decline from 7.5 to 7.3 percent of the average family's income.

Health Care

The cost of an average family's medical care will drop by 20 percent, from 10.1 percent of income to 8 percent. Beginning in the

EFFECTS OF INFLATION

Product	1970	1980	1990	2000	2010
Hamburger (1 lb.)	.89	1.99	4.50	10.50	22.75
Bacon (1 lb.)	.75	2.25	3.00	7.50	12.00
Lettuce (head)	.35	.89	1.50	2.75	5.00
Corn (ear)	.04	.20	.70	1.20	2.50
Can of soup	.13	.43	.89	1.50	2.75
1 doz lg eggs	.59	1.09	3.00	7.50	18.00
Loaf of bread	.29	.89	1.75	3.75	8.00
Quart of milk	.29	.69	1.25	2.59	5.75
Coffee (1 lb.)	.85	2.89	7.00	12.50	25.00
Paperback book	1.00	2.25	4.95	12.50	22.00
Newspaper	.15	.25	.60	1.50	2.75
Magazine	.75	2.00	5.00	15.00	30.00
Movie ticket	1.50	4.00	8.50	17.50	33.00
Gallon of gas	.30	1.00	4.00	2.00	2.00
Postage stamp	.06	.15	.38	.90	2.25
Candy bar	.05	.25	.65	1.50	2.50
Package of gum	.05	.20	.50	1.25	2.00
Coca Cola (12 oz.)	.15	.45	1.00	2.25	4.75
Subway ride	.35	.60	2.25	7.50	20.00
Hotel room	30.00	75.00	200.00	500.00	1200.00
Calculator	175.00	65.00	60.00	55.00	50.00
Woman's dress	25.00	60.00	130.00	275.00	500.00
Man's suit	125.00	215.00	400.00	650.00	1000.00
Man's shoes	25.00	55.00	125.00	275.00	500.00
Pantyhose	2.00	2.25	3.00	4.00	5.50
Man's haircut	1.75	5.00	12.00	25.00	40.00
Woman's cut and set	8.00	30.00	60.00	100.00	225.00
Cup of coffee	.10	.40	1.00	2.00	4.50
Ten-speed bike	90.00	190.00	350.00	600.00	1000.00
American compact car	3,100.00	5,200.00	12,000.00	30,000.00	70,000.00
Three room apt. rent	130.00	550.00	1,500.00	4,000.00	10,000.00
Three BR house	30,000.00	75,000.00	250,000.00	600,000.00	1,000,000.00

early 1980s, timolol and other new drugs will vastly reduce the danger of heart attacks. Near the end of the century, interferon and other biological products will improve and simplify cancer treatment.

AND THE SALARIES TO MATCH:

Job	1970	1980	1990	2000	2010
Secretary	$ 6,000	11,000	25,000	45,000	95,000
Advertising executive	25,000	45,000	100,000	185,000	375,000
Factory worker	10,400 ($5/hr)	25,000 ($12/hr)	52,000 ($25/hr)	98,000 ($47.50/hr)	197,600 ($95/hr)
Public high school teacher	8,000	15,000	28,000	58,000	110,000
Subway conductor	9,000	·17,000	35,000	72,000	135,000
Major league baseball player (average skills)	20,000	50,000	100,000	185,000	330,000

SOURCE: 1970 and 1980 figures, U.S. Bureau of Labor Statistics

At a more basic level, the public will benefit from being better prepared to prevent diseases. Deeper understanding of the causes of cancer will finally bring about significant reductions in smoking. Increased awareness of the workings of the whole body will keep Americans exercising and dieting—and away from drugs.

Institutions will help this process. Health maintenance organizations will encourage preventive medicine. By the end of the 1980s, many experts predict that the United States government will adopt a national health insurance plan because of public pressure to contain medical costs. Unlike the health plans of the 1980s, this national health insurance will discourage expensive hospitalization and, like Canada's health insurance, will provide incentives for cheaper, and often better, care at home or in out-patient facilities.

Purchase	Income % 1980	Income % 2000	$ Amount 1980	$ Amt. 2000
Housing	21.3	19.1	3,301	4,316
Food	20.7	19.6	3,208	4,429
Clothes	7.5	7.3	1,162	1,650
Health Care	10.1	8.0	1,565	1,808
Transportation	15.6	12.6	2,418	2,847
Disposable Income	24.8	33.4	3,844	7,550

Average Family Income: 1980: $15,500   2000: $24,600

Transportation

Personal transportation outlays will drop from 15.6 to 12.6 percent of the typical family's income by 2000. Cars will continue to get smaller and more efficient. The bicycle, with improved transmission and drive-shaft systems, may replace second cars in many families. Revitalized mass transit should also reduce the need for cars because it will become more convenient to ride than to cope with driving. The money for these improvements will come largely from private business, which will make mass transit a profitable enterprise and ensure that workers will be able to commute to their jobs. Finally home computers will elimi-nate much of the need for transportation, whether to go to work or to go shopping.

Emerging Job Markets
and New Careers

The technological revolution that will prevail in the last two dec-ades of this century will create new jobs and professions unheard of as recently as five years ago. An understanding of sophisticated informa-tion and communication systems as well as an increased technical expertise will be demanded of workers entering newly developed markets. As robots and other machines begin to replace manual labor-ers, the need for trained people to monitor these robotic and computer devices will create millions of jobs. The "Help Wanted" sections of newspapers throughout countries in the developed world will carry multiple listings in many of the following new labor fields.

Telecommunications Consultants

The "gold rush" growth of the telecommunications industry will create thousands of jobs in which experts will have to process and analyze inordinate amounts of information. Selecting and evaluating transmission and receiver systems in telecommunications will fall at first to outside business consultants, who will in time be replaced by corpo-rate officers and telecommunications departments.

Alternative Telephone Technologies Consultants

During the 1980s and 1990s, telephone technology experts will be increasingly called upon to help companies and individuals choose from a multitude of alternate phone systems. The breakup of A.T.&T. will create increased competition among regional telephone companies and will lead to many alternative telephone systems.

Office Networking Technologists

As interactive computer systems take hold in the office, there will be a vital need for technicians, engineers, designers, and ergonomics experts. When such advanced systems are in place, they will require supervision personnel, operator training programs, and maintenance and repair technicians.

Robot Marketing

The sales of robots to firms and individuals could soar into the millions within two decades. This business phenomenon will create the need for expert marketing personnel as well as a highly informed robot sales force. Since there will be more than a thousand different kinds of robot, their proper distribution and use will be key to industrial growth within a company. Whether IBM or another international conglomerate can dominate the marketing of this robotics field remains a question only time can answer.

Urban Security Force

The prospect of increased crime, fluctuating unemployment, and renewed inner city growth will call for increased use of private, corporate, and governmental security forces. Many of these security positions will be highly technical in nature. Security personnel will use computer scanning, complex listening devices, and other forms of electronic surveillance and control. Highly-specialized security officers will actively try to prevent computer crime, which could become a well-developed criminal art.

Copyright Law Analysts and Aides

Electronic printing, facsimiles, microfiche, hard copy printers, disks, tapes, drums, and other technological gadgets will create enormous turmoil in the field of copyright law. The need for interpretation, analysis, case study, and case preparation will greatly expand this branch of law, creating increased opportunities for legal consultants, brief writers, caseworkers, etc.

Computer Graphics Designers and Engineers

The need to design products, machines, packages, buildings, and even cities using computers will open up a new work discipline with many specialized branches. The combination of computer-aided design and computer-aided manufacturing (CAD/CAM) will offer tens of thousands of job opportunities for persons trained in engineering, design, and computer programming. Individuals expert in all three of these skills will be in an enviable employment position.

Data Bank Managers

As libraries and files are combined into data files and banks, the need for data managers will increase dramatically. As information specialists, they will oversee the structuring of information storage and retrieval. They will need combined training in computer memory and storage systems and in the programming of the particular business or discipline within which they work.

Bionics

Medicine's increasing ability to replace limbs, organs, and other human parts will effectively create jobs for many bionics inventors, engineers, designers, market experts, etc. Bionics as a discipline will require a background in biology, electronics, physics, mechanical engineering, and ergonomics.

Tele- and Cable-Shopping Installers

The transition from in-person shopping to cable or teleshopping will require thousands of technicians to install and maintain such systems. Sales and marketing of these services will also call for large numbers of trained persons.

Solar Array Technicians

The thousands of acres of solar panels in space will have to be maintained and supervised by thoroughly trained technical staffs. This work will demand a rudimentary knowledge of piloting, space travel technology, high-tech tool use and repair, and general judgment and reliability.

ADDITIONAL JOB LISTINGS AND CATEGORIES:

Cryogenics laboratory assistants
Genetic engineering salespeople
Computer games programmers
Space traffic control officers
Aerospace designers
Simulations specialists
Clone doctors and nurses
Teleconferencing coordinators
Automatic factory security
Organic computer inventors and
  engineers
Hybrid airship operators and pilots
Office area assistants
Debugging specialists
Laser beam operators
Holograph designers
Digitizer technicians
Maser specialists
Silicon mining experts
Space geographers
Fiber optics technicians
Voice-activated computer repair people
Computer museum directors
Technology transfer monitors
  and specialists
Remote-nursing technicians
Sports engineers
Biological historians
Software coding experts

Charged-couple device
  technicians and designers
Abstract writers
CAT scan technicians
Space shuttle repair and
  maintenance staff
Magnetic train developers
Industry control center technicians
Automatic drafting programmers
Robot retrainers
Video systems engineers
Microwave marketers
Computer art specialists
Automatic tunneling experts
Deep-well explorers
Submersible crews
Underwater archeologists
Bio-farming experts
Organ replacement surgeons and
  nursing specialists
Obesity control consultants
Mutation experts
Artificial intelligence scientists
  and engineers
Sonar applications sales people
Bullet train managers
Materials recycling technicians
Speech compression technology
  engineers

Vanishing Skills
and Occupations

By the end of the century, many skills that once were vital to business will be obsolete. Jobs that we still take for granted in today's economy will join the steamboat pilot and the blacksmith on history's discard heap.

JOBS TO BE OUTMODED BY TECHNOLOGY

Factory and Manufacturing-related

Machinists (lathe, milling, grinding, stamping)
Finishing (deburring, spraying, polishing)
Inventory (longshoreman, warehouseman, inventory clerical)
Fitters, riveters, cutters
Machine loaders and parts handlers
Packers

Office-Related Jobs

Typist and standard secretary (exclusive of executive secretary)
Mailroom personnel
Art room staff (paste-up, letterer, graph maker, draftsman)
File clerks
"Paper" librarians

Miscellaneous Jobs and Careers

Small farmers
Convenience stores (dry cleaning, general store, small real estate broker)
Newspaper workers and deliverers
Door-to-door salespeople
Toll and ticket booth operators
Bank clerks
Traditional telephone operators

The most significant trend in jobs and careers over the next twenty years will be the shift from "formation"-type jobs (manufacturing factory work, office typing, and clerical duties) to "information"-type jobs (technical machine processing supervision, programming, and systems analysis).

The American economy will witness the demise of the blue-collar worker as automation and robotics take over. The rapid elimination of most manual factory jobs will take place by 2000. Traditional blue-collar employers, like General Motors and U.S. Steel, have all too rapidly begun this process. The swollen unemployment rolls in industrial states like Michigan already attest to this development.

Office and service jobs, on the other hand, will increase, but only for those who are prepared to increase their technical efficiency. Automation in the form of robots, super-copiers, and information networks will replace many of the low-skilled and semi-skilled jobs so prevalent in the economy of the early 1980s.

SKILL	WHEN IT WILL VANISH	WHAT WILL OUTMODE IT	WHAT WILL REPLACE IT
Data Card Puncher	1990	Computer punch cards will vanish and punch card operators will go with them. Magnetic media will completely wipe out this old form of computer storage.	Software engineers who will be able to manipulate the blips on magnetic computer storage files will be the workhorses of the next century.
Farmworker	2000	There will always be farming, but by 2000 the farmworker as we know him or her will be disappearing. The farm will grow increasingly complex and, with computer control and robotic harvesters, there will be no need for the unskilled laborer to do back-breaking field work.	The future farm will be a place for people who know mechanics and gene-splicing; electronic technicians, bio-engineers, and programmers. Indeed, some day the human farmworker may be simply the fellow with the phone number of the robot repairman.
Grocery Cashier	2000	Humans at grocery checkouts make mistakes, gossip, get tired, and demand raises and vacations. New technologies can handle these jobs with aplomb; humans will be expendable.	Laser scanners instead of people already add up purchases. They will soon be able to deduct the cost directly from bank accounts. Cash registers will be found only at the few remaining "mom and pop" grocery stores.

SKILL	WHEN IT WILL VANISH	WHAT WILL OUTMODE IT	WHAT WILL REPLACE IT
Linotypist	1990s	The first use of computerized printing and typesetting occurred in 1963. The computer revolution was a way not only of cutting costs, but also of putting control of publication totally in the hands of the white collar members of the word business.	By 1980, most newspapers had broken the lino-type operators' unions and had scrapped their old presses. New offset presses and spotless, computerized composing rooms took over. By 2000, they will be universal, and the linotype operators will be retired, retrained, or doing the makework jobs given them as part of the settlement that computerized newspapers made. The linotype will become a museum piece.
Machinist	2010	Once the symbol of American industrial might, skilled machine workers will be done in by cheaper foreign competitors and the coming of robots.	More industrial work will be handled by newly developed nations, whose workers will not yet balk at the drudgery, dangers and pollution inherent in their jobs. Here, robots will make the tools and fix the machines.
Short-Order Cook	2020	The need for speed will do in short-order cooks. Computer-controlled machines will be able to do their job faster and cheaper, with fewer mistakes and virtually no waste.	The kitchen will contain a computer-controlled microwave system that can mix and heat ingredients with perfect efficiency. The food will come faster, the stools and booths will fill and empty more often, making restaurant owners more money.

SKILL	WHEN IT WILL VANISH	WHAT WILL OUTMODE IT	WHAT WILL REPLACE IT
Steno Worker	2020	The expansion of computer power, along with the speed of fiber optics, will overwhelm the information handling ability of human office workers.	Integrated office systems will create, store, and retrieve documents in seconds. Future secretaries will be computer programmers.
TV Programmer	2010	Since 1950, the television programmer has held one of the most powerful jobs in the United States, for he exercised control of the most powerful information medium, television. But by 1980, cable television had already begun to erode the mass market. By the mid-1980s, cable television will penetrate enough of the market to make cable a true mass medium. Producers, promoters, advertisers, entertainers, and finally the audience will desert over-the-air television for cable. Broadcasting will become "narrowcasting."	There will be no need in 2000 for a programmer to devise and develop a show that can simultaneously reach both the lowest common denominator and the largest audience. Fiber optics and satellite technology will give cable viewers dozens of channels to choose from. This expanded market will allow programs to be directed at even tiny audiences. Indeed, the television system's biggest problem may be finding enough programs to fill air space that will have expanded thirty times. Nor will there be a need to schedule programs rigidly to gain the maximum audience. Shows will air when and wherever there exists an audience, once or a thousand times, not unlike Broadway shows.

20 OCCUPATIONS TO AVOID IN THE 1980s

Occupation	Percent growth in employment, 1978-1990
Farm supervisors and laborers	25.4
Shoemaking machine operators	20.0
Railroad car repairers	18.8
Farmers and farm managers	17.2
Graduate assistants	16.5
Loggers	16.0
Private household workers	15.4
Secondary school teachers	12.9
Taxi drivers	12.6
Weavers	11.2
Railroad brake operators	10.3
College teachers	10.1
Dressmakers	8.3
Railroad conductors	6.6
Cannery workers	2.5
Compositors and typesetters	1.9
Postal clerks	0.3
Textile operatives	1.4
Clergy	1.7
Laundry workers	2.4

SOURCE: *Monthly Labor Bulletin*, August 1981.

Where America's Energy Will Come From

A Look at Trends to 2050

Fossil Fuel. Fossil fuel will dwindle steadily over the next thirty years as new energy sources become operative and the supply of crude oil diminishes. By 2010, high prices and decreasing supply will limit the use of fossil fuels to old buildings, cars, and airplanes, and for specialized lubrication functions. As the antiquated gas and kerosene vehicles go out of service and old buildings are demolished, fossil fuel use will continue to dip.

Solar Heat. Solar heat is a technology that may be of limited value. When first introduced in the 1970s, the use of sunlight to heat buildings directly was seen as an energy panacea, but solar heat will become merely one component of America's energy mix. The need in most climates for back-up systems to solar heat will reduce interest in the system. Solar heat will also prove impractical for most commercial uses. The energy form will probably reach its peak as a viable source by 2000.

Solar Electricity. Solar-generated electricity, unlike solar heat, will become more useful and effective in the years to come, despite initially modest expectations. Development of the cheap, reliable silicon-based voltaic cell in the late 1980s should spur development enormously. Of even greater importance will be the creation of the synthetic photosynthesis cell, which generates an electric current from sunlight in much the same way plant leaves do. Prototype models are already being tested. Small, flexible, efficient, and cheap solar electrical units should become steadily more popular.

Hydroelectric Power. While energy consumption will expand enormously in the next three decades, the amount of hydro power consumed will decrease proportionately. The primary reason is that few strong sites remain in America for dam development. However, isolated rural ranchers and farmers will make use of tiny water-wheel plants that use small amounts of moving water to generate a usable current. This will be a new development in the hydroelectric field. These torque units will enable rural areas to generate electricity from even the most sluggish streams.

Geothermal Energy. Geothermal energy will never be more than a secondary energy form, but improved understanding of geothermal engineering should increase its use. Hawaii and the Pacific Northwest plan to take advantage of favorable local conditions to generate most of their energy from underground streams. Most of America's geothermal development will occur in these two regions.

Tidal Power. Hawaii is pioneering the use of tidal shifts for power generation in America. Large oil companies along the Gulf Coast may soon follow suit, creating offshore power supplies for their derricks and platforms. Experts project that tidal power could eventually provide up to 5 percent of America's energy, as much as 25 percent in areas like Louisiana and southern Texas.

Wind Power. Wind power, like solar heat, is a technology that may not prove as promising as once anticipated. Still, large installations in Hawaii, Washington, Wyoming, Vermont, and the experimental offshore stations just beyond Nantucket should generate significant amounts of power by 2050. The limitation here is that only the massive stations will prove practical. Smaller units simply lack the consistency and dependability needed to become economically viable.

WHERE AMERICA'S ENERGY WILL COME FROM

Source	% of U.S. Total 1979	% of U.S. Total 2050
Fossil fuels	90	49
Solar (heat)	0.5	2
Solar (electric)	--	20
Hydroelectric	5	2
Geothermal	0.5	4
Tidal power	--	1
Wind power	--	1
Enzyme bioproducts	--	10
Fusion	--	9
Nuclear fission	4	1
Gasohol	--	1

SOURCE: 1979 figures, Statistical Abstract of the U.S. 1980

Enzyme Bioproducts. The stranglehold of fossil fuels in American energy development will be removed by the successful use of enzyme technologies which can build up the same complex hydrocarbon chains as petroleum refining. The enzyme bioproduct will most likely be introduced in conjunction with a product like motor oil, but totally synthetic hydrocarbons should spread steadily to areas once monopolized by oil. By the turn of the century, enzyme products will be used in plastics, fertilizers, paints, and fuels. Genetically engineered enzymes will be built up from simple hydrogen, oxygen, and carbon and fashioned into virtually any desired molecule. The future for this energy source appears almost limitless.

Fusion. The percentage of U.S. electricity supplied by fusion nuclear power plants may not be overwhelming by 2050, but the impact of this source—in which hydrogen atoms are mashed together, releasing vast amounts of power—could become significant since, theoretically, 9 percent of America's electricity needs could be supplied by only two fusion power plants. The extraordinary amounts of power each fusion plant will be able to produce suggest the importance of the new technology. Fusion will most likely become the dominant form of large-scale electrical power generation in the twenty-first century.

Fission. The development of fusion power and other energy sources could all but eliminate fission power plant construction in the first half of the next century. But nuclear power technology as practiced today will be obsolete even before fusion emerges as a dominant energy source in America. This decline will result from two primary factors: the brief useful life-span of a fission plant; and the spiraling price of uranium. By 2000, many fission plants built before the 1980s will already be out of service.

Gasohol. Gasohol as an energy source has potential for greater use than the statistics would indicate. The anticipated pressure for increased food production, however, may limit the amount of land that can be devoted to gasohol grains, which are developed mainly in farming regions. In time, gasohol may provide the fuel to run farm machinery, cars, and civic vehicles in farm-belt regions. But bioenzyme technology has the advantage that it produces usable fuel without the pollution problems or sacrifice of farmland inherent in gasohol.

Five Fastest-Growing National Economies: 2000

Despite turbulent politics and persistently chaotic economic histories, Third World countries will have the fastest growing economies over the next two decades. The five countries presented here will have economic downswings, but their raw materials and abiding desire to become modern, post-industrial nations will push them ahead overall.

Brazil

Population 2000: 205 million
Growth rate GNP: 8.2%

Brazil will continue its aggressive exploitation of its vast natural resources in order to fuel a booming economy. Every year, companies in the Amazon jungle will deforest an area the size of Kansas, ensuring that Brazil will become a major source of the world's lumber and paper. The 18 billion tons of iron ore in the Carajas region—the world's largest iron ore reserve—will supply iron both for industry and export.

Other companies will delve into the immense reserves of bauxite, copper, diamonds, gold, tin, nickel, and scores of other minerals. Newly cleared land will provide pastures and farmland.

Brazil will continue to encourage foreign investment in industry but may discourage foreign land speculation in the Amazon following its cantankerous relationship with American billionaire Daniel Ludwig. Ludwig, an American speculator, was forced in early 1982 to sell Jari, his plantation and industrial center that equaled in size the combined areas of Rhode Island and Connecticut, following fifteen years of unprofitable investment. The government nonetheless will probably continue to give foreign firms a helping hand by keeping both labor unions and anti-pollution laws weak. The auto-manufacturing industry, the ninth-largest in the world in 1981, will continue to grow rapidly, along with the steel-making and petrochemical industries as well as other businesses too dirty and costly for the developed nations. The arms trade, encouraged by a right-wing government, will also add needed currency to Brazil's economy.

Several factors may cloud Brazil's economic future. A Brazilian official boasted in the 1970s that "the Amazon will be for us what oil is for the Arabs." Some observers may remember such comments and will compare the desertification of the Amazon with the depletion of oil reserves and the ensuing political turmoil that is likely to beset the Mideast. Another problem could be the resentment created when foreign nations continue to exploit Brazil's resources and rulers, a situation that could conceivably transform the pro-American Brazilian nation into a hostile giant. Finally, there is the persistent problem of the impoverished Brazilian peasants—some 10 million landless people—whose collective voices will grow louder as the rich industrialists, the military, and the government reap immense financial rewards from one of the last untamed land masses remaining on earth.

Nigeria

Population 2000: 154 million
Growth Rate GNP: 6.2%

Oil will be the backbone of Nigeria's growth by 2000. Any disruptions in the Mideast will make oil more valuable and boost Nigeria's position as the most stable and affluent nation in black Africa. Nigeria will derive tremendous economic gains from this oil bonanza. The government will use this money to expand industry. Nigeria will develop its natural gas resources, and its petrochemical and chemical manufacturing industries will become among the largest in the world.

South Korea

Population 2000: 53 million
Growth Rate GNP: 10.1%
South Korea will shake off its current energy problems to maintain its reputation as a haven for capitalists. The densely concentrated population will force the government to impose strict conservation measures. Solar energy, tidal power, and wind power will help free the nation from expensive imported oil.

The conservative government, braced by the United States, will ensure that workers will go about making steel, building ships, and assembling machines without being distracted by strikes and protests. At the same time, the government will push for higher living standards to defuse any revolutionary stirrings. The increased output of radios, televisions, and even autos will give an added boost to the economy.

China

Population 2000: 1,093 billion
Growth Rate GNP: 9.6%
China's awesome natural and human resources could make it one of the fastest-growing countries of the world. With a population estimated at more than a billion, China will have sufficient labor for its own needs and may export laborers all over the world. Unlike the natural resources of much of the world, which by 2000 will be diminishing in some cases, the resources of this vast country will be virtually untouched.

China will indeed be ahead of the rest of the world in the crucial field of energy management. Developed nations like the United States will find conservation painful and disruptive. Many Third World nations are liable to waste their resources because the people are unskilled or the leaders are impatient to build airfields and superhighways. Disciplined, resourceful, and hard-working, the Chinese have long practiced conservation. The replenishing of soil through the use of natural fertilizer, a project ordered by the late Chairman Mao, is but one of the practices that will make China a model for other nations by 2000. Increased incentives for personal profit will also fuel the economy.

Mexico

Population 2000: 126 million
Growth Rate GNP: 5.8%

Mexico's severe financial problems will ease as the temporary oil glut of late 1982 and 1983 is replaced by tightened energy supplies in the 1990s. Once more, Mexico's oil will be vital to the United States, and its natural gas will supplement Russian supplies that keep the homes of Europe heated. Population control will help stabilize the country somewhat, although people will continue to pour in staggering numbers into Mexico City, swelling the metropolitan area of the city to over 31 million by 2000. These people will form an immense and cheap labor pool for Mexico's expanding industry.

Mexico's prosperity will be further buttressed by American support. The United States will realize that, in spite of ethnic and economic friction, Mexico is one of America's most useful allies.

As in the other countries of the Third World, rapid growth, hard-pressed workers, the abrupt break from tradition, and the unsettling effects of rising expectations—all side effects of a growing economy—could be the main threat to Mexico's political and economic stability.

New Industries
of the
Twenty-first Century

Fifty years ago, most of the companies at the top of today's "Fortune 500" did not exist, while others were mere fledgling firms. The time had not yet come for companies like IBM or RCA to achieve prominence. In the same way, tomorrow's leading industries are not known today. Here is a sampling of some industries that may lead the economy of the future.

Enzymatics

Enzyme processing will revolutionize the field of chemistry. Enzymes will be able to duplicate the reactions of petroleum refining, plastics synthesis, and high-temperature reagent processes. Combining with genetic engineering, a field that creates novel and potent strains of enzymes for various jobs, enzymatics will command the lion's share of the multi-billion dollar fuel, plastics, and specialty chemical markets by mid-twenty-first century. Little-known companies now exploring these fields (for example, Engenics of Palo Alto, California) may be industrial giants by 2050.

Portable Diagnostics

The agony of not knowing what disease or illness one has will be virtually eliminated in the early twenty-first century by the growth of portable diagnostics. Using sophisticated protein chemistry, tiny laser and chemical test crystals, and other small but potent techniques, a group of entrepreneurial engineering firms will create pocket-sized kits for testing virtually any serious set of symptoms. Patients will be able to screen themselves for diabetes, hypoglycemia, blood fats, pollutant poisoning, allergies, incipient arthritis, potential stroke, and virtually every kind of cancer. All of these tests will be made at home. These kits will work like today's home pregnancy tests—as initial screening procedures to confirm or refute suspicions before a costly trip to the doctor is needed.

Holographic Viewing

The perfection of the holographic cassette will open up this long-awaited market. The cassette will contain a loop of high-density videotape that contains an interference pattern formed by bursts of laser light. This tape will recreate three-dimensional images at speeds that correspond to the frame resolution time of new fast-acting video screens. The three-dimensional visual images will flash into view as the cards of a shuffled deck do, creating the illusion of three-dimensional motion.

When first introduced, the cassette will be one-color with sound on a second tape that must be played separately. By the turn of the century, sound will be included on the video tape, and by 2010, full-color, stereo sound cassettes will hit the market. Home television viewing, art object storage, and home movies will be revolutionized by this laser system.

Space Pharmaceuticals

In the germ-free, gravity-free, vibration-free atmosphere of space, drug companies will be able to manufacture drugs currently unknown to man. Within a decade or two of the opening of the first space pharmaceutical plant, link-ups between computers and space pharmaceutical factories will allow for the manufacture of individualized drugs.

The computer will research the patient's body chemistry and design the perfect drug for his or her case. The space platform will draw from an on-hand supply of organic molecules, synthesize the needed chemicals from these molecules, and then blend them according to medical instructions. Daily transports will carry the medications to earth.

Natural Process Engineering

Specialty engineering firms centered in the American West and along the coasts will use natural processes to create temporary buildings or to change the face of any given environment. Using high-tech cloud control, these companies will be able to create a literal wall of water to cool workers in a desert. By using matrices of plastic wires that attract materials that cling together by electrical force, they will be able to create living reefs in the form of buildings. Using wind engineering, they could shape artificial dunes for temporary sand shelters. People will resort to permanent artificial structures only when they want a dwelling to last for a lifetime. Short-term shelters, therefore, will be created through nature. By 2000, small professional firms will handle as much as $1 billion in natural design work and will create such projects throughout the world.

Bio-Implantation

Using computer modeling, genetic engineering, and complex body scanning, bio-implantation firms will fashion biological analogues for lost body parts or non-functioning organs. Instead of using a metal or plastic prosthesis device, the individual will receive a biological implant that corresponds in every respect to his body chemistry. If a man loses a foot, he will get a new "flesh and blood" foot. Even if his liver, the toughest organ to replace, fails, he will receive an artificial liver that might exceed the performance of the original. These replacement parts will still need to be surgically implanted or mechanically attached, but they will look and act exactly like the real organ. Many will even work under control of the recipient's brain. By the early twenty-first century, spin-off companies from the University of Utah's bioengineering lab and from UCLA and MIT programs will build $2.5 billion of new human pieces.

Human-powered Vehicles

Invention of vehicles that enormously magnify the power of human muscles will slowly supplant the car in the inner city and will ultimately revolutionize city travel. Cam-driven, super-lubricated wheels, located beneath membrane frames that weigh just a few pounds, will allow human drivers to maintain speeds of thirty miles per hour for more than an hour without getting out of breath. Whereas a bicycle requires the driver to pedal with the whole leg, these vehicles will work from a simple back and forth movement of the feet, requiring as little exertion of energy as the pressing of a clutch.

The industry may be hampered at first by liability problems, for such new-fangled vehicles will share the road with larger automobiles. Some cities could conceivably ban cars in the late 1990s. With the cost of traditional automobiles rising even faster than the rate of inflation, many people will not be able to afford them by 1990. The consumer response to human-powered vehicles will become steadily more positive. By the middle of the next century, human-powered vehicle unit sales will exceed those of autos.

By the first decade of the next century, major auto manufacturers will seriously enter the human-powered vehicle market. Eventually the manufacturing of private autos may be nearly abandoned as economic conditions favor the manufacture and operation of human-powered vehicles.

Robot Population
by Country: 2000

Japan

The typical factory worker in Japan may be a robot by 2000. The system will be so all-encompassing that robots will be used to manufacture and repair other robots.

The automotive industry will have the greatest number of robots in operation, closely followed by the appliance-manufacturing field. The electronics and watch-making industries, however, will be the first to rely solely on robot workers. By 2000, the Japanese car will be so enhanced with computer gadgets that it will be virtually a robot in itself. As robots become more efficient and as their development progresses, one out of ten robots will be replaced each year. This would ensure that over one million robots will be manufactured in Japan annually.

The Japanese will also lead the world in development of household robotics. A household robot will be about as common as a television. The robot's primary functions will relate to entertainment and communication, acting as a tape deck, telephone, video player and recorder, two-way television unit, security system, games center, word processing unit, and general multi-media center. In today's dollars, such a machine will cost between $9,000 and $10,000, equal to the cost of a standard car.

By 2000, the Japanese will be leaders in space robotics. The Japanese will design and implement space factories, and their robots will be used to repair satellites and undertake space mining.

United States

By 2000, robots will be used extensively in offices, service industries, and manufacturing. The following occupations are fated to become obsolete as a result of robots: bank tellers, supermarket checkout clerks, movie theater ticket operators, car wash workers, and stock clerks.

Short-order food preparation also appears likely to be overtaken by robotics. These firms could implement a robot food-serving system as early as 1985. Gas stations also will be totally serviced by robots. While the tank is being filled, a credit card will be put in the machine to register payment and complete the transaction.

Blue collar and service industries will be the most severely affected by the robot influx. Factory assembly lines will become a nostalgic notion of the past.

In contrast to Japan, robots will not be used as extensively in the American home. Widespread use of robots will prevail only among the upper and upper middle classes.

The United States will continue to maintain a leading position in space robotics. Robot probes will be used to explore other solar systems. If new life exists in other solar systems, first contact may be made by robot "diplomats."

USSR

The Soviets will standardize the robot industry. Widespread use of rudimentary robots in manufacturing will prevail by 2000. Although the Soviets will have more robots in industry than any nation other than Japan, their robots will be far less sophisticated than those in either the United States or Japan.

Use of robots could create increasing political and psychological tension in Russia as workers enjoy more leisure time. How they will use time they have never had before is a question with which policymakers will have to wrestle.

Applications of the robot in the Soviet home may be limited, since government officials may be reluctant to give most people easy access to a computer. Information could become harder to control. Books, tapes, and records could easily be stored and hidden from the eyes and ears of bureaucrats if robot/computer use became prevalent.

In the application of computers and robots, the Soviet Union may lag as much as ten years behind the United States.

West Germany

The West Germans will likely produce the best-engineered robots in the world. They will be used in virtually all industries. But the Germans will retain a combination of manual and robotic workers, since they pride themselves on their fine craftmanship. Use in the home may be limited, reflecting an essential conservatism in German living standards. Robots will primarily be used in developing greater industrial productivity and exportation of goods.

France

As the first people to develop a national policy on the application of robots and computers, the French will be highly advanced in the use of robots in commerce and industry. The main hindrance to France's assumption of international leadership in this field would be if the French insist on using a unique computer language and standards, preventing matchups with robots manufactured in other countries. Overall, however, French developments in the robotics field will be highly sophisticated.

ROBOT POPULATION BY COUNTRY: 2000	
Japan	11,000,000
United States	7,500,000
USSR	5,600,000
West Germany	3,600,000
France	1,620,000
Italy	1,600,000
East Germany	1,000,000
United Kingdom	820,000
Sweden	650,000
Brazil	550,000

Italy

Italy will create excellent technology in robotics and automation, and will continue to display great talent and innovation in their products. The first so-called "Da Vinci" robot or engineer will be developed in Italy. This robot will be able to solve engineering problems and come up with new ideas. Chief Italian robot industries: plastics, cars, furniture, clothing, household appliances.

East Germany

East Germany will be a leader in the use of robotics in Eastern Europe. The East Germans will have some of the most sophisticated automotive factories in the world. Robots will be used for simulation purposes in studying and perfecting sports activities.

United Kingdom

The United Kingdom will continue to develop major innovations in robotics. However, the possibility of strong labor union action against robotic automation could delay the widespread introduction of robots into factories. In any case, the advances made by British scientists will continue to be applied for greater gains by the international robotics industry.

Sweden

By 2000, Sweden will have a largely automated robot society, one that will extend to the factory, office, and home. This vastly increased quantity of free time for all citizens will stimulate the development of new leisure activities. Every industry will be dominated by robots: furniture, paper, automotive, printing, and other heavy manufacturing industries.

Brazil

Brazil will be an emerging country in the robotics field. Applying the technological advances of other countries, Brazilian industrialists will make use of foreign scientific innovations in the areas of automobile manufacturing, agriculture, lumber, and mining. Robots will be put to work in areas of the Amazon unsuitable for humans. Brazil will stand in the forefront of robot application in Latin America.

The Automated Office

Transformation of the office into a paperless world began in the early 1980s, motivated by two principal forces: computer applications to business information processing, and the growth of telecommunications systems and products. The office revolution has changed not only the methods of getting work done and handling information but has also radically altered the roles and functions of all personnel in the office, from the highest strata of corporate management to the lowest clerical positions.

Computers have been an integral component of the paperless office concept. They provide workers and managers with vast storage files that take up virtually no space, as well as a tool for solving virtually any problem. Through office networks, all of a firm's employees can be tied into a huge computer that can handle all their requests simultaneously. With *modems* (modulator-demodulators), computers can talk over telephone lines with computers at distant sales offices or overseas branches.

As the rules for directing computers to solve problems grow more sophisticated and the machines themselves become more varied, the flexibility of office computers will expand. Already, networks can include either simple terminals, which can do nothing except transmit information back and forth from the worker to the central computer, and "smart" versions that can solve several basic problems on their own. They can feature executive tiering, so that requests from the work stations of more senior employees get priority response from the computer. They can provide color graphics, limited speech recognition, a wide array of printing options, links to office photo-copying systems for document creation, and dozens of other options.

The future will bring still more possibilities. Here are just a few.

Electronic Mail

The transfer from paper mail to electronic computer-delivered mail will take at least two decades to implement. The advantages of electronic storage of information and the speed of computer message delivery will act as major forces to create this technological revolution. In electronic mail, messages are typed into the computer, which instantly sends the letter to its destination and files all requested copies. The recipient gets the message—either on his screen or through his printer—when he asks his computer for the mail. First, internal corporate messages will go electronic, then, by 1990, high-speed computer advances will make inter-office electronic mail cost-effective. The post office will be forced to compete; first class mail may be mostly electronic by 2000.

Data Banking

Within twenty years, the storage of office information will constitute one of the largest businesses in the world. Systems devised to store, sort, and retrieve information dependably will stagger the mind. As of 1981, the number of office documents produced in the United States alone amounted to 72 billion pieces a year. By 1991, the volume will increase to 250 billion pieces. However, more than 50 percent will be stored in digital computer form in electronic information banks. And by 2000, more than 93 percent of the 1 trillion pieces of business information generated will be in digital form. The average manager by then will have instant access to more information than in a thousand Libraries of Congress.

Teleconferencing

The dismal record of the early picture phone will stand in contrast to the successful growth of the teleconferencing industry for office functions. The teleconference may first catch on as a way to reduce the cost of in-person meetings among far-flung executives. The additional advantages of sophisticated corporate presentation control with teleconferencing and the capability to record entire conference proceedings will lead to still wider use. Sales teleconferencing will set new precedents, doubling the already prosperous business by the mid-1990s.

Supergraphics

Computer stations that create intricate graphics will become a principal tool of future business. Large scale graphics, originally conceived for computer chip design and engineering, will be successfully applied to the field of real-time corporate scanning. Such a system would make it possible for an executive to see any number of business variables displayed in relation to one another through colored moving images. The executive will be able to expedite vital decisions by seeing how changes in any variable transform the picture of every other facet of business.

Automatic Translations

Machines that comprehend human speech will spur the development of automatic in-office translation services for businesses and institutions. Any language spoken, typed, or drawn from computer memory will be automatically translatable into any other language of choice. It can then be used on the computer's videoscreen, transmitted to another computer, or turned into a document.

The Voice-Activated Typewriter

The voice-activated typewriter will automatically display words and images as a speaker pronounces them. VAT will increase executive productivity enormously by decreasing by millions the number of typists in offices worldwide.

New Office Landscape

The invention of the programmable sound "silencer" that eliminates noise far better than brick or stone will increase the use of open landscape office designs. Full walls will be used for symbolic or status purposes only. Microcomputerized office machinery will fit into conventional furniture, and files will consist of compact computer discs stored in basement recesses. Plants, art, and display presentations will take over the space once filled with file cabinets, typing tables, copying machines, and other paper handling equipment and furniture.

Electronic Blackboards

Specially designed digitizing surfaces will be laminated onto tables, conference walls, and podiums. These surfaces will display drawings, charts, or text for transmission, storage, or immediate display. The user will be able to draw on them with an "electronic" pen or stick a prepared image into a reading machine that will reproduce it on the board. These systems will hook into existing telephone or telecommunications networks for remote transmission anywhere in the world.

Fax

Automated facsimile devices will be made more efficient. Rather than running hundreds of pages of copy per minute, they will achieve a rate of tens of thousands of pages per second. Together with computer memories, they will make letter generation, memo distribution, and other paper chores faster and easier.

Videodiscs

An increasing number of businesses may elect to store documents, reference materials, employee files, and other permanent information on videodiscs. Since these record album-sized storage plates are encoded with a laser, they fit in neatly with laser-based fiber optic networks that could conceivably become the basis for most future information transmission. The disc's capacity is incredible. Each side of a videodisc can store at least 54,000 pages; new developments may raise that capacity by a power of ten. Already, Toshiba has a disc document storage, retrieval, and printing system on the market. By the 1990s, compact laser disc storage will be common.

Ten Leading "OMNI 500" Companies in 2000

Big business will grow even larger over the next few decades, as mergers and acquisitions continue to be the easiest way to buy into new markets. There will be occasional bursts of entrepreneurial energy as frustrated baby-boomers realize that there is not enough room at the top and will strike out to start businesses of their own. However, for the most part, the major corporations of today will try to ride new technologies and new services into market dominance by taking over smaller, financially profitable, technology-oriented companies.

Telecommunications services, energy, and genetic/biological engineering will probably be the significant growth areas over the coming years, and the "Fortune 500" of today will look quite different from the "OMNI 500" of tomorrow. Here is a look at what ten leading companies might look like at the turn of the century.

The OMNI 500 is based on projected profitability over asset base and possible mergers to occur before 2000.

Warner-Amex Compunications Services

The biggest and most profitable corporation in the OMNI 500 will be Warner-Amex Compunications Services. "Compunications" is a coined word to describe the fusion of computations and communications. Warner-Amex, which has had a few limited ventures in the cable television field, is expected to consummate a complete corporate merger in the late 1980s. It should be a perfect fit. American Express has a large quantity of investment capital and a high-quality customer base; Warner Communications has the marketing skills and a pulse on the public's taste. Better yet, Warner has Atari, the phenomenally successful electronic games/personal computer company. Atari could become the single largest revenue source in the Warner-Amex constellation, given the incredible popularity of video games. The company is expected to make breakthroughs in computer research that will make programming a computer as easy as conducting a conversation with it, while hardware developments adapted from the Japanese will make Atari's computers as cheap as their hand-held games.

Warner's television and movie inventors will create movie-games, which give customers the ability to create their own films using video simulacra of great stars and sets of the past. Computers will integrate the many variables into a creation of the individual's design. The system will enable the ordinary consumer to feel like Otto Preminger or Billy Wilder, even though the results may not approach the calibre of Hollywood's great directors.

Using their cable and satellite assets, Warner-Amex will develop their own communications networks for their extensive customer base in order to provide such services as home banking, electronic mail, and cross-continental video games. Warner-Amex is the most promising company on the OMNI list. With assets in hardware, software, entertainment, business, and communications networks, it will be the ultimate media company in an age dominated by information.

Citicorp

The second OMNI 500 company is the multinational behemoth Citicorp. Best-known as a bank, the corporation will nonetheless move quickly to take advantage of deregulatory moves. It will thus expand into the business and financial services marketplace on an international level. With the removal of interstate banking restrictions, Citicorp will acquire both banks and banking machine networks to blanket the country with access points to Citi's services. And with satellites acting to link transactions instantaneously, Citi will become the nation's leading banker.

Using its technological base and its enormous contacts, the company will extend its expertise overseas and will become the major financier of many multinational corporations in underdeveloped nations in need of capital. The key to Citicorp's success will likely lie in its ability to predict and forecast economic developments through the use of computer programs that will develop economic plans, suggest major investments, and track world cash and capital flows. An advanced computer system will enable Citicorp to act simultaneously as a conservative banking concern and as a risk-taking, entrepreneurial operation. Citicorp's substantial wealth and its ability to deploy such funds will make the bank a surrogate government of sorts by the middle 1990s.

A.T.&T.

A.T.&T. will be a company that will profit from legal deregulation. For years restricted to providing only basic telephone service, "Ma Bell" could become a bigger computer manufacturer than IBM. Each one of A.T.&T.'s phones already contains a series of multi-function computer chips. In fact, A.T.&T. really no longer sells phones; it sells computers that also happen to be phones. Its computer phones are slightly different from other computers such as Apple's or IBM's in that they are designed around the telephone network.

This means that A.T.&T.'s computers are already designed to communicate with one another all over the world. Today, they carry human voice messages, but with slight upgrading they will be able to transmit any kind of data anywhere. A.T.&T.'s network will no longer be a web of twisted pairs of copper wires; it will be a fine-spun mesh of fiber optics capable of transmitting thousands of TV pictures, conversations, and computer data simultaneously. So popular will this total information networking become that A.T.&T. will be hard-pressed to keep up with demand.

A.T.&T. will also begin to offer radio-phone service enabling consumers to carry a portable phone. Such a network system will use communication satellite systems extensively. Although other companies will offer alternative networks to A.T.&T.'s—indeed, many cable companies will carry voice and data communications—A.T.&T. will be the leader in the field of network services.

Finally, A.T.&T. will rise as a formidable competitor in the business equipment market, offering office systems and computer services to major companies that will need resources on a scale that only such a large corporation could provide.

Exxon

Exxon will retain its position as a leading corporation in 2000. Exxon will invest in natural resources that will range from shale and coal to geothermal energy to solar cells.

In the latter half of the 1980s, Exxon will most likely move to de-emphasize its huge petroleum holdings and concentrate on attacking the energy situation through alternative methods. Heavy investment will inevitably follow.

Exxon executives and analysts are keenly aware that the future American energy situation will change dramatically. Many households, for example, will purchase their own energy-supply devices, be they fuel cells or solar cells, and will decrease their dependence on centrally supplied power. This decentralization of demand will bankrupt many smaller utilities and create cash flow crises in the larger concerns. In addition, conservation efforts and the substitution of telecommunications for transportation (shop-at-home, electronic banking, working at home through the computer terminal, etc.) will reduce demand for petroleum to the extent that profit margins in that area will decline.

Energy, in short, will no longer be the dominant industry in American life.

By investing all across the board, however, Exxon will manage to avoid facing unprecedented lows. It will have hedged its bets. But spectacular highs seem just as remote. Although Exxon's industrial greatness may decline with the passing dependence on one source of energy, its role in providing technologies that decentralize the energy supply will make the corporation an integral part of the expanding information society.

IBM

IBM is a time-honored institution, as rooted in the American tradition as any corporation. It will, of course, still be the major computer company in 2000, but it will also offer a wide array of smaller computers for individual consumers. By virtue of the crazy-quilt nature of the telecommunications/computer marketplace, IBM will find itself competing against A.T.&T. on the high end of the spectrum and against Warner's Atari on the low end. The result is that layoffs may be likely, enabling the company to stay lean against both domestic and Japanese competition.

IBM will evolve in the next twenty years from being principally a hardware house to a corporation that will provide high-speed data communications services through its Satellite Business Systems subsidiary. IBM will also become the largest publisher and provider of computer software in the world, offering dozens of computer languages. Many will be based on artificial intelligence techniques. Catalogs will become a chief selling device, complementing the IBM salesman. Consumers will order new programs that will be shipped electronically into their computer.

While IBM will continue to do well in gross sales, it could find its margins declining both in the United States and abroad. Competition will squeeze the computer giant. It is even likely that IBM will become more of a software provider than a hardware manufacturer. The return on investment for hardware development will diminish in the future.

Mobil

Mobil will become the merger king of industry, acquiring and scuttling subsidiary companies at a pace that will astound and confound Wall Street analysts. Unwilling to exist solely as an energy company, the Mobil conglomerate will use its considerable cash flow from oil to buy its way into whatever growth markets it desires. Though Mobil's primary interests may remain in energy, its money will be channeled into whatever industry offers the best rate of return. Mobil's biggest problem will be in seeing its planned mergers through, for it will be forced to fight hard for takeovers and will be thwarted many times.

General Motors

Once the biggest company in the world, General Motors's sheer size will keep it near the corporate top despite the decline of the Detroit automobile monopoly. Maintaining its position, however, will require adjustments to accommodate a changing economy.

Japan has already begun to dominate the international automobile industry, and Third World car manufacturers, such as those in Brazil, have yet to be reckoned with.

Eventually, the company will make small, fuel-cell-powered cars for local travel and buses for mass transit in congested urban areas, but the success of its products will no longer be used as a yardstick to measure the U.S. economy. General Motors will remain profitable for many years, but by 2010 the Detroit giant could vanish from the leading ranks of corporate conglomeration.

Cetus and Genentech

In contrast to General Motors, Cetus and Genentech are where the future is being born. The two genetic engineering concerns may merge in the early 1990s and pool their laboratory resources. The merger could hold awesome implications for an industry that has yet to mature. Someday, genetic engineering may replace telecommunications and computers as the dominant world industry.

Whether they combine or remain separate entities, Cetus and Genentech will create pharmaceuticals that will effectively cure diabetes and suppress the cancer tendencies in smokers. Genetic engineering will eventually make heart, lung, kidney, and even liver transplants routine surgery, since the genetically engineered organs should never pose implant problems.

In the agricultural area, Cetus/Genentech will develop several strains of grains that will take root in the harshest, most arid soils on the African continent. These grains, by the early years of the new century, will provide nourishment for millions of people. Animals will become meatier as a result of genetic tampering, creating a healthy surplus of meat from both poultry and livestock. All of this will encourage increased growth of the genetic engineering industry.

While progress will come slowly throughout the 1980s and early 1990s, the wide-ranging applicability of genetic engineering will become evident when the techniques become cheap enough for commercial use.

Time Inc.

With an acquisition like NBC (which RCA may sell to get itself out of financial straits), Time Inc. could position itself prominently in the techno-logical sphere of the media world. While steering clear of interactive media (versus, say, Warner-Amex), Time Inc. will be a dominant force in news and entertainment. It will own a broadcast network, an interna-tional satellite link that it will use to launch international programming, and an efficient structure for creating specialized print and video publi-cations according to market demands. By the twenty-first century, mag-azines will represent the smallest fraction of Time Inc.'s business.

Johnson & Johnson

In an industry characterized by guarded conservatism, Johnson & Johnson will assert itself as an aggressive conglomerate and will embrace new pharmaceutical possibilities. The pharmaceutical compa-ny, for example, will be a leader in developing space drug manufac-turing. It will sponsor the first space drug factory in the late 1980s. The unique products made there will give Johnson & Johnson footholds in dozens of new drug markets.

The company will also jump into the field of genetic engineering. Johnson & Johnson was to be a full partner in DNA Research, E.F. Hutton's ill-fated genetic firm, so the company will surely turn up else-where in this emerging business as a primary force. Willing to take more chances by putting its money into controversial techniques, John-son & Johnson will dominate in future drug development. Its involve-ment in the slowly emerging field of mood drugs, drugs that will effec-tively and safely alter human mind states, will take hold around the turn of the century.

6 TECHNOLOGICAL LIFESTYLES

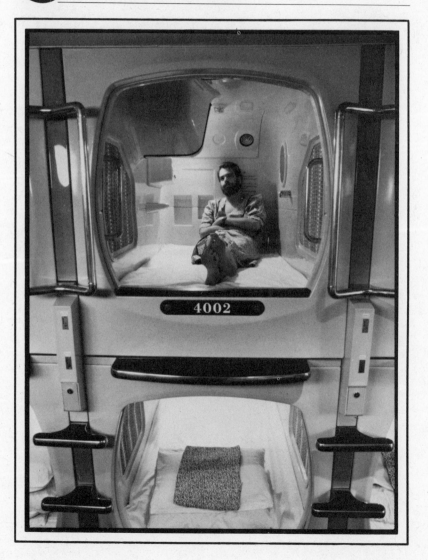

6 TECHNOLOGICAL LIFESTYLES

How will the extraordinary technological advances of the future affect our personal daily lives? Will they change the way we work and the way we play?

One of the major fronts of technological development is the rapid transmission of information made possible by the computer revolution. We gain access to new information each passing day. Sooner than many believe, our homes and offices will offer us virtually limitless choices of information, making our jobs simpler and our lives easier.

This explosion of information technology will open the door for new forms of entertainment and altered ways of learning. It may make music, literature, and the visual arts more accessible to the entire population. On the other hand, we may find all this information psychologically overwhelming and difficult to absorb. We might also discover that our new ''information society'' violates individual and collective rights. Cherished privacy may indeed vanish.

Still, the tools of our future are already advancing from the laboratories into our homes and offices. Will we take advantage of the opportunities they present? To some extent, we surely will, but their promise seems ambiguous as we move into an age of information abundance.

That's Entertainment: Movie Trends

The American film industry has resisted change for decades. Despite improvements in film stock, color, and sound, the movies basically remain as they were fifty years ago. But changes are appearing on the horizon, less so in story concept than in the areas of marketing and production.

The increasing availability of cable, pay-TV, and home video will make the movie theater, as we know it, obsolete. High ticket prices will reduce the number of larger theaters and will bring a demise to the Saturday dinner and movie dating custom. Instead of grabbing a meal at the local steakhouse and then heading down for a flick at the Bijou, the typical couple of the near future might pop a steak into the microwave oven and settle down to an evening of taped video entertainment.

Here is a survey of future entertainment.

Film

At present, all motion picture film stocks are made of silver and petroleum compounds. Silver has become more expensive in recent years, and its demand by other technologies will continue to drive up the cost of prints for movie theaters. This will further contribute to the theater industry's already troubled economic state.

Before film is made obsolete, researchers will extend the life of movie prints by making tougher plastic bases and emulsions less reliant on silver. Already, one Japanese firm has demonstrated its success with color films that are reproduced electrostatically (like Xerography), rather than by conventional photo methods.

Screens

Responding to the success of home video and pay-TV, the film industry will come up with new gimmicks in an attempt to lure lost audiences back into theaters. Corporate movie moguls and theater executives will create new techniques and dust off some old ones. Although we would like to predict the time frames for these events, fads are difficult, if not impossible, to forecast.

• A new 3-D craze may arise, but will die for the same reasons the technique faded in the 1950s—poor picture quality, shoddy low-budget productions, and the inconvenience of wearing special glasses to watch the films.

• Systems for 3-D movies employing stereo techniques that eliminate the need for special viewing glasses may be developed, but might not make it out of the laboratory stage due to high costs and the financial risks involved.

• Cinerama-like panoramic movie screens may make a comeback, too, but will similarly disappear. The scope and scale has already proven unsuitable for almost any movie story, save for the occasional movie spectaculars—biblical epics, science fiction extravaganzas, and broad-horizon westerns. The fact that such projects make up only a small percentage of the total number of movie releases will make broad-screen installation unprofitable.

• Holograms are laser-created three-dimensional images. The technique has been around since the mid-1960s. Originally, holograms were limited to non-moving images, but refinements in the field have introduced limited motion and color. In the future, perhaps by the end of the century, a practical holographic movie system may be created. In a holographic movie theater, the audience may see the actors and action played out in front of and around them—life-sized and life-like. These theaters will have no screens; the holograms will recreate themselves in free space.

The enormous financial capital needed to perfect this system may stifle development or postpone its introduction until well into the next century.

Video theaters that utilize new, high-definition video projectors instead of conventional film projectors will be used to exhibit both motion pictures and live events. These theaters are likely to be linked by a network of communications satellites, making possible the transmission of a movie to many theaters from a single source. The rising costs of producing and shipping individual prints of movies will encourage the rapid establishment of these video theaters.

Sound

Advances in sound technology will first reach the home through consumer high fidelity systems with the development and marketing of sophisticated digital recording and playback systems. Movie theaters will need to respond to this competition by creating new movie sound systems that are fully digital and use as many as ten to twenty separate channels. These digital audio systems will be built around computer encoding and playback techniques that will offer noise-free reproduction that is far more accurate than any sound system available at present. Movie-goers can anticipate seeing the first of these major audio advances by the late 1980s. Digital research began in the United States and Japan during the early 1970s and is already so advanced that these improvements in the movie theater could be easily achieved within the next ten years.

Sound systems capable of reproducing sub-audial frequencies—sounds that are felt more than heard, creating rumbling physical effects—have so far been limited to a few films like *Earthquake*, *Midway*, and *Rollercoaster*. This sound capability will be integrated into the newly designed digital sound systems. Filmmakers will learn to use this capability in dramatic ways. The moviegoer in, say, 1988, might feel the protagonist's heartbeat, the impact of a train wreck, or the full force of a summer storm, adding a new physical sensation to an experience that had previously been limited to sight and sound.

Production

Tomorrow's movie studios will be designed specifically to accommodate the use of computer and video techniques. Instead of film cameras, ultra high-definition video cameras will record picture and sound in digital computer memories. It is possible that dramatic performances, even actors' lines, will be altered, via computer synthesis, yielding a perfect first "take" every time. Some actors, specifically character types, might be totally synthesized. One actor's performance might easily be combined with another person's distinctive physical look or voice. By using computer synthesis, a director would be able to marry the acting skills of Laurence Olivier to photographic images of Abraham Lincoln.

With these techniques available, editing a motion picture will consist of combining live-action scenes with synthesized or recorded backgrounds in order to place the actors on location anywhere in the world. In this way, expensive location filming will be eliminated or, at least, used infrequently.

These computer graphic techniques are presently in their infancy, although advancing rapidly in the United States and Japan. The advantage of recording motion pictures into a computer memory is that the movies can be "packaged" in any existing or future format—electronic or photographic. The films can therefore be subsequently released as a home video product, distributed by satellite to theaters and homes around the world, or even be projected onto a theater screen using scanning lasers.

Special Effects

The excellent image quality associated with motion picture film will not be lost. In fact, computer graphics and imaging systems will surpass present definitions of quality, each frame being composed of tens of millions of *pixels*, or individual picture elements.

Digital techniques will enhance special effects as well. Miniature props, such as spaceships, trains, and historical buildings, need no longer be built, but need only be described to the graphics computer. In this way, any "camera angle" view of an object can be created and combined with other elements in a scene. Instead of sculpting or painting in clay or canvas, a special effects artist will visualize his creation on a cathode ray tube and produce revised versions almost instantaneously at a director's request. Graphics artists will become computer-graphics specialists. Traditional painters or animators will contribute in limited areas where their creative skills can still give a unique touch to films. The movie studio's back lot, already obsolete, will be revived only in the mind of a computer.

Movies in Theaters

The number of motion pictures made expressly for theaters will be eclipsed by production for television, pay-TV, and home video media.

Today's theater designs will evolve into two distinct types of movie theaters. The large multiple theaters commonly located in suburban malls and shopping centers will be remodeled to produce a single, giant auditorium suitable for lavish spectacles with enormous public appeal. More intimate boutique theaters will be the popular outlet for smaller, personal dramas and films with specialized audience appeal. Foreign language and avant-garde movies will be a staple of these boutique theaters.

The cost of going to a theater to see these technical extravaganzas will increase exponentially due to the soaring costs of maintaining, heating, and cooling large public auditoriums. The new, sophisticated hardware required for their presentation will also contribute to the high cost. In theaters showing these spectaculars, the cost of admission will be comparable to that of a live performance. By the end of the century, movie tickets could run as high as thirty dollars (in today's dollars) for major blockbusters such as *Star Wars: Chapter 8*. The economy of the the small boutique theaters, however, will be maintained because of their reliance on video and other electronic techniques. Old equipment will still be used to show classic films. Perhaps those old movies will be the only ones available to theatergoers at ticket prices under ten dollars.

Other Movie Trends

What has succeeded in Hollywood's past will work best in its future.

• Cartoons, westerns, and love stories will still constitute the predominant hits of the twenty-first century.

• Future audiences, unfamiliar with classic films like *Citizen Kane, Gone with the Wind, Casablanca,* and *The Godfather,* will see these enduring tales remade with the stars of the future. This will continue a revivalist tradition that has long been in existence in Hollywood and on the Broadway stage.

• Instant classics will be created by increased Hollywood hype and intensive advertising. Aggressive marketing techniques will also be used in the promotion of pay television and home video media.

• Old-time movies—black and white films from the 1930s, 1940s, and 1950s—will be electronically colored by computer techniques for a generation unfamiliar with the medium of black and white photography.

• Trends at the theater concession stand may come and go, but popcorn will remain America's favorite movie-going snack.

• Movie studios will continue to become electronic entertainment conglomerates. With their vast financial resources, these will be the only organizations capable of funding the giant spectaculars of the future. The trend is already exemplified by Universal, Paramount, MGM, and Warner. Smaller experimental movies, on the other hand, will flourish with the availability of video to independant producers.

• Though the techniques and technologies of movies are certain to change, movies will always be called movies.

Television
Transformations

The television industry, long dominated by commercial broadcasting networks, will undergo radical changes by the end of the century. New programming will become amazingly diverse, while new forms of video media will free viewers from the traditional restrictions of network scheduling.

Video Recording

The ubiquity of home video tape recording systems will be the most perceptible movement of the shifting television scene, at least during the next decade. Videocassette recorders (VCRs) will continue to be the most attractive and economical systems for consumers, and manufacturers will learn how to build the devices less expensively and more reliably. They will increasingly be regarded as mass market appliances rather than luxury items. These machines are central to the idea of video-on-demand since they allow an individual or family to tailor an entire week or more of television to their tastes.

The use of home video recorders for this type of "time shifting" will cause major problems for broadcasters who must predict to their advertisers which market will be watching which program at a specific time. Fans of daytime television programs, for example, will watch soap operas when their schedules permit—probably in prime-time—utterly skewing ratings and confusing advertising plans.

HOME VIDEO PROJECTIONS
U.S.A., 1980 - 1990

	1981	1985	1990	Projection 2000
Homes using television (in millions)	80.6	85.4	93.9	in excess of 100
Cable TV households (in millions)	10	28	46	55
Percentage of all television households using cable	29.8%	32.8%	49%	55%
Homes with pay-TV (including pay-cable and subscription TV) (in millions)	10	16.5	30	42
Percentage of all television households using pay-TV	12.4%	23.4%	37.8%	42%
Videocassette recorders in homes (in millions)	2.1	6	13	20
Videodisc players in homes (in millions) (125,000)	0.125	3.5	7.5	18

SOURCE: 1981 figures, Motion Picture Association of America

The most optimistic projections show that sales of video recorders will steadily increase throughout this decade, leveling off at approximately 20 million by the end of this century in the United States. Sales of videocassette recorders in other countries still outpace American consumption. These recorders are also bringing video programming to countries without broadcast television, specifically underdeveloped and remote areas of the world, making them "videocassette societies."

All-in-one video camera-recorder combinations (video movie cameras) will be introduced by the mid-1980s, but their relatively high cost may prevent them from achieving the popularity that personal photography products now enjoy, at least during this decade. The key to acceptance will not be in producing an electronic movie camera (it already exists), but in developing peripheral tools—editors, special effects devices, multiple camera switchers—that will give individuals the flexibility and production power now available only to professionals. Home movies will become self-produced television programs, enabling, say, a Boy Scout troop to record its adventures in the field or a group of community activists to make programs espousing their particular point of view.

Miniature videotape systems and tape formats are certain to emerge by the end of the decade, but this miniaturization will only represent a refinement (as opposed to an innovation) of present technologies. Truly new systems will be fully digital, complete with non-mechanical storage in solid-state memory. This means that all images will be converted into patterns of numbers that are stored electronically in compact computer memories. Video, however, needs enormous amounts of cheap memory, so these systems will most likely not be introduced until early in the next century when economical, large-scale memory microchips will be available.

Another solution to digital video and nonmechanical storage may be found in exotic memory schemes—a cube of crystalline structure that could be laser-scanned, for example. Already in the laboratory stage in the United States and Japan and planned for introduction in the 1980s is a plastic card the size of a microfiche that can store both digital audio and video information that will be read by a moving laser beam.

Videodiscs

Videodiscs—records that play pictures as well as sound—have not caught the public imagination as planned. The reasons behind this failure are twofold: the manufacturers' inability to produce hardware and software at promised low prices; and the lack of new programming suited to the medium.

There are several types of videodiscs. Some are played with needles, whereas others are scanned by lasers. Laser-scanned "optical videodiscs" offer innovative programming opportunities such as their ability to display still frames, store bilingual or multiple sound tracks, and be accessed by a microcomputer. These laser discs, in contrast to needle-tracked videodiscs, make them the ideal medium for interactive and participatory programming.

Laser-scanned optical videodiscs will gain the most momentum during this decade as the costs of players drop with the introduction of a crucial component, the solid state laser. The capability of the optical videodisc to combine speech, video, still pictures, and computer data on the same disc will make the disc an increasingly attractive method of information storage. One key development in optical videodisc technology in this decade will be a compression technique now known as sound over stills, in which alternate frames (one disc side can store 54,000 frames) are devoted to still photographs and digitized audio, yielding many hours of sound and thousands of individual pictures.

Finally, the development of a disposable floppy optical videodisc will create video supplements to magazines and books, and even video advertisements bound into the pages of national newsmagazines.

Direct Broadcast Satellites

Direct broadcast satellites (DBS) will be operational by the late 1980s. As their name implies, these satellites will broadcast dozens of channels of television programming directly to homes. Like present-day telecommunications satellites, DBS units will follow the earth in geostationary orbits, but they will not require today's giant dish antennae for reception.

They will instead use high-power transmitters and broadcast in the high-frequency 12 gigaHertz band so that home receivers can use small parabolic dish antennas and inexpensive receivers. The leading company in this expanding field is Comsat, based in Washington, D.C. It will most likely be the first corporation to provide this new satellite service.

Particularly important, the DBS satellites will use "spot beams," highly directional signals that aim broadcasts regionally and can be redirected under instructions from the earth. In this way, new networks will be able to tailor their programming to the diverse tastes and varying time schedules of different regions.

Earth station receivers for these satellites are being designed to be sold at comparatively low prices. Industry projections place future prices at $300 to $600, or about one-tenth the present cost of today's backyard satellite receivers. Direct broadcast satellites are expected to bring expanded television viewing to rural areas where cable television is prohibitively expensive to install. Ranches, farms, and isolated communities will be the first to benefit.

Direct broadcast satellites will also offer the opportunity to redesign television standards, possibly establishing a new class of high-definition broadcasting. The danger in this scheme is that these satellites could seriously jeopardize local television stations by undercutting their dependable viewership should commercial networks choose to use DBS. Cable, too, could be threatened if the advertiser-supported networks that today come over the cable decide to broadcast these same services via DBS.

Cable Television

If present trends continue, cable should emerge as the true winner of the new television sweepstakes, primarily because of its ever-growing channel capacity and overall economy to viewers. Already in about 30 percent of American homes, cable penetration should exceed 50 percent during the next decade. This audience strength—more than 45 million homes wired to cable—would provide an adequate subscriber base to threaten the present dominance of the three commercial networks in the United States.

Such facts are not lost on the networks, of course, and each network has already begun to diversify by establishing new programming services for cable. It is possible that, as the cable industry grows, the networks' cable services may become their chief activity, surpassing broadcast TV. Present network services may be left with "lowest common denominator" programs, live news, and some national sporting events. In short, the best programs will go to cable, at least for their first run.

In addition to conventional television programming and entertainment, the cable industry will expand with the addition of ancillary services.

• Cable lines will be leased to corporations and financial institutions for data transmission use.

• Public utilities will read energy and water meters by tying them into cable systems.

• The popularity of cable-based security systems may not grow dramatically, but these systems will be incorporated into new buildings, luxury condominiums, and apartment developments.

Just as national pay-TV services provided a boost to cable television companies (both in terms of increased subscribership and revenues) during the 1970s, "pay-per-view" programming will be a major profit area for the television industry in the 1990s. Most cable systems will have the electronic capability to deliver programs selectively, so that premium or event programming can be restricted to subscribers willing to pay. Popular pay-per-view programs will include premieres of major motion pictures (simultaneous with their theatrical debuts), performing arts events created especially for the medium, and most regular season sporting events. Events may even be priced according to demand. A world championship boxing match may cost, for example, ten times more than an ordinary Saturday afternoon baseball game between the Cincinnati Reds and the St. Louis Cardinals.

By combining this pay-per-view capability with two-way, interactive cable TV, viewers will be able to place bets on horse races and participate in national lotteries or gambling tournaments. Governments will be able to tax revenues through legalized interactive cable gambling, thus reducing the importance of the numbers runner or the local bookie.

Hardware

New television equipment standards, such as a high-definition television screens using twice the present number of scanning lines, will require new television set designs capable of receiving many different types of high-tech broadcasts. Conventional television sets will also benefit from a makeover. Flat cathode ray (picture) tubes and liquid crystal screens will make pocket-sized sets practical. Digital light emitting diode matrices will make crisp-imaging, wall-sized screens possible. Presently available projection TV sets will improve and become cheaper, but their success could be challenged by more advanced laser projection systems.

The current U.S. standard of 525 scanning lines per television will remain for many decades to come. Too much new video hardware—video games, video recorders, disc players, and home computers—has been developed under this present-day system. A new high-definition television displaying 1,125 scanning lines will make higher quality video images feasible by the early 1990s and will compete with present television systems. CBS, Sony, and Matsushita are all working toward developing this system as a new global standard.

Personal Electronics

Consumer advances of the last ten years have included home computers, pocket calculators, electronic games, and digital watches—

items that have all revolutionized the electronics industry. Just when consumers thought that there were no new twists on old ideas, 1981 spawned a new craze: the Sony *Walkman* headsets, a personal, carry-along electronic music machine.

Other electronic trends are soon to follow. One may need to wait a few years for these electronic marvels, but here are some ideas with fanciful names that are likely to become reality in the decades ahead.

• *Walkman-Sans-Headphones*, or "phoneless" headphones, will combine an innovation in audio technology—a miniaturized digital playback unit— with the bone-conducting sound reproducer. This bone-conducting sound unit will produce audio when attached to any head bone by creating a subtle vibratory pattern that the ear will recognize. It will enable listeners to enjoy high-quality sound while on the run.

One Japanese firm has already developed bone conductor hearing aids built into conventional eyeglass frames. While these reproducers are not yet capable of full high-fidelity sound, future refinements in technology could make this experimental gadget a reality soon.

• Biofeedback-controlled games will become the most popular electronic game of the twenty-first century. While player success with pinball machines was related to manual dexterity, this biofeedback machine will require the player to generate alpha and delta brainwaves on demand. As you hold this electronic pocket game in your hand, its sensors will constantly monitor your galvanic skin response (GSR) and pulse rate. As the new games become more exciting, the machines will play harder. Great self-control will be demanded.

While such a device is many years from the marketplace, improvements are rapidly being made in biofeedback detection and measuring techniques. A new generation of electrodes and sophisticated computer programs could provide the sensitivity required for such games. Will people stare at those wearing electrodes on their scalps? Outsiders may never even notice the gamesters when these sensors are disguised as a jogger's sweatband.

• A true pocket computer will combine a small personal computer with a full-color liquid crystal television set. The small size of this new unit—one can hold it in the palm of a hand—will necessitate an alternative to the "QWERTY" typewriter keyboard. In its place will be touch sensors positioned around the edges of the device. You might "type" on it by gripping the sides in different ways. The tiny, full-color liquid crystal video display will improve on the standard desk computer that used cathode ray tubes. This one, quite naturally, will double as a functional TV set.

There is every reason to believe that such devices will be widely marketed in the 1990s. Their internal memories will have enormous capacity, perhaps even eliminating the need for floppy disks or tapes.

As for the TV screen, liquid crystal and flat-screen television sets are somewhere between prototype and production stages at most major electronics companies. The pocket computer device will be a logical extension of an industry trend toward combining electronic functions, which has already inspired calculators that play music and game-playing digital watches.

An electronic ''instant camera'' will revolutionize the camera industry early in the twenty-first century, if not before. It will be equipped with an all-electronic imaging system, one that will enable viewers to press the shutter button and then decide whether or not they want a photographic print. The camera will retain the precise image that is to be developed. If Junior stuck out his tongue, one may want to destroy the image. Photographers will be able to test the color image in advance. If one person in the desired photograph blinked, he can be electronically removed from the shot. The camera will also be able to make enough copies for everyone at the party.

Major international camera and electronics manufacturers are working on the principles underlying this camera or on variations on it. Prototypes of these computer imaging systems have already been displayed, but a marketable product requires considerable computer memory and a high-definition, solid-state sensor array. These developments are still more than a decade away.

• Hologames will make videogames obsolete within twenty-five years. Some models will be played on a three-dimensional, table-top playing field. Others will be worn like helmets and will be played in the space around your head. The holographic images created by these games could make ''zapping'' the alien attackers unnervingly believable—much too realistic for the squeamish. Possible dangerous psychological consequences created by the effect on children of such realistic game-playing may require investigation.

One videogame manufacturer has already developed a method to mass produce holograms very cheaply. But manufacturing has been postponed, presumably to improve image quality. Totally realistic holograms, however, are at least a decade away. The holo-helmet game, thus, remains just a dream at present.

• A personal electronic bio-monitor will become a household commodity within two decades. When worn on the wrist, this medical item will measure pulse rate, blood pressure, and body temperature. Another feature will be a small aperture on one side, an item to be known as a ''breathalyzer.'' The breathalyzer will let someone know whether it is safe to drive home after a night on the town. An oral probe offers other features, including fertility projections for women.

Most functions of this kind of device are already miniaturized and computerized, waiting to be combined into a single product.

Even though an eager market exists for this commodity, obstacles remain. Researchers believe that such self-diagnosis items will arouse the opposition of physicians' groups like the American Medical Association, since these devices will inevitably reduce the number of patients' office visits.

Electronic
Nightmares

As new communication devices and systems grow in number, so does the potential for their abuse. However, it is unlikely that George Orwell's vision of 1984 will become a reality, at least in part because his prophetic novel has already warned society of the dangers of a technological society.

Still, the issue of invasion of privacy via electronic means will command more attention as we approach the twenty-first century. Ironically, debates about these sensitive topics may only occur after such abuses have been unleashed on the public.

Here are just a few scenarios involving electronic intrusion, both individual and collective, that could occur as a result of new communications technology. If these schemes seem far-fetched or overly paranoid, bear in mind that each is already possible.

Instant Opinions? During the 1980 presidential campaign, ABC television offered viewers an opportunity to give their opinions about who they felt was the winner of one particular debate between Ronald Reagan and Jimmy Carter. This "vote" was tabulated with the aid of a national telephone circuit called Dial-It. Realizing the dramatic effect of such instant polling schemes, political groups could easily skew these results, either purposely or accidentally, and affect future national political campaigns. An instant poll like this one could also be taken during times of national controversy or crisis (a nuclear dispute or an international hostage-taking incident, for example), forcing legislators or other public officials to accept hastily made, emotional decisions by the people. Public hysteria, whetted by these sophisticated electronic polling devices, could reach such a crescendo that politicians could be forced to declare a war. Colonial legislators specifically designed the U.S. Constitution to limit the power of such rash public sentiment.

The Easy Sell. A local auto dealer, plagued by sagging sales, stumbles upon the solution to his problems: his friend is a computer operator for a bank. With limited access to charge card accounts affiliated with the bank, the friend creates a small but useful computer program that spots and collects information on the number of auto repairs billed to each account. The program then isolates and identifies which card holders are having auto problems and generates a list of potential customers for the auto dealer. Using this list, the dealer can make his contacts and close his sales without the customers' knowledge that they were computer-selected for this petty scheme. The variations on this scenario, and the dangers to consumers, are countless.

Junk Mail Nightmare. With the proliferation of sophisticated computer mailing lists, individuals will find themselves the recipients of hundreds—not just dozens—of solicitation mailings. Junk mail dilemmas will increase substantially, as these mailing companies grow in number and their mass storage capacities expand. Individuals will have no clue to how their names moved from list to list and no easy way to have them removed. These traded lists could create an almost hopeless tangle of irrecoverable personal information.

Computer Harassment. You are involved in a dispute with a collection agency. The agency contends that a bill has not been paid and, of course, you insist it has. Annoying dunning letters appear regularly in your mailbox, but you do not respond. One morning, the telephone rings, and a disembodied voice asks for you by name. Confused and curious, you answer, not realizing for a few minutes that the voice on the other end is actually computer-synthesized. Nor are you aware that your voice and responses are now being stored in digital memory.

You have just received the telephone equivalent of a registered letter. Your recorded responses, probably along with a computer voiceprint, will be used in a civil suit as proof of your acknowledgement of the debt.

Far-fetched? Not at all. Computer-dialed telephone calls are presently being used in many kinds of direct-telephone advertising, and telephonic "dunning" is now being developed. Imagine what the government could do with this—"IRS calling. Did you cheat on your taxes?" Or an employer—"Good morning, are you really home sick?"

The Purloined Letter. Computer piracy is rapidly joining the ranks of major crime statistics in the world. Software computer companies in California's Silicon Valley, for example, guard their technological secrets from both competitive national companies and foreign spies.

Here is a computer piracy scenario that may likely occur at the corporate level.

An executive suspects that his company's new marketing strategy is the target of intra-corporate espionage. Analyzing his office for the source of repeated "leaks," he spots dozens of insecure locations. Word processing files (on magnetic floppy disks) can be quickly and easily duplicated. Electronic interoffice mail can be read from terminals in the central computer room. Copying machines are everywhere, so memos can be copied during regular office hours without suspicion.

The executive considers his options. A confidential business plan is about to be filed with the home office. Security is a must. He decides to avoid the word-processing department and prepares the document himself. To protect himself further, he also decides to send the document to the home office via a telephone-linked facsimile machine. Placing his typed sheets in the machine, he picks up the telephone, drops the information in a cradle, and pushes a button marked "send."

In another room in the office, a similar procedure takes place, clandestinely. Someone else picks up an office phone and drops it into the cradle of his facsimile machine, connects to the same office line, and pushes a button marked "receive." Indeed, the message reaches the home office, but a third, pirated version is made simultaneously.

Gotcha. A hard-working citizen enjoys all of the conveniences offered by electronic banking and personal financial management. His personal bank account is an EFT (Electronic Funds Transfer) account, to which he can have access by using his bank credit card at "money machine" terminals. At home, he uses his personal computer to study his few investments and to transfer funds between these investments and his EFT account. He never sees his weekly paycheck, because it is directly deposited by his employer. He enjoys the flexibility and benefits of the system—until the nightmare begins.

A misplaced decimal point in his year-end EFT account statement indicates that he has earned thousands of dollars more than he actually has. The error is quickly corrected by his bank, but years later, during a routine IRS tax audit (computerized, no doubt), it mistakenly shows up again. This leads the IRS to attach his accounts—both EFT and brokerage accounts—pending resolution of the case in court.

What is our citizen left with? Only his plastic cards, which no longer activate his account. He has become a victim of the "cashless society"—an account number without recognition.

This is perhaps the most paranoid of all fantasies involving breaches of personal privacy, but a common one nonetheless. Most EFT plans have been established with scrupulous attention to personal rights.

Computer systems, however, can be incredibly complex. The programs that drive them are equally intricate, and programmers sometimes make mistakes, producing "bugs" or operating errors. Locating these mistakes in simple systems is difficult, but future systems—particularly ones as large as a nationwide EFT system—could lead to bugs that don't become apparent for years.

If and when such an error does occur, the unthinkable might become a sudden reality, and an unsuspecting person could easily end up a helpless victim.

The Technological
Home of
the Future

Domestic life of the future has always been a popular area of speculation. Futurists and writers in Sunday magazine supplements have told us that our future homes will be spacious and that life will be leisurely. We will sit before wall-sized screens that will bring the world to us, while robots will perform our daily household chores.

Future home life may be even more attractive than these projections indicate, though not as colorful. If present trends persist, personal residences will probably be smaller, not larger. Most people won't have room for those giant video screens, though television sets will become the display terminals for an enormous number of new products and services. Domestic machines of the future will be endowed with more capabilities than the robots of science fiction stories, though these machines will not be nearly as amusing as their fictional prototypes.

The most popular "information utility" of our present world will probably remain the most potent information force of the future—the telephone. But the future telephone will provide much more than mere telephone service, and our reliance on it may become even greater that it is today.

The Yankee Group is a Cambridge, Massachusetts, market research and consulting firm that closely follows technological developments that will affect our home life. Here are some of the ways domestic life may change, according to their researchers.

Home Information Delivery

Videotex is the generic name for systems that use computer graphic displays to bring information into the home using telephone lines, broadcast, or cable television. Yankee Group analyst Robert Wells predicts that presently-proposed videotex systems are limited and are, in fact, "an experiment in sensory deprivation for people who are used to real life, or even ordinary video." In order for these systems to succeed, he says, they will need to go beyond the visual delivery of information and will have to include other sensory experiences such as sound.

Electronic information delivery systems will enable consumers to transact their business in the home. These systems will also function as popular games and electronic mail services. The most popular types of information delivered will be "perishable information" such as weather, traffic conditions, current news, and stockmarket quotations.

Electronic newspapers will be versions of the news rewritten especially for these electronic systems. They will need to differ from standard newswriting before the public will accept them. A new style of electronic newswriting will thus emerge, one based on abbreviated sentences and compressed information.

There are other types of information that will be most efficiently communicated by sound. Audio-only methods of delivering vital information are called *audiotex*.

One such new medium will be listener-customized radio, designed not for music but for delivery of pertinent information. With such a service, each individual news item or piece of information may be identified by computer code prior to being broadcast. Using a programmable radio to recognize these identifications and an audio cassette recorder to record only desired information, the listener may create a program of information tailored to his or her needs. A racetrack bettor, for example, could get complete summaries of race results and a breakdown of the day's handicap odds, while a stockbroker could request a detailed appraisal of the latest transactions on Wall Street or the price of gold in Zurich. The audio cassette will be convenient because it can be listened to while driving or riding to work or home, or even while jogging.

Teleshopping

Shopping from home will become a reality, though the products most easily sold in this manner are likely to be purely electronic products such as digital music and computer software. Information-based products like these do not require physical delivery to the door. Yankee Group researchers, however, believe that consumers will need high-resolution color video pictures, rather than computer graphics, to be motived to buy. The major catalogue houses will be the first to adopt electronic teleshopping catalogues, in part to reduce the costs of manufacturing and mailing tens of millions of catalogues. Cable television companies, rather than telephone-based videotex systems, will provide this catalogue service, paid for by the companies. Shopping via toll-free telephone numbers and television advertising will increase dramatically in the future.

Telebanking

Electronic Funds Transfer has already become a commonplace transaction for consumers in the United States. Millions of Americans already pay their bills and do most of their banking using such systems. This constitutes a major revolution in American economic culture and is the harbinger of the cashless society that awaits us in the future. Such systems are also well under way in Great Britain and Japan. The popularity of EFT is certain to grow. Prospects for the future include nationwide "cash management systems" geared to home terminals or computers.

These systems will link brokerage, bank, and credit card accounts. Customers will pay bills, shuffle cash from one investment to another, and get expert analyses of their budgets and future financial projections through the press of a key.

Telemanagement

The development of workhorse domestic robots seems unlikely for at least several decades in the United States, though an increasing number of home appliances are being designed with microprocessors that will control their timing and function. Once a microprocessor has been built into an appliance, it costs little more to design it so that it can communicate with other devices in the home or with a central controlling system.

Home appliances that will most likely be linked to a central telemanagement system operated either under manual, program, or remote control include television sets, microwave ovens, clothes washers and dryers, furnaces, air conditioners, coffee pots, and dishwashers.

The missing link is the standardization of a universal domestic data base, a control port for each home appliance. An international committee consisting of representatives from the United States, Japan, and the European countries has already been formed to create such a universal standard, and it is expected to be adopted before the end of the decade. One new appliance might be a hand-held keypad, similar to today's channel controllers for remote-control TV sets. This keypad will be used for control, not just of the living room television set, but of all home appliances using the domestic data base.

A device generating the same universal command codes and linked to these appliances by a home computer will allow complete control of the home under this program control. Another coder generating audio equivalents of these commands will control the appliances, or even change a master home management program remotely via telephone. Even though one may be away on a business trip or vacation, one will be able to check the status of a home burglar-alarm system or be able to water the lawn through remote control.

Some "smart appliances" of the future may not even need to talk to the central computer. A microwave oven preparing one course of a dinner, for example, may give directions to the stove to coordinate other elements of the meal that should be served at the same time. This will enable the homemaker to plan the meal from the factory or office. In the past, the housewife was generally expected to do the family cooking. Cooking will become a more sexually egalitarian responsibility when meals will be prepared by women and men from their place of work.

Telephonics

The recent agreement by A.T.&T. to sell off its local telephone networks came about largely because the huge corporation wanted the freedom to take advantage of the deregulation of the communications industry and participate in new and profitable communications businesses.

One new business for A.T.&T. will be the manufacture of information data bases, available for consumer and professional use. These will include the establishment of a nationwide videotex system during this decade.

Other new areas of activity will come from A.T.&T.'s entrance into the fields of computer equipment and consumer electronics. The company will invent and develop personal products such as high-definition television receivers (with built-in phones, of course), internal security devices, and personal computers. It will also sell business computers and telephone equipment, as well as products made by other electronics manufacturers.

A.T.&T. will also move from providing conventional telephone services to offering new services resulting from the upgrading of its nationwide system of wires and switches. Messages spoken into a telephone, for example, will be stored in digital memory and forwarded to the intended parties. Digital data might be typed into a home computer at one end, sent over telephone lines, then delivered as electronically synthesized speech. A.T.&T. might also create a service bureau to offer data processing to businesses and professionals as an alternative for those not wishing to buy their own computing hardware.

One reason for A.T.&T.'s development of new information services and products is the continuing erosion of its share of the market for long-distance telephone calling. Competition to Bell from other long-distance services—ITT City Call, MCI, and Southern Pacific's Sprint service—represented a loss of only ten minutes of annual revenues to A.T.&T. in 1974. By mid-decade, this equivalent loss will represent thirty-one days of revenue, predicts Howard Anderson, president of the Yankee Group and a leading authority on A.T.&T.

A.T.&T. is also aware of the threats posed to its dominance by cable television and other emerging telecommunications companies. For this reason, it will continue to upgrade its system to include more digital switching systems and fiber-optic trunk cables. By rapidly improving its hardware, strengthening the programs that run its behemoth system, and inventing attractive new consumer and industrial services, the corporation believes it can prevent new companies from gaining an edge over it.

New services are likely to include forwarding and electronic "delivery" of both voice and digital data, and access to specialized and timely computer programs (such as tax computation and preparation). A.T.&T. will also enter the consumer electronics business, selling high-tech products in addition to telephone accessories such as answering machines and computerized dialers.

By moving from basic voice communications to new data services for corporations and individuals, the phone company will become the information company.

The Changing Classroom

1980s

The most visible educational development of the 1980s will be the widespread introduction of automated teaching devices. The most promising of these is a teaching system that will marry the medium of the videodisc to the microcomputer. Such systems will permit massive amounts of audio-visual information to be introduced to students at their own rate of learning.

Inner-city public schools will continue to deteriorate, and education may essentially disappear from the lives of millions of urban youths. Truancy will rise. Schools will be forced to deal with unprecedented violence and threats to teachers. This trend will continue throughout the decade, or until the basic structure of these schools is reviewed and overhauled. Look for a rebuilding of urban school systems, possibly by corporations and industries, which will step in as a last resort with a solution to these problems, to keep from losing workers.

Education of children will focus more on "life skills"—personal financial accounting, the responsibilities of renting or owning property, basic civil law, and other topics required for survival in an increasingly complex society. Spanish will increasingly become a primary language in many urban school districts.

More adults will choose to continue their educations or complete abandoned degree programs. Educational curricula that teach skills for beginning a second career will also gain in popularity. It is likely that junior colleges and technical schools will be the main centers for such continuing education. They will change rapidly and often to accommodate the needs of the adult population.

One reason for the resurgence of popularity of adult education will continue to be a purely social one: Schools are meeting places for an increasing number of single adults.

1990s

This decade will be marked by advances in the individualized education of children. Educational programs will begin to be tailored to the individual biological differences among children. As these individual needs are diagnosed, children will receive an education program specifically designed to enable them to learn better and faster.

Among the major biological differences that will be considered are:

• Biological cycles that determine different times of mental, physical, and intellectual efficiency.

• Sensory styles that account for basic perceptual differences.

Accepting the fact that biological cycles vary from child to child, for example, classroom times will change so that all children will no longer be locked into today's early morning-to-mid-afternoon school schedule. Children who reach their daily intellectual peak in late afternoon or early evening will attend classes scheduled for them.

Sensory styles affect the way humans perceive sensory stimuli. Persons identified as "sensory reducers" tend to reduce the level of stimuli with which they are presented. Those who amplify the visual and auditory stimuli are called "augmenters." It is quite likely that these differences will be accommodated by different classroom teaching styles. Augmenters will be taught by teachers with low-key personalities and quiet voices. Reducers will accept and require a much higher level of stimulus from their teachers.

It is quite likely, too, that automated-teaching systems—systems that link the microcomputer with video devices—will develop so that physical and neurophysical responses by children to teaching material can be monitored. Telemetry devices measuring pulse, galvanic skin response, respiration, and even brain waves will aid teaching computers in the pacing and presentation of these automated lessons. Such developments could be widely adopted in the classroom in the latter part of the 1990s, but lack of funding may impede technological transformations in American schools.

2000 and Beyond

During the next century, many of the responsibilities of traditional schooling will be transferred to parents. The mass availability of video and computer hardware will bring the classroom into the home. The chief purpose of schools and classrooms will be to socialize young people and introduce them to one another. By necessity, and even without long classroom hours, the worldwide literacy rate will rise.

A major alternative to the traditional structure of education could be an intellectual apprentice system. Under such a system, any member of society—a manual laborer, a journalist, a musician, an academic historian, a shop clerk, or a mechanic—could become a teacher. These people would simply choose to devote part of their time to the teaching of the young. Students wishing to eschew the classroom for this kind of apprentice system would have their portion of the publically funded school budget returned to them as credits (a kind of educational scrip, perhaps) with which teaching "masters" could be paid.

Education during the next century is certain to center around the learning of skills rather than the accumulation of abstract information. Rote learning of historical dates and facts, for instance, will be useless, since it will be much simpler to demand the information from a computer database.

Learning drugs—aids to memory and cognition—will further help in the education of both children and adults. This type of chemical learning aid, however, are not likely to be adopted until the middle of the twenty-first century.

Computerized Music

The ability to compose and perform music has traditionally required great discipline, skill, and dexterity. Today, modern man seldom hears music played live. Music is recorded, and symphony orchestras are electronically amplified in live performance. Soon, with the aid of new instruments and computer technology, making and playing music may become almost instinctively simple.

Key to the development of electronic music was Lee De Forest's invention in 1915 of a simple oscillating circuit capable of generating a wide range of electronic tones. In 1923, the oscillator was coupled to a vertical antenna by Leon Theremin to create the electronic musical instrument that bears his name.

In 1929, Lorenz Hammond developed the electronic organ based on oscillating circuits. This represented the first marriage of the familiar piano keyboard to an electronic instrument. The advent of magnetic audio tape recording provided new ways to make and produce electronic sounds during the 1950s. The next decade saw the development of electronic music synthesizers based on voltage-controlled oscillators which greatly expanded the range and types of generated sounds.

Digital computers and cheap new synthesizer designs now offer novel approaches to music and are the chief tools of our musical future. Today, most personal computers are able to make sounds of one form or another. These same computers can also be used with some electronic music synthesizers.

By linking these machines to a pianolike keyboard, it will become possible to enter compositions, store them in digital memory, and play them by controlling the synthesizer with the computer.

According to Professor Marvin Minsky of the Massachusetts Institute of Technology's Artificial Intelligence Laboratory and other experts and observers, these are some of the likely developments in the world of music.

• The use of the microcomputer with the piano keyboard is the first step toward a ''composer's assistant'' computer. This system will accept as input music that will be entered either by using the piano keyboard or by singing into the machine. Music will then be transposed to other keys and assigned a voice or instrument. Each individual voice may then be edited in much the same way word processors can edit manuscripts. When the composer is pleased with the results, he may request the machine to print out a copy of the score.

Such future systems will blur the boundaries between composer and musician and between musician and conductor. Even children will be able to compose without years of manual training on a musical instrument.

• As computer hardware becomes cheaper, more powerful, and more widely available, it is likely that systems will be developed that can compose new music. Several primitive prototypes of this kind already exist. One developed at M.I.T. improvises jazz horn solos, for example. Sometime during the next century, though, we may see systems that can "listen" to a group of works by a single composer, analyze their structure, and then compose new pieces in the same style. Such a system could analyze Bach concerti, then proceed to create a new composition in Bach's style.

• Electronic musical synthesizers will become considerably more powerful and will replace traditional instruments in the education of children (though most experts agree that traditional instruments will never be replaced in performance). By the end of this decade, electronic music instruments with the power of a minicomputer and the sophistication of today's finest synthesizers could be available to the masses for the price of a pocket calculator. In addition to synthesizers using piano keyboards, horn synthesizers—blown exactly like their brass counterparts—and electronic woodwinds will also be developed.

One development that commands special attention in this field is the computerized equivalent of the player piano. Some versions available currently allow complex compositions to be read from printed bar codes (like the price coding on supermarket products). These compositions are stored directly in the synthesizer's memory and then played back. Some programs also allow various musical elements—the melody line, for instance—to be isolated and played manually along with the programmed accompaniment. The logical extension of this idea is an electronic symphony orchestra in which the musician can choose to play any role, be it conductor, first violinist, or piano soloist.

• New kinds of careers and career requirements in music are very likely to emerge. Many of tomorrow's composers might need to be expert computer programmers. Music teachers will need not only great manual dexterity, but also the engineering background to explain the hardware architecture of these musical computers. Synthesizer virtuosos—the "one-man-bands" of the future—are almost certain to replace many cocktail pianists and cabaret organists.

• Finally, a new breed of musical psychologist could prove invaluable in environments where a continuous background of music exists. Already, companies like Muzak are using music to stimulate productivity in factories and sales in supermarkets. Musical psychologists might be able to quantify the influence of such subliminal stimuli of music on consumer buying patterns.

One question remains unanswered. Will traditional musical skills—the manual ability to play the violin or piano, for example—be threatened when conventional instruments exist side-by-side with new music systems? Or will these musical computers lure a new generation to the arts and create a new golden age of composition and performance?

Publishing's Future

The invention of movable type began the publishing industry. Throughout the centuries, innovations in printing techniques and hardware enabled that industry to grow and new trends to appear.

Roll-fed web presses replaced sheet-fed presses and allowed newspapers and magazines to be printed in mass numbers. Individual, hand-set type elements gave way to linotype. Today, the system of movable type and letterpresses has been replaced by photo typesetting and offset lithography.

The increased scarcity of raw materials, particularly wood pulp, and their rising costs, will force publishers to re-evaluate traditional publishing technology throughout the remainder of this century. Public resistance to higher book prices, both in mass market and hardcover editions, has already forced many publishing companies to reduce their lists and staffs substantially. As cover prices for traditional books continue to escalate, houses will have to adopt alternative methods of publishing or else go out of business.

Printing Technology

The most influential new force in publishing will be the computer. These machines can be used to enter text matter, create images of words on paper, and store entire pages of a book, newspaper, or magazine. Finally, computers will give the proper instructions to new printing presses that will not require plates.

Here is an outline of how publishing companies and printing plants will operate in the near future.

• Authors will enter their text either on a computer terminal linked by telephone (or other type of cable) to a publisher's central computer. These writers will most likely use their own word processors. Although word processors have rapidly become commonplace in offices, they will move into the hands of professional writers by necessity. The increasing mechanization of publishing will require that writers buy and use word processors to increase their productivity and have their texts be compatible with publishers' computer systems.

• Manuscripts on paper may all but vanish, since text will be shuttled between writer and publisher in this electronic method. Dialogue between writers and editors will also take place electronically, and each will be able to see and make revisions to a manuscript instantly, while linked to a central storage computer. Of course, an old-fashioned editor, unwilling to work off a screen, will be able to get a computer printout of a manuscript, on which he or she will be able to make corrections.

• Once the text is written and edited, designers will visualize, create, and lay out pages on a video screen. Photographs and other graphic elements will be digitized—reduced to numbers in solid state memory—so that they can be cropped, enlarged, or enhanced, and then integrated with text set in type on the pages. The typesetter's job will be virtually eliminated, with the computer able to transform the author's text into justified galley pages at the flick of a key.

• Offset lithography printing plates will be made electronically, from the information in computer memory. This technology, however, will slowly begin to disappear during the next century as lithography is replaced by ink-jet printing and electrostatic presses. Ink-jet printers create images on paper by painting each page with precision, high-speed ink sprayers. This type of printer (it cannot be described as a press, since no impression is actually made) will not use printing plates or type. It can also be programmed so that a single ink-jet printer can produce all the pages of a book sequentially, eliminating the need to sort or collate individual sheets of paper. Electrostatic printers, essentially scaled-up and high-speed adaptations of Xerox copiers, will not require plates, or even ink. They will print pages by scanning with a computer-controlled, needle-thin beam of laser light.

• Color printing, too, will change, first with the widespread use of lasers to create color separations and printing plates. By the next century, it appears likely that ink-jet printers and electrostatic presses will replace conventional lithography for high-quality color reproduction.

Book, Magazine, and Newspaper Publishing

The major concern of the next century might not be, "Can Johnny read?" but rather, "Can Johnny afford to read?" Simply put, the cost of buying books and magazines will continue to spiral, chiefly due to the costs of paper and manufacturing. Here's what may happen.

Hardcover Editions. Hardcover books won't entirely vanish, but their very high prices will mean that only the affluent will be able to afford to buy important new novels, major historical works, and art books. This development is not a surprise to publishers and booksellers, who have already adjusted to a limited hardcover audience. It is quite likely that even the smallest hardbound volume will cost between twenty and thirty dollars by the end of this decade.

These high costs will mean that more books will be initially published as either quality trade or mass market rack-size paperbacks. Book titles chosen for hardbound publication will be those titles that will primarily appeal to the buying public who can afford them.

Paperbacks. The mass market paperback industry will need to find ways to keep prices down. Paperback houses are encountering stiff public resistance to books priced at $3.95 or $4.95. So-called bestselling blockbusters in today's book world may sell between 1 and 3 million copies, down from 4 to 8 million a mere decade ago. A bestselling pulp novel may now change hands four or even five times, because friends are more likely to exchange their books than buy new ones. Most of the major paperback houses, troubled by huge returns, high production costs, and dwindling profits, are producing their own hardcover lines, thereby developing their own authors and avoiding the huge advances that they once routinely paid to hardcover publishers for reprint rights.

Despite such innovations, original works of popular fiction, diet books, and other staples of mass market publishing could cost ten dollars or more during the next decade.

Reference Books. Encyclopedic works, reference books, and how-to texts will simply be too expensive to purchase as books. Many of these will be more economically produced through electronic delivery and packaging, rather than paper publishing. Videodisc, with its ability to store large numbers of individual frames (approximately 54,000 per side), is, at present, the most likely medium for packaging this kind of material. Computer databanks and home videotex services will also make these types of reference data available to readers who need to consult the information, but not necessarily own it.

Magazines. These periodicals are in for troubled times during the next two decades. Coupled with rising editorial and production costs, dramatic increases in the cost of distributing magazines will challenge magazine publishers. Alternatives to mailing copies to subscribers will need to be found, and the number of regional printers—each simultaneously printing the same issue of a magazine—will probably increase.

Magazine publishers will also continue to move from the print media to electronic publishing, making monthly video programs—equivalents of their magazines—available using cable television or videocassette or videodisc rental. Flexible, thin plastic videodiscs, similar to today's throwaway phonograph records, should also appear during the next decade as an audio-visual complement to printed magazines. These floppy videodiscs could contain mini-documentaries, excerpts from current films, plays, or musical performances, and even glossy entertainment or information-oriented advertising.

Newspapers. Daily newspapers, unfortunately, will continue to vanish during the rest of this century. The coming years will see smaller newspapers go out of business in many medium-sized cities, forcing their readers to rely on the remaining major city papers for regional news. Even the largest of city tabloids will not avoid financial crises.

The surviving big-city papers will pay more attention to readers outside their immediate urban market. They will cover suburban and statewide issues more thoroughly. Newspaper chains will proliferate throughout the United States, since publishers can tailor different editions of the same paper for diverse local markets.

The newspaper business, however, will not disappear. It will not be replaced by "electronic newspapers," home information, and videotex services. In fact, there could be a gradual rediscovery of the newspaper, largely because of electronic information delivery. Readers who have abandoned the newspaper may return to it, finding that a paper is convenient to carry and can be read anywhere. There is also a serendipitous element to newspaper reading; readers are often attracted to incidental news items, human interest features, and less significant information. New electronic systems of the future will only provide readers with the information that they specifically want.

Reference Works

Many standard reference works are already available through computer database services, among them *The Encyclopedia Britannica*, *Index Medicus*, and many of the Standard and Poor's financial publications. Other works likely to be available on-line or on videodisc by the end of the century include:

The World Almanac & Book of Facts (976 pages)
Webster's Third New International Dictionary (3663 pages)
The U.S. Government Manual (annual, approximately 950 pages)
Rand McNally Commercial Atlas (approximately 650 pages)
City directories and telephone directories (annuals of
  various lengths)
The Physician's Desk Reference (2047 pages)

Consumer Reports Buying Guide (annual, approximately 400 pages)
The McGraw-Hill Encyclopedia of Science and Technology (15 volumes)
Broadcasting Yearbook (annual, approximately 1800 pages)
The New York Times Film Reviews (11 volumes)
The Grove Dictionary of Music and Musicians (20 volumes)
The Praeger Encyclopedia of Art (5 volumes)
Benezit Dictionary of Painters, Sculptors, Designers, and Engravers (10 volumes)

Sports in the Twenty-first Century

The greatest development in sports over the next thirty years will be the combination of computer technology with increased emphasis on the selection and training of athletes as currently practiced by East Germany and other Soviet-bloc countries. Specialization of athletes within a sport will continue as it has for the past three decades, leading to increased performance. Along with this growing trend toward specialization, there will also be a decline of multi-talented athletes.

The East German style of selection and training relies on the following simple but strict rules.

• Begin games to assess the skills of children at the age of five.

• Note children's aptitudes for particular sports.

• Send the child at the age of ten to a special school that trains him completely, both physically and mentally, to excel in his or her chosen sport.

• Strict supervision and control becomes the essence of these sport schools, extending to diet, type and amount of exercise, and sleeping habits.

• Train athletes to develop total self-discipline. Those athletes who fail to follow the demands of their coaches do not succeed, while those who respond obediently will win.

This total dedication to one activity—the developing of muscles and mind for one set of actions—leads to success in speed, strength, and endurance contests. Employing these methods, the East Germans and Soviets have captured most of the important prizes in recent years in men's cycling, women's swimming, women's track and field, and weight lifting.

The application of these training methods in Western nations will remain limited for the forseeable future. The West will maintain a substantial advantage in computer technology that may offset the authoritarian programs of the Soviet-bloc countries. Sports scientists in this country already use computers to analyze athletes' techniques, and the practice will grow dramatically in the next few decades. Computer experts will hone their skills to the point where they will be able to prescribe bold new techniques to athletes who wish to improve their performances. The new technology has already made an important impact in track and field, and more sports will be dramatically affected in the future.

Sports Records Likely to be Attained through Specialized Training or Use of Computers

Baseball: 65 home runs in one season by a designated hitter.
160 stolen bases in one season by a
"designated runner."
175 walks in one season, 40 percent of
them intentional.
110-mile-per-hour fastball

Football: 1,000 yards in one season will become a
commonplace, as new training methods have
already made football a specialized sport.
New milestone: 1,500 yards.
Longest field goal: 75 yards.
Highest lifetime average gain: 5.4 yards.

Running: Sub-3:45 mile by 1988 (mile times have been
declining since 1954 by 1 second every 2 years)
Sub-3:40 mile by 2010.
3:30 mile (estimated maximum) by 2030.
8.5-second 100-yard dash by 2030.

Swimming: (men's) 100-meter freestyle in 45 seconds.
400-meter freestyle in 3:47.
1,500-meter freestyle in 14.50 minutes.

The Shape of Things to Come

Dr. Marvin Clein, chairman of the Physical Education and Sports Science Department at the University of Denver, and John Keefe, a graduate student in Clein's department, developed a computer program to predict the physical dimensions of athletes who could be expected to perform at certain levels. Their findings for football field-goal kickers are summarized below.

Kicker's Height	Kicker's Weight	Distance Ball can be Kicked
5'10"	180	60 yards
6'6"	250	75 yards
7'6"	383	85 yards

Clein and Keefe also used their computer to make some predictions about pitch speed in baseball. They arrived at their findings by selecting an ideal model and "exploding" him to larger proportions.

Pitcher's Height	Pitcher's Weight	Speed Ball Can Be Pitched	
6'3"	210	105	mph
6'4"	218	107	mph
6'5"	227	108.5	mph
6'6"	236	110	mph
6'8"	255	112	mph
6'10"	274.5	115	mph
7'0"	295	117	mph

Trends in Sports Medicine

Corrective Surgery. Athletes will submit to operations intended not to repair human anatomy but to improve on it. In the next century, doctors will routinely move tendons, tailor cartilage, and redesign joints on healthy athletes. These techniques will be particularly beneficial to baseball pitchers, tennis players, football running backs, and others prone to career-shortening injuries directly related to the stresses of normal athletic activity.

Electronic Implants. Selected athletes will be fitted surgically with solid-state chips that will provide electrical stimulation to the nerves controlling important muscles. The chips will enable the athletes to exercise all of their muscle fibers with a minimum of exertion and in a fraction of the time now required. The technique is already being used by weight lifters and will soon spread into other areas. Long distance runners may use the technique to strengthen seldom-tested fibers and thus enhance endurance.

Bionics. Early in the twenty-first century, sports scientists will begin their first serious experiments with bionics. The research will begin as the logical extension of surgical techniques developed over the previous decades, and it will be first applied in the treatment of injured athletes. Eventually, other athletes will be fitted with more sophisticated devices intended primarily to improve performance beyond human range. A great ethical debate may arise over the propriety of tinkering with the human body, but new developments will proceed in spite of it.

Drug Abuse. Drug and hormone abuse among athletes, often at the direction of team physicians, could become increasingly common, and athletes will become more adept at keeping abuses undetected. New drugs will be developed specifically to enhance athletic performance. Harmful side effects, possibly including cancers and sterility, may frequently be covered up. Some young Soviet athletes have already been found to have growth disorders and other ailments.

Future Changes in Athletic Playing Surfaces

Football. Football fields will be lengthened and widened to increase offensive flexibility and reduce the strategic significance of placekickers. Football goal posts will be narrowed. Despite the link now obvious between artificial playing surfaces and certain kinds of traumatic injuries, grass will never make a comeback in professional football.

Basketball. Basketball courts will be enlarged to reduce the claustrophobia induced by recent trends in player size and speed. Goals will be raised.

Baseball. The pitcher's mound will be lowered a few inches by 1995, as it was in the late 1960s, to counter a league-wide batting slump brought about by increases in pitch speed. The composition of the ball itself will be altered several times before the turn of the century.

Track. Running tracks will be "tuned" to increase runners' times and reduce injuries. The tuned track, which was developed by a pair of scientists at Harvard, gives runners a 3 percent boost by returning energy that would be dissipated on harder surfaces. The scientists estimate that an outdoor track built according to the same principles would enable milers to improve the world record by seven seconds. Such a track will be built in the near future, perhaps for the 1988 Olympic games.

Future Changes in Athletic Equipment

Football. Football helmets will be made of synthetic material that deforms on impact to protect both the wearer and the "victim" in spearing and butting with the head. An impact energy-absorbing substance known as Sorbothane is being tested to put in helmets.

A brace that protects knees from lateral stress without inhibiting movement will be in widespread use in the 1990s. Use of the braces will bring about a dramatic reduction in knee injuries and extend the careers of running backs significantly.

Baseball. Before the close of the century, baseballs will be dyed yellow or orange to increase visibility. Aluminum bats will be allowed in major-league competition.

Sailing. Hulls will be both lighter and more durable than ever, fashioned out of graphite and Kevlar-reinforced plastics. Fiberglass, once inexpensive to use, is made from petrochemicals and has become unaffordable. Sails will be made from plastic Kevlar/mylar laminates.

COMPARISONS AND PROJECTIONS FOR TRACK AND FIELD PERFORMANCES (men's)

	1950	1980	2010
Long jump	26'8 1/4"	29'2 1/2"	29'2 1/2"
High jump	6'11"	7'8 1/2"	8'4"
Pole vault	15'7 3/4"	18'8 1/4"	20' (graphite pole)
Shot put	58'10"	72'8"	83'
Discus throw	186'11"	233'5"	260'
Javelin	258'2"	310'4"	350'
Hammer throw	196'5"	263'6"	325'

The Only Current Major Athletic Record That May Never Be Broken

Bob Beamon's record-shattering 29 foot, 2½ inch long jump at the 1968 Olympics in Mexico City may never be topped. Beamon's jump, which was nearly two feet longer than the previous record, was the equivalent of eleven centuries worth of improvement in the event, based on comparison with an existing record from ancient Sparta. A sports scientist who has studied Beamon's jump with a high-speed camera and a network of computers says the only area in which Beamon fell short of perfection was his angle of attack. If his take-off had been one degree steeper, Beamon might have added an inch or two to his effort. Beating him will require an absolutely flawless jump.

Modern Baseball Records Unlikely to be Broken

- .426 batting average in one season (Napoleon Lajoie, 1901).

- 2,130 consecutive games played (Lou Gehrig, 1925-1939).

- .690 lifetime slugging percentage (Babe Ruth, 1914-1935).

- 511 lifetime wins for a pitcher (Cy Young, 1890-1911).

- 41 wins in a single season for a pitcher (Jack Chesbro, 1904).

- 190 runs-batted-in in one season (Hack Wilson, 1930).

- 56 game consecutive-hitting streak (Joe DiMaggio, 1941).

- 3 feet 7 inch, 65 pound player, the smallest batter ever to appear at the plate (Eddie Gaedel, 1951).

The Future of Women's Athletic Performance

Women's records, particularly in running events, will continue to improve at a dramatic rate. Women runners have already achieved records superior to top marks set by men as recently as the middle 1970s. The best women runners today are faster than all but a tiny fraction of all the men who have ever run. Within the next ten years, early athletic training for females will become more widespread, and women's accomplishments will approach men's in events where neither sex has a pronounced anatomical advantage. As women become more active in sports, new athletic events will be created to capitalize on gender-related strengths.

The Political Future

As science comes to play a larger role in all sports, political tensions will be aggravated by conflicts between nations with different technological capabilities. Western nations will attempt to impose controls on the training of amateur athletes elsewhere in the world, and Olympic boycotts by significant groups of nations will be commonplace, leading to a major reorganization of the Olympic games by early in the next century.

Fickle Fashions

Clothes designers say that predicting fashion styles in the coming decades is like trying to anticipate how people will feel and think. Historically, fashion has often reflected the politics and economics of a given society. Still, many prominent designers detect cycles in fashion tastes. Classically-influenced designers maintain that a beautiful, well-constructed piece of clothing will always withstand the passage of time. Others feel the future will bring about dramatic changes in clothing.

According to leading European and American designers, here are what models may be wearing on fashion runways in the future.

1990

Bill Blass, a well-known American designer of the 1970s and 1980s, predicts that a new crop of body-clinging suits will come into fashion by 1990. These lightweight one-piece jump suits will become popular as the weight of clothes becomes an increasingly important factor in choosing garments.

Many designers believe that black will become a more popular color in informal wardrobes. No longer will black be restricted to religious and formal attire.

Hats, continuing their seven-year cycle of popularity among both men and women, should be back in style by 1990. Many men, American designers predict, may wear stylized versions of cowboy hats.

2000

Clothing designers believe that garments will become more functional and will serve as protection against weather extremes. Some clothes in 2000 may be made of year-round computerized fabrics. The wearer will be able to adjust a few dials, and a cooling/heating system will change the temperature of a fabric. In winter, wires woven into cloth will generate heat. This type of garment exists already in the U.S. military, and the concept can be found today in many homes. In fact, the electric blanket may influence fashion in the future.

Another heat source for clothes in 2000, according to fashion designer Willi Smith, will be a solar belt pack. The belt, with controls, will regulate the amount of solar energy that filters through clothing.

Other designers mention the idea of body paints as a kind of overall underwear for protection against cold weather. Manufactured in an assortment of colors and textures, these paints would also decorate the body.

2010

Fashion designers say light and color will be transmutable elements in future fabrics. When one enters a room, one's clothing could change color to match the decor. Outdoors, clothes could turn white or be camouflaged by the local landscape. Some designers even foresee clothing color changing according to the way a person feels at a particular moment. Anger might turn a shirt red; depression might turn it grey; tranquility, blue, perhaps; happiness, yellow.

Psychology may become a part of the fashion world if light and color can adjust to a person's environment in 2010. People could radiate or display their emotions through their clothes, making it impossible to mask feelings. "To wear one's emotions on one's sleeve" could have a literal meaning.

Fashionable clothes may decline in popularity. Personal clothes that are well-made for protecting the body and enhancing the personality may dominate the market. In an age of ultrasophisticated technology and automation, clothing may remain one of the last realms of personal expression.

Well-made clothes of natural fabrics may be in short supply by 2010, but in high demand by the affluent. The prevalence of synthetic fabrics will make natural materials, such as wool and cotton, luxury items in this age.

Science and Technology in Fashion

Science and technology will transform our wardrobes. Future clothing will cost less because of advancements in industrial technology.

Although a creative mind will always remain at the forefront, clothing design is on the way to being computerized. Already, European fashion designers are weaving technology into fashion. With the help of computer experts, they program fabric selection, length, size, color, and style into a computer. The output allows designers to experiment with many alternatives on a video screen before the actual garment is finally manufactured.

Fashion "tech-notes" of the future:

• Seamstresses and tailors may see their jobs disappear. Garments may be fused or even glued together.

• If air pollution goes unchecked in many urban areas, special synthetic veils may be worn as air filters.

• The decline in availability of natural furs may prompt a new industry of genetically engineered animal furs. Mink and rabbit could be interbred to make the fur coats of the future. New generations of foxes could be genetically altered to provide thicker pelts and richer colors.

• Paper and other "disposable" clothes may become popular, expecially for children who outgrow and ruin clothes rapidly.

Fashions for Men

Fashion experts say that men will finally become more aware of their bodies in the coming decades and may even dispense with the pin-stripe suit, button-down collar, and traditional tie. They see men's fashion heading in the direction of sportswear. Cosmetics in the form of skin creams and colognes have recently become male grooming staples and men may even begin to wear subdued make-up. Styles

FUTURE MENSWEAR

	At home	At the office	On the town
1990	old, loose clothes jeans; T-shirts	pin-stripe suits ties; jackets	tuxedoes; suits in pastel colors
2000	one-piece body suits	body suits with ties; sports jackets	tight-fitting body suits revealing male body; make-up
2010	temperature-controlled body suits	body suits with special packs for job (i.e., intercom, tools, pen)	body paints; handbags; make-up

that have been considered taboo for centuries, such as a wide variety of pastel colored clothes, will gain wide acceptance. Shoulder bags are already a common male fashion accessory in many cosmopolitan areas.

Menswear will be freed from the gender-based restrictions that have prevailed in the past. Clothes will be looser and bodies barer. Dress codes will be lifted in most professional settings, yet clothes will always be used as a determinant of wealth and social status.

Fashions for Women

The most important development in women's fashion, designers anticipate, will be what women will wear on the job. As business styles become more conservative and sexless, evening and casual wear will become more glamorous and sexy. Designers say women will mask their femininity at the office but will boldly reassert their femininity in the evening.

FUTURE WOMENSWEAR

	At home	At the office	On the town
1990	old, loose clothes; jeans; housecoats	conservative skirts; jacket suits	tight-fitting, sexy dresses
2000	body suits; sexy clothing	pant suits; more unisex-styles	wide variety of colors in very revealing body suits
2010	temperature-controlled body suits	body suits and pant suits with job packs; few skirts or dresses	color-changing body suits; old-time dresses

Toy Technology

Toy trucks will no longer be pushed but programmed to drive under the coffee table, around the sofa, and into the next room. Arcade games will become standard with most television sets. Dolls, once lifeless creatures, may walk and talk better than some of their owners. Chess computers, the size of basketball courts when first designed, will be hand-held and capable of defeating many humans.

The microprocessor, the "computer on a chip," is the basis of this transformation. It spurred the growth of electronic games in the 1970s to a multi-million dollar industry.

Not surprisingly, game company officials say future electronic games will be based on age-old games that are continually popular. Electronic toys like *Simon* and *Super Simon*, based on an old children's repetition game, or electronic backgammon, chess, and even baseball, are the kinds of computer games children and adults will play with in the years ahead.

Playing in the Future

• Video games have become the new national pastime in the United States, and their popularity is spreading around the world. In the late 1970s, Japan experienced a severe yen shortage because too many coins were being gobbled up by video arcade machines. In West Germany, people spent $88 million during the 1981 Christmas season on home video consoles and cartridges. In Australia, arcade games rack up $182 million annually. Manufacturers of these games expect the trend to continue with video games being installed in the most remote areas around the globe.

• Electronic game companies are planning to market a variety of hand-held games in the future, perhaps by the early 1990s, that have sophisticated programs. For example, a football version will have small, distinct, programmable players. The figures will execute a play according to how the controlling person sets up a scrimmage. The human operator will be able to tell the quarterback how far to drop back, where to pass, or when to run with the ball. Offensive tackles, runners, and the entire defensive team will have their individual plans, just as in a real football game. And all the action will take place on a screen the size of your palm.

• By the early 1990s, game companies plan to market wristwatches that can play dozens of games from chess to hockey. Such a watch will also function as an alarm clock, stopwatch, and calculator, while communicating its information to the owner in a clear, computerized voice.

• During the 1980s and 1990s, electronic games will move from public arcade arenas to private living rooms. Home video manufacturers say the most popular home video games in the future will be the "blast them before they blast you" challenges. The good guys against the bad guys has been a favorite theme of games for centuries.

• Gamesmen point to a new demographic phenomenon that will continue to develop in the future. A large percentage, nearly one-third, of the people who play video games are adults, and that figure is going to increase.

• As the technology behind electronic video games progresses, there will be hundreds of options, decisions, and maneuvers confronting human players with each particular game. Manufacturers say that as electronic challenges become more sophisticated, psychological problems posed by man-versus-computer confrontations may take on greater significance.

• Fantasy and role-playing games will also continue to attract more players in the future. These games are successful because they rely totally on the imagination of the players. They are especially entertaining for adults and college students who play out fantasy roles during social gatherings. Many spin-offs of the original role-playing game, *Dungeons and Dragons*, exist today, and many more will be created in the years to come. Some experts say the introduction of computers into fantasy games will make them even more successful. Computer programs will help simplify the bewildering sets of rules that accompany the games.

Robot Games

Looking toward the twenty-first century, game companies are toying with the idea of robot games. Technology will continue to advance at an increasing rate, but man's baser instincts will not change. One of these instincts, the lust to see "the kill," may be revitalized in a game of the future, Gladiator Robots. This would be a violent game for the very rich and decadent. Patterned after the pagan Roman circus, future elitists would buy and program demolition robots equipped with a variety of weapons. People and their robots would get together in a carnival atmosphere and pit one robot against another for a metallic duel unto death, or a "thumbs down" decision.

Computer Dealers

Game experts believe that computer robots will eventually act as card dealers. These robots, infallible and fair, could be especially useful in gambling casinos. Misdealing will never occur if a machine spits out each player's hand. The most time-consuming and frustrating part of a game like poker is the figuring, the adding, and the keeping track of who hasn't anted. This process will change when a player has a keyboard terminal instead of chips in front of him. A player's calls and raises could be punched into the terminal, and the computer's voice could tell players whose turn it is to bet and what the total of the pot is at any given time. That is, of course, if the computer doesn't have an ace hidden up its slot.

The Growth
of Tourism

Tourism will burgeon into one of the world's largest industries over the next few decades with travel networks expanding into the remote regions of earth and space. Already central and southern Asia, as well as South America, are developing major tourist facilities. Charter expeditions to Greenland, Alaska, and the arctic frontiers are gaining popularity. Tourism experts predict that the trend will continue in the future, climaxing with sub-ocean and orbital hotel tour packages in the mid-twenty-first century.

This expansion will be due to faster modes of travel that bring about cheaper fares, new destinations, and increased leisure time. Tourist industry research from the late 1970s outlines the following possibilities for tourism in the future.

	1990	2010	2030
Travel mode:	Supersonic and subsonic jets; trains and cars still popular	Vertical/short take-off and landing craft; ultra-high speed trains.	Common, tiny private aircraft; computer controlled land vehicles.
Travel speed:	500-1,500 mph	500-3,000 mph	500-6,000 mph
Destination:	Frequent weekend commutes to far-away cities.	Extensive world-wide travel to remote areas	Wide global accessibility, but space is still a luxury.
Fare:	New York City to Paris-$200, or 6.5 cents per mile.	Five cents per mile. Some free travel.	Five cents per mile; much public assisted travel.

* 1981 dollars

Getting Away from It All

The explosion of tourism in the coming decades will also be attributable to higher incomes and the psychological need for escape from an increasingly technological world. Family members will have greater options of separate vacations, each person going somewhere that is suited to his or her particular tastes and needs.

Specialized environments will fulfill leisure requirements. The success of Disneyland and Disneyworld will encourage the growth of high-tech clubs, theme parks, and holiday retreats. Groups like Club Med will gain more members in the future by creating real-world "Fantasy Islands" for stress-knotted urbanites. These clubs will provide one-price packages to resorts advertising the leisure life. Access to conventional money, telephones, newspapers, and televisions can be eliminated to provide psychological relief from the trappings of society, while computer simulators and psycho-planning can create analogues for any desired environment or experience.

Share-a-Condo

Another current leisure phenomenon that travel experts say will flourish is the growth of condominium sharing. In such a situation, several people purchase a condominium in a resort and use it at specified times of the year. Realtors maintain that this time-sharing technique gives people a permanent vacation home at a fraction of the cost of keeping up a second house or even a modest cabin. With house mortgage rates hovering between 15 and 20 percent, sharing presents vacationers with an affordable alternative to sole home ownership. Real estate investors are funneling money into condo-sharing construction projects, and their profitable results ensure that these developments will proliferate.

Following are the ten best places to share-a-condo in 2000 according to Pan American Airlines.

1. **Caribbean Islands.** Many facilities have been in operation since the 1970s.

2. **Southern Florida.** Residents of northeastern states flock each winter to their places in the sun.

3. **Southern California.** Condo-sharers appreciate the year-round good weather.

4. **Costa del Sol along the Mediterranean Sea.** The southern coasts of Portugal and Spain provide inexpensive refuge.

5. **Swiss, Italian, and Austrian Alps.** Ski resorts attract many Americans and Europeans who in the past could not afford the accommodation prices.

6. Rocky Mountains in Canada and the United States. The North American mountain range has its own fair share of skiers.

7. Islands in the South Pacific Ocean. In particular, sections of the Fiji islands have become major condo-sharing communities for Oriental vacationers.

8. Australia and New Zealand. Along the Great Barrier Reef, condos are built with underwater rooms and spectacular aquatic views.

9. Hawaii. The Hawaiian islands are dotted with hundreds of condominium communities.

10. Fantasy Land. Theme cities like Disneyworld have many transient residents.

Space Vacations

Sometime in the early twenty-first century, probably by 2010, the first space vacations will become reality, say NASA officials. Although cramped and physically taxing, short stays in space aboard a space station should prove very alluring because of the danger—largely an illusion—and sheer excitement. At first, space tourism will be more of a novelty vacation. As space development continues and the fares decrease, astronomy and photography hobbyists will become the first serious space tourists.

By 2030, honeymoons for newlyweds may be available in special settlements on the moon. Such honeymoons may feature sex in zero gravity, a unique experience many couples may find too intriguing to pass by.

Undersea Explorers

Travel experts believe that undersea vacations will also become available in the next century. The world's first underwater hotel is now being built in the Grand Cayman Islands. It promises to be luxurious and safe, offering scuba divers a haven below the ocean. In the future, we may be able to vacation in the depths of the ocean canyons in worlds as alien from our own as the moon.

7 WORLD VITAL STATISTICS

7 WORLD VITAL STATISTICS

Assuming that mankind can avoid its most terrifying nightmares—nuclear accident or attack, cataclysmic war, or global ecological breakdown—the world population will exceed 6 billion by 2000. Population experts predict that this rapid growth will persist throughout the next century, stabilizing at 10.5 billion around 2110. Knowledgeable futurists consider this exponential population growth to be the most crucial factor determining man's future on this planet.

In the United States, growth will be slower but nonetheless significant. By the end of the century, the population of the U.S. should exceed 260 million. Ultimate stabilization at just over 300 million people should occur around the middle of the twenty-first century.

What do these figures actually mean? Globally, the questions take on starker significance. Can the earth's resources feed, clothe, house, and educate a population almost two and one-half times the size of earth's present 4.4 billion? Can new sources of raw materials and energy be discovered and exploited in time to address the problems of an overpopulated planet?

In short, will we face a grim, impoverished future? Or will scientists and technicians through their research usher in a future era of plenty?

World Population Totals

From Stone Age to Space Age

Historical demographers estimate that the total world population around the end of the Stone Age in Europe (about 7000 B.C.) stood between 5 and 10 million people. By the dawn of the Christian Era, the human number had risen to about 300 million. At the beginning of the modern age in Europe, seventeen centuries later (1650), the population had risen again to about 500 million, representing a growth rate in world population of little more than 20,000 people per year.

After 1650, the course of human population growth changed radically. It took ninety centuries for world population to increase from 10 million to 500 million. The next 500 million in growth took only a century and a half. And the largest explosion was yet to come.

The population soared from 1 billion in 1800 to 1.6 billion in 1900, and then to 2.5 billion in 1950. This unparalleled growth of 900 million occurred despite two devastating world wars.

The next burst of population growth, from 2.5 to 3.6 billion, occurred over a much shorter span of time, in just two decades between 1950 and 1970. Finally, the 1970s witnessed by far the fastest growth yet, from 3.6 to 4.4 billion. Thus, the growth of the last forty years has roughly equaled the growth of the entire previous history of mankind.

The Future Prospect

Our world population growth rate is beginning to decelerate, but the gross totals continue to mount inexorably. Eighty million new human beings are born each year. Even the most conservative forecasters project a total world population of around 6 billion by the turn

Between now and 2110, according to the UNFPA projections, regional populations will grow as follows:

South Asia	1.4 billion to	4.1 billion
East Asia	1.2 billion to	1.7 billion
Africa	400 million to	2.1 billion
Latin America	400 million to	1.2 billion
Europe	450 million to	500 million
USSR	265 million to	380 million
North America	248 million to	320 million
Oceania	23 million to	41 million

of the century. Thus, while 1.9 billion people were added to population totals in the last three decades, an almost equivalent number should be added during the next two decades. This ominous population explosion has far from run its course. The United Nations Fund for Population Activities (UNFPA) projects eventual population stabilization, but not before the year 2110 when the world population will have expanded to some 10.5 billion.

Almost 90 percent of the world in 2110 will be living in areas that comprised the less developed Third World nations of 1980. The more developed, industrialized nations will face a decline in their share of total world population, from 24 percent in 1980 to 13 percent in 2110. Unless these Third World areas can develop economically at a rate at least equivalent to their population growth, they will face the grim consequences of overcrowding and increased poverty, disease, famine, and, ultimately, social chaos. In the global village of the future, these problems will be impossible to isolate. The leading countries of the Western world will no doubt have to deal increasingly with Third World problems.

The chart on page 241 gives future population projections for the world's 30 largest countries.

Declining World Birth Rates

People are having fewer babies than they used to in all parts of the world. Estimates suggest that still fewer babies will be born in the future. United Nations predictions of global population growth have twice had to be revised downward during the past five years and now stand at 1.73 percent per year. The notable exception to this downward trend is sub-Saharan Africa, the scene of so much famine and brushfire warfare in recent years. But even in this impoverished and disrupted region, the birth rate will have fallen by the turn of the century.

The United States Census Bureau projects the drop in birth rate (live births per 1,000 population) between 1975 and 2000, region by region, as follows:

- The world rate will drop from 30 to 26.
- The African rate will drop from 47 to 38.5.
- The Asian and Oceanian rate will drop from 34 to 26.
- The Latin American rate will drop from 37 to 29.
- The Soviet and Eastern European rate will drop from 18 to 16.
- The North American, Western European, Japanese, New Zealand, and Australian averaged rates will drop from 15 to 14.5.

WORLD'S THIRTY LARGEST COUNTRIES, RANKED BY SIZE OF POPULATION (in millions)

1960		1980		2000	
China	682.0	China	956.8	China	1189.6
India	436.9	India	775.7	India	1036.7
USSR	214.3	USSR	266.7	USSR	311.8
USA	180.7	USA	222.2	USA	260.4
Japan	94.1	Indonesia	151.9	Indonesia	221.6
Indonesia	92.7	Brazil	126.4	Brazil	212.5
Brazil	71.5	Japan	116.4	Bangladesh	153.3
Germany, Fed. Rep. of	55.4	Bangladesh	88.7	Nigeria	148.9
UK	52.6	Pakistan	82.4	Pakistan	145.0
Bangladesh	51.4	Nigeria	77.1	Mexico	132.3
Italy	50.2	Mexico	70.0	Japan	128.9
Pakistan	45.9	Germany, Fed. Rep. of	60.9	Philippines	83.4
France	45.7	Italy	58.0	Vietnam	79.4
Nigeria	42.4	UK	55.9	Thailand	76.1
Mexico	36.4	France	53.5	Turkey	69.4
Vietnam	34.0	Vietnam	52.3	Iran	65.4
Spain	30.3	Philippines	51.0	Egypt	64.7
Poland	29.6	Thailand	47.7	Italy	61.0
Philippines	27.6	Turkey	45.3	Germany, Fed. Rep. of	59.5
Turkey	27.5	Egypt	42.0	France	57.3
Thailand	26.4	Iran	38.1	UK	56.7
Egypt	25.9	Korea, Rep. of	38.0	Ethiopia	55.3
Korea, Rep. of	24.7	Spain	37.4	Burma	55.1
Burma	22.3	Poland	35.8	Korea, Rep. of	50.8
Iran	21.6	Burma	35.3	South Africa	47.8
Argentina	20.6	Ethiopia	32.6	Zaire	46.4
Ethiopia	20.1	South Africa	29.3	Spain	43.4
Romania	18.4	Zaire	28.3	Colombia	42.5
Yugoslavia	18.4	Argentina	27.1	Poland	41.2
Canada	17.9	Colombia	26.9	Afghanistan	36.7

SOURCE: United Nations, World Population Trends and Prospect by Country, 1950-2000: Summary report of the 1978 Assessment (ST/ESA/SER.R/33), New York, 1979.

The Aging of the Human Race

On the average, the world population is slowly aging, a trend that has been in process in industrial countries for several decades and that seems to have begun in much of the Third World. According to United Nations Fund for Population Activities (UNFPA) projections, the global median age will have risen to 25.3 years by 2000, up almost 3 years from the 1980 median age of 22.6. In less developed regions, the median age will increase from 20 years in 1980 to 23.2 in 2000; in more developed regions, the increase will be from 31.4 to 35.7.

Region by region, the median age will rise as follows:

Africa	17.7 years to 18.5 years
Latin America	19.3 years to 21.4 years
North America	30.1 years to 35.6 years
East Asia	24.3 years to 31.1 years
South Asia	18.7 years to 21.9 years
Europe	33 years to 36.6 years
Oceania	26.5 years to 30.1 years

The nation with the highest median age in 2000 will be Luxembourg at 40.6 years, closely followed by Switzerland and West Germany at 39.6 years each and East Germany at 39.1 years. The youngest populations will live in the African nations of Malawi (16.5 years median age), Kenya and Nigeria (16.7 years), and Niger (16.8 years).

World
Urbanization

BY 2000, more than half of the earth's population will be living in cities, most of the people compressed into the sprawling, expanding urban metropolises of the Third World. This massive influx will pose extraordinary challenges for Third World governments and their citizens. The cities of the industrial world will also face severe problems. Older cities, such as London and Rome, show distinct signs of decay. The world's cities, centers of both growth and decay, will become the sites of the most important social and political battles of the years to come.

The World's Largest Cities

Over 3,000 years ago, the world's three largest cities were located in the great river valleys of the Nile and the Tigris and Euphrates Rivers—the Egyptian cities of Thebes (100,000 people) and Memphis (74,000) and the ancient Asian metropolis of Babylon (54,000).

One thousand years later, Rome had become the largest city with almost 600,000 inhabitants. By 1,000 A.D., the leading giants had become Cordova, Spain, and Constantinople (both around 450,000). The first city to top 1 million inhabitants was the Chinese capital of Peking, late in the eighteenth century.

Region by region, between 1980 and 2000 the percentage of people living in cities will increase as follows:

Africa	29 percent to	42.5 percent
Latin America	65 percent to	72 percent
North America	74 percent to	81 percent
East Asia	33 percent to	45 percent
South Asia	24 percent to	36 percent
Europe	69 percent to	77 percent
Oceania	76 percent to	83 percent
USSR	65 percent to	76 percent

It was only with the arrival of the Industrial Revolution that the process of urbanization accelerated rapidly. In England, the first center of industrialization, the imperial capital of London reached 2.3 million by 1850, 4.2 million by 1875, and the incredible size of 6.5 million by 1900. In that year, twenty metropolises boasted 1 million-plus populations, a number which tripled during the next four decades.

World urban growth has soared even more dramatically since 1950. Between then and 1975, the total number of metropolitan dwellers in the world more than doubled. Even more alarming, urban demographers project that the 1975 total may triple by the year 2000. At the beginning of the next century, the metropolitan area of Mexico City is expected to be the world's largest city with a population of 31.6 million.

According to UNFPA projections, the percentage of the world's people living in cities will rise from 41 to 51 percent during the next twenty years. The figure was 19 percent in 1920. The rate of change will vary widely by region. While many older cities in North America will have stopped expanding, Third World cities will continue with an unprecedented and unchecked growth rate. Throughout the Third World, the percentage of population in cities will increase from 30.5 percent today to 42.5 percent by 2000, contrasting with a figure of 12.6 percent in 1940.

The world's poorest regions are urbanizing most rapidly. For the entire half century from 1950 to 2000, Africa will establish the pace among the eight major world regions with a 981 percent increase in city dwellers, from 32 million in 1950 to a projected 346 million by 2000. South Asia will be second, with a 652 percent increase to 790 million by the century's end.

Urbanization will progress most slowly in Europe and North America, continents that are already largely urbanized. The most urban nation in the world in 2000 will be the United Kingdom (94 percent urban), and the most rural will be Burundi in central Africa (only 4 percent urban).

TEN MOST POPULOUS URBAN AREAS IN THE YEAR 1980

1. New York-northeastern New Jersey	20,400,000
2. Tokyo-Yokohama	20,000,000
3. Mexico City	15,000,000
4. Sao Paulo	13,500,000
5. Shanghai	13,400,000
6. Los Angeles-Long Beach	11,700,000
7. Beijing (Peking)	10,700,000
8. Rio de Janeiro	10,700,000
9. London	10,200,000
10. Buenos Aires	10,100,000

TEN MOST POPULOUS URBAN AREAS IN THE YEAR 2000

1. Mexico City	31,000,000
2. Sao Paulo	25,800,000
3. Tokyo-Yokohama	24,200,000
4. New York-northeastern New Jersey	22,800,000
5. Shanghai	22,700,000
6. Beijing (Peking)	19,900,000
7. Rio de Janeiro	19,000,000
8. Greater Bombay	17,100,000
9. Calcutta	16,700,000
10. Djakarta	16,600,000

SOURCE: United Nations, Patterns of Urban and Rural Population Growth, 1950-2000, 1979

By 2000, United Nations demographers project a grand total of 82 cities in the 4 million range, 61 of them in today's less developed regions. Furthermore, of the 191 world cities over 2 million (there were 30 in 1950), two-thirds will be located in today's less developed regions. Of the 440 cities over 1 million (there were 77 in 1950), again 2 of every 3 will be located in today's Third World. Not in the foreseeable future, and probably never again, will the majority of the world's largest cities be found in today's industrialized nations as they were as recently as twenty years ago.

These burgeoning Third World cities face the stiffest challenge of all in meeting the employment and basic service needs of newcomers from the rural countryside. They come in a flood, pursuing the bright lights of the twentieth century, and settle in shantytowns that ring such cities as Djakarta, Calcutta, and Mexico City. The shantytowns, along with their host of attendant problems, grow larger and more unmanageable every year. The urban horrors that Charles Dickens described so vividly in ninteenth century London will seem slight compared to the ills that await Third World cities in the coming years.

Future Wealth
and Poverty

Fortunately, global economic expansion has managed to outpace the rapid population growth of the past two decades. Between 1960 and 1975, while world population grew at a 1.9 percent average annual rate, world aggregate income grew an average of only 4.7 percent a year, and individual income grew just 2.8 percent annually over the same period.

Income gains have varied widely from one country to the next, and problems of severe poverty and extreme inequality of wealth persist in many areas. Even the more optimistic experts project almost half a billion poor by 2000. Ironically, population is growing fastest in these impoverished areas. The populations of the thirty-six least developed countries, now totalling almost 300 million, are growing at a yearly rate of 2.7 percent. If this rate holds steady, the population totals will double the current total within one generation.

On the whole, the gap between less and more developed countries widened during the 1960s and 1970s, as average annual per capita income in the more developed economies grew 3.1 percent compared to 2.9 percent in the less developed countries.

Per Capita GNP Estimates (1975) and Projections and Growth Rates (1985,2000) by Major Regions and Selected Countries and Regions

(Constant 1975 U.S. dollars)

	1975	Average Annual Growth Rate 1975-85	1985 Projections	Average Annual Growth Rate 1985-2000	2000 Projections
		percent		*percent*	
WORLD	1,473	2.3	1,841	1.5	2,311
More developed countries	4,325	3.2	5,901	2.5	8,485
Less developed countries	382	2.8	501	2.1	587
MAJOR REGIONS					
Africa	405	2.2	505	1.4	620
Asia and Oceania	306	2.7	398	2.3	557
Latin America	1,005	2.6	1,301	1.8	1,715
USSR and Eastern Europe	2,591	2.4	3,279	2.1	4,472
North America, Western Europe, Japan, Australia, and New Zealand	5,431	3.4	7,597	2.6	11,117
SELECTED COUNTRIES AND REGIONS					
People's Republic of China	306	2.3	384	2.3	540
India	148	1.5	171	0.8	191
Indonesia	179	4.1	268	3.1	422
Bangladesh	111	0.6	118	0.1	120
Pakistan	138	0.4	144	0.1	142
Philippines	368	3.2	503	2.3	701
Thailand	343	3.0	460	2.2	633
South Korea	507	3.5	718	2.7	1,071
Egypt	313	2.9	416	2.2	578
Nigeria	367	3.3	507	2.2	698
Brazil	991	2.2	1,236	1.6	1,563
Mexico	1,188	2.0	1,454	1.3	1,775
United States	7,066	3.3	9,756	2.5	14,212
USSR	2,618	2.3	3,286	2.1	4,459
Japan	4,437	3.1	6,023	2.5	8,712
Eastern Europe	2,539	2.6	3,265	2.2	4,500
Western Europe	4,653	3.7	6,666	2.7	9,889

SOURCE: Global 2000 Technical Report

The Global 2000 Report to the President commissioned by former President Jimmy Carter projects that the average slice of the world's wealth obtained by each individual will increase to $2,311 (in 1975 currency) by the year 2000, up from $1,475 in 1975—a healthy increase of 53 percent in per capita world gross national product (GNP). Again, however, the projection indicates widely disparate gains.

For instance, while the United States per capita annual GNP will more than double, from $7,066 in 1975 to $14,212 in 2000, the per capita annual GNP of Pakistan will grow only from $138 to $142. On the whole, for every $1 increase in per capita annual GNP in the less developed countries, there will be a $20 increase in the more developed countries.

Feeding the
Future World

As late as the 1950s, the world's non-industrialized regions maintained agricultural self-sufficiency; only the industrial regions needed to import food. The picture has since changed drastically. Today, population growth is outstripping food production in many of the poorest Third World areas.

Regionally, the picture of available calories in relation to population varied as follows:

More developed regions	32 percent surplus
Less developed regions	4 percent deficiency
North America	31 percent surplus
Northern, Western, and Southern Europe	32 percent surplus
Australia and New Zealand	27 percent surplus
Eastern Europe and USSR	35 percent surplus
Africa	9 percent deficiency
Latin America	7 percent surplus
Asia (estimated)	4 percent deficiency

On the whole, global food production continues to run ahead of world population growth, but the gap between these rates of growth has narrowed since the early 1970s. Declining food production in Africa and Asia, the two fastest growing continents, accounts for the increased problems.

In all other major regions, food production continued to gain ground in the race with population growth as more land was brought under cultivation. The agricultural work force grew in number (0.5 percent average annual growth worldwide), and productivity of both land and workers increased (almost 2 percent average annual growth worldwide). As a result, world food supplies exceeded world nutritional requirements by an estimated 7 percent in 1974.

Food Production

According to United Nations projections, nearly 1.5 billion additional persons will live in today's Third World nations by 2000. Feeding these people will necessitate strong, continuous gains in food production, especially in land productivity because available land, with the exception of tropical Africa and Latin America, is running short.

Fortunately, such strong continuous productivity gains do seem likely. The Global 2000 Report to the President projects a 2.2 percent rate of annual increase in world food production between now and 2000. This projection roughly extends the rate of the past thirty years, corrected for fluctuations due to weather and natural disasters and including the well-publicized "Green Revolution" of the early 1970s.

Global Solutions to Hunger Problems

To feed the world of 6 billion people in 2000, world governments must affect certain improvements in food productivity. Some of the keys to improved production include the following.

• International fisheries must be cooperatively managed to avoid disastrous overfishing.

• Nontraditional marine species, such as the Antarctic krill, must be used as future sources of vital protein.

• Aquaculture must be further exploited. A 1976 Food and Agriculture Organization world conference on aquaculture concluded that with adequate investment, we could achieve a five to tenfold increase in aquacultural production by the year 2000. (Aquaculture produced 6 million metric tons in 1975.)

• Agricultural output on existing land must be maximized through use of more and better fertilizers, pesticides, herbicides, equipment, and irrigation.

• More land must be brought under cultivation. However, land use experts caution that agricultural lands will probably be extended by only 4 percent more by the year 2000 and that much of this expansion will be into marginally fertile land.

• Developed countries must increase agricultural aid to their less developed neighbors. Such aid currently totals $5 billion, but the FAO projects need for a figure over three times that amount by 2000.

• Research and development in the area of closed-cycle (greenhouse) agriculture, currently being conducted by corporations and universities, must be expanded. The potential advantages of closed-cycle agriculture include elimination of pollution from runoff of fertilizers and pesticides, economy of land use, elimination of the supply fluctuations that inevitably result from weather and climatic vagaries, and extension of the growing season to twelve months through the use of artificial light and climate control.

With strong efforts in these areas, the FAO estimates that the world can increase its food production by almost 4 percent annually during the closing decades of the twentieth century.

The food problem can be solved. In fact, a recent study at the University of Waginingen in the Netherlands based on the new FAO/UNESCO world soil maps concluded that the earth could potentially produce 32 billion tons of grain each year—twenty-five times the present production level. It is all a matter of increased investment, improved management and technology, and land and economic reform. The human race holds within its grasp the potential to feed its hungriest citizens. The great question remaining is whether or not we will choose to shoulder the burden of responsibility.

The United States
Population Projections

On May 1, 1981, the huge population clock in the main lobby of the vast United States Commerce Department building in Washington, D.C. registered a total of 229,440,000 Americans, a striking contrast to the 3,929,000 counted in the first census in 1790.

U.S. Population Totals

The United States' growth has been steady—5 million people in 1790; 23 million in 1850; 76 million in 1900; 151 million in 1950; 227 million in 1980. The nation's history has been one of a continually expanding population. This trend of expansion will continue into the future, although it will be marked by events and growth patterns apart from the past.

AMERICAN POPULATION TOTALS: 1790-2000 (in thousands)

	1790	1900	1980	2000 (Projected)
U.S.Total	3,939	75,995	226,505	259,869
NORTHEASTERN STATES				
NEW ENGLAND				
Maine	97	694	1,125	1,405
New Hampshire	142	412	921	1,113
Vermont	85	344	511	586
Massachusetts	379	2,005	5,737	6,842
Rhode Island	69	429	947	1,117
Connecticut	238	908	3,108	3,386
MIDDLE ATLANTIC				
New York	340	7,269	17,557	17,961
New Jersey	184	1,884	7,364	8,425
Pennsylvania	434	6,302	11,867	12,317
NORTH CENTRAL STATES:				
EAST NORTH CENTRAL				
Ohio	--	4,158	10,797	11,051
Indiana	--	2,516	5,490	5,731
Illinois	--	4,822	11,418	11,923
Michigan	--	2,421	9,258	10,148
Wisconsin	--	2,069	4,706	5,545
WEST NORTH CENTRAL				
Minnesota	--	1,751	4,077	4,561
Iowa	--	2,232	2,913	3,131
Missouri	--	3,107	4,917	5,346
North Dakota	--	319	653	732
South Dakota	--	402	690	748
Nebraska	--	1,066	1,570	1,851
Kansas	--	1,470	2,363	2,540
SOUTHERN STATES:				
SOUTH ATLANTIC				
Delaware	59	185	595	689
Maryland	320	1,188	4,217	5,436
Virginia	822	1,854	5,346	6,768
West Virginia	--	959	1,950	2,076

North Carolina	394	1,894	5,874	7,226
South Carolina	249	1,340	3,119	3,893
Georgia	83	2,216	5,464	6,840
Florida	--	529	9,740	14,394
EAST SOUTH CENTRAL				
Kentucky	74	2,147	3,661	4,290
Tennessee	35	2,021	4,591	5,183
Alabama	--	1,829	3,890	4,425
Mississippi	--	1,551	2,521	2,763

AMERICAN POPULATION TOTALS: 1790-2000 (in thousands)

	1790	1900	1980	2000 (Projected)
WEST SOUTH CENTRAL				
Arkansas	--	1,312	2,286	2,690
Louisiana	--	1,381	4,204	4,486
Oklahoma	--	790	3,025	3,449
Texas	--	3,049	14,228	17,167
WESTERN STATES: MOUNTAIN				
Montana	--	243	787	977
Idaho	--	162	944	1,195
Wyoming	--	93	471	527
Colorado	--	540	2,889	3,892
New Mexico	--	195	1,300	1,636
Arizona	--	123	2,718	3,822
Utah	--	277	1,461	1,775
Nevada	--	42	799	908
PACIFIC				
Washington	--	518	4,130	4,161
Oregon	--	414	2,633	3,070
California	--	1,485	23,669	27,309
Alaska	--	--	400	544
Hawaii	--	--	965	1,193

Demographic Projections

As the nation approaches the third millenium, the United States' demographic center will gravitate increasingly southward and westward.

In 2000, the Western Census region will show a significant growth rate of 18 percent, while the Southern region will record an even larger gain of 23 percent. In the same time period, the Northeastern and North Central regions will grow by only about 8 percent.

Other highlights:

• Of the nine geographic subdivisions of the four great Census regions, the Mountain and South Atlantic divisions will show the largest gains at 30 percent each.

• The slowest growing regions will be the heavily industrial Middle Atlantic (5 percent growth) and East North Central states (7 percent growth). Population growth in the states surrounding the Great Lakes will be minimal.

• With a projected population of 48 million by 2000, the South Atlantic division, a largely coastal area that extends from Delaware to

TEN MOST POPULOUS STATES (in thousands)

1980		2000	
1. California	23,669	1. California	27,309
2. New York	17,557	2. New York	17,961
3. Texas	14,228	3. Texas	17,167
4. Pennsylvania	11,867	4. Florida	14,394
5. Illinois	11,418	5. Pennsylvania	12,317
6. Ohio	10,797	6. Illinois	11,923
7. Florida	9,740	7. Ohio	11,051
8. Michigan	9,258	8. Michigan	10,148
9. New Jersey	7,364	9. New Jersey	8,425
10. North Carolina	5,874	10. North Carolina	7,226

TEN LEAST POPULOUS STATES (in thousands)

1980		2000	
1. Alaska	400	1. Wyoming	527
2. Wyoming	471	2. Alaska	544
3. Vermont	511	3. Vermont	586
4. Delaware	595	4. Delaware	689
5. North Dakota	653	5. North Dakota	732
6. South Dakota	690	6. South Dakota	748
7. Montana	787	7. Nevada	908
8. Nevada	799	8. Montana	977
9. New Hampshire	921	9. New Hampshire	1,113
10. Rhode Island	947	10. Rhode Island	1,117

SOURCE: U.S. Census Bureau

Georgia, will overtake the East North Central division (44 million) for the first time in over a century to become the most populous division. The South will also become the nation's most influential political area, bringing a legislative power to the states south of the Mason-Dixon line not seen since the days of the Civil War.

• The New England (14 million) and Mountain (15 million) subdivisions will remain America's least populous.

Births and Baby Boomers

There were 3,598,000 babies born in the United States during 1980, nearly 4 percent more than in 1979. This marked the fifth straight year of increasing birth rates. Why the upswing?

ANNUAL NUMBER OF BIRTHS IN AMERICA: 1940 to 2000
(in thousands)

Year (July 1 - June 30)	
1940-1945	2,903
1945-1950	3,555
1950-1955	3,949
1955-1960	4,274
1960-1965	4,171
1965-1970	3,621
1970-1975	3,319
1975-1980	3,314
1980-1985	3,882
1985-1990	4,008
1990-1995	3,868
1995-2000	3,676

SOURCE: U.S. Census Bureau

The key to this, as to so many trends in the United States today, is the dramatic baby boom that followed World War II and continued into the early 1960s. Women born during those boom years are now between eighteen and thirty-four, the prime childbearing years. In 1980 almost 33 million American women fell within this age range, an increase of 13 million over 1960. By 1985, they should number about 34 million. Thereafter, the number of women in the prime childbearing age range will decline slowly to about 30 million by 2000.

As a result, the population of the nation will continue growing for the rest of the century, though at rates that are unlikely to reach those of the great post-war baby boom.

American Lifespan

The worldwide population explosion of recent centuries has certainly been influenced by a successful reduction in mortality rates. It is not that more people are being born, but that more people are surviving longer. In the United States, the death rate has dropped almost 50 percent since the turn of the century, while average life expectancy has increased 57 percent.

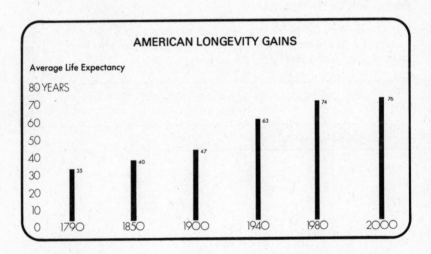

The Final Tally

When all the demographic credits and debits have been tallied, the United States is currently growing at a rate of a little under 1 percent a year. This is considerably slower than, for example, the 3 percent

THE COMPONENTS OF AMERICAN GROWTH

United States	around 1900	1980	(Projected) 2000
Population	76 million	226 million	260 million
Growth rate	2.3%	1.2%	1.0%
Birth rate (per 1000 people)	32	19	18
Death rate (per 1000 people)	17	9	9
Life expectancy	47	74	76
Immigration rate (per 1000 people)	8	2	1

According to the United States Census Bureau, the population growth rate will probably drop as follows:

1980-1990	.9% annually
1990-1995	.7% annually
1995-2000	.6% annually

annual rate of the first fifty years of the nineteenth century or even than the 2 percent annual rate being registered in 1900. This decline in the growth rate will continue in the years to come.

Although the rate of population growth will decline, the population totals will nonetheless rise for the remainder of the twentieth century and on into the twenty-first, until Zero Population Growth is ultimately achieved around mid-century. By 2050 the United States Census Bureau predicts that the U.S. population will level off at 315,000,000 people.

The Graying of America

The typical American at the turn of the century will be a white, middle-class, thirty-five-year-old, white collar worker with at least some higher education and earning a salary in the range of 20 to 30 thousand dollars a year. She (that's right, she) will be less likely to live in a traditional nuclear family household, although the odds will still favor such arrangements. At any rate, the typical future home, statistically speaking, will contain 2.4 persons.

The post-war baby boom will largely determine who dominates the United States population in the final years of the twentieth century. As the baby boomers grow older, the median age of the general population will increase from today's 30.2 years to 35.5 years by the turn of the century.

This "graying of America" will affect every aspect of our culture—from clothing styles to housing patterns to advertising campaigns. Among the potentially serious problems, planners foresee that by 2030, 20 percent of our population will be age sixty-five or older, a situation that could severely strain America's ability to provide for its aged.

The situation poses the gravest problems for America's politicians who will have to restructure the Social Security program. In 1930, for example, only 4 percent of the American population were over sixty-five, while in 2030, over 20 percent of all citizens will be sixty-five or older. The fact that these elderly citizens who receive benefits will grow at twenty times the growth rate of the American labor force strongly indicates that the Social Security program is already in a state of shambles. One way of restructuring the program will be to raise the retirement and benefit age from sixty-five to seventy, an act of legislation that is likely to take effect before 2000.

U.S.POPULATION STATISTICS: 2000

		% of total population
Total U.S. population	260,378,000	100.0
Male population	126,588,000	48.6
Female population	133,790,000	51.4
Caucasian population	218,913,000	84.1
Non-Caucasian population	41,464,000	15.9
By Age: 0 to 21	80,404,000	30.8
21 to 65	148,152,000	56.9
65 and over	31,822,000	12.2
Median age of the U.S.		35.5
Median age of males		34.1
Median age of females		36.8
Median age of Caucasians		36.4
Median age of non-Caucasians		31.0

SOURCE: U.S. Census Bureau

The Sex Ratio

Although the longevity gap between females and males will narrow as sex roles become less differentiated and as women work throughout their lives, women will continue to outlive men by several years on the average. The ratio of 51.4 women for every 48.6 men at the end of the century will be more heavily weighted among the older population cohorts. In fact, among those sixty-five years and older, there will be three women for every two men greeting the dawn of the new millenium.

The median age of whites in 2000 (36.4 years old) compared to that of blacks and other races (31 years old) will reflect not only better prospects for long life but also a lower fertility rate among whites. While whites will constitute 89 percent of the population aged sixty-five and over, blacks and other races will constitute fully 18 percent of youths aged thirteen and under.

The United States population by 2000 will be larger, older, and proportionally more non-Caucasian and more female. While the total population will grow 14.6 percent, the female population will expand by 17 percent, and the black and other minority populations will increase by almost 36 percent.

Families and Households

Since 1950, the overall population growth of the United States (50 percent) has been rapidly outstripped by the growth in the number of households (84 percent). During the same three-decade span, the average household size declined from 3.46 to 2.75 persons. This trend toward smaller households became particularly evident in the 1980 census. For example, the borough of Manhattan in New York City became the first national county to average less than 2 people per household unit, with the exception of one leper colony in Hawaii.

The "typical" U.S. household is considerably more difficult to define today than it was in earlier times. In 1950, 78 percent of American households fit the traditional pattern of mother, father, and children. This percentage dropped to about 61 percent by 1980, and should

AMERICAN FAMILY CHARACTERISTICS: 1995		
	1980	1995
Total (in millions of families)		
number of family households	59.3	72.1
Headed by husband and wife	49 (83%)	56.7(79%)
Headed by woman no spouse present)	8.6 (15%)	13 (18%)
Headed by man (no spouse present)	1.7 (2%)	2.5(3%)
Age of householder (family head):		
under 25 years	3.7 (6%)	3 (4%)
25 to 29 years	6.5 (11%)	5.6(8%)
30 to 34 years	7.5 (13%)	9.0(13%)
35 to 44 years	12.0 (21%)	18.9(27%)
45 to 54 years	10.3 (18%)	14.0(20%)
55 to 64 years	9.2 (16%)	8.9(13%)
65 to 74 years	5.8 (10%)	6.8(10%)
75 years and older	2.6 (5%)	3.6(5%)
Average family size (household)	3.25 persons	2.94 persons
number under 18 (living in household)	1.03 persons	.94 persons
number 18 years and over (living in household)	2.22 persons	2.00 persons

SOURCE: U.S. Census Bureau

continue its decline to about 55 percent by 1995. The remaining 45 percent in that year will exhibit more diversity than ever, with notable increases in the number of "nonfamily" households and single parent families.

MARITAL STATUS OF ADULTS AGED 14 YEARS AND OLDER
(in millions)

	1955	1979	1995
TOTAL	107	170	197
MALE	51	81	94
Single (never married)	9 (17%)	25 (31%)	25 (27%)
Married (spouse present)	38 (75%)	49 (60%)	55 (59%)
Separated, divorced, or widowed	4 (8%)	7 (9%)	14 (14%)
FEMALE	56	89	103
Single (never married)	7 (12%)	22 (24%)	22 (21%)
Married (spouse present)	38 (68%)	49 (55%)	55 (54%)
Separated, divorced, or widowed	45 (20%)	18 (21%)	26 (25%)

SOURCE: U.S. Census Bureau

8 THE FUTURE CALENDAR

8 THE FUTURE CALENDAR

No one can tell with certainty what lies ahead or exactly when specific events will occur, but mass achievements in science and technology can be charted with reasonable accuracy. Many experts in astronomy, geology, meteorology, sociology, and space sciences foresee a predictable scenario for future developments. Add to this the factors of inevitability, common-sense supposition, and historical markers, and one ends up with an agenda for the years to come.

Astronomy is a discipline governed by cycles. Satellite orbits, the paths of planets, comets, and meteors are cyclical in nature and can therefore be predicted, in some cases to the day and hour. The cycles of our galaxy have changed little through recorded history and are not about to change drastically in the foreseeable future.

As a geological science, earthquake forecasting is only in its infancy. But quakes, volcanic eruptions, and other earth phenomena do tend to occur periodically rather than sporadically. Once a major tremor has struck along an active fault line, it is only a matter of time before another strikes. Granted, it is generally a matter of decades or centuries before the buildup of seismic pressure reaches a point where geologists can say an earthquake is imminent, but the inevitability of such a quake or volcanic eruption exists nonetheless. When geologists do warn us that an event is going to happen, the odds are good that the occurrence is not far off. And their ability to pinpoint the exact moment and location of the quake will grow tremendously over the next few decades.

Although meteorological forecasting is not exact, temperature extremes, foul weather, and even Ice Ages have occurred on a cyclical basis in the past. There is no reason to suppose they will not continue along a similar course. Although meteorologists are admittedly making educated guesses, they agree upon certain probabilities, such as when a drought or cold period is due that will afflict different regions on earth in the future.

Sociology and psychology, or, more specifically, the study of how humanity will deal with rapid technological growth, cannot be precise either. But social scientists can try to predict what effect each major innovation will have on people's lives and thus speculate: What will civilization be like in 1999, 2008, 2020, and 2037?

The conquest of space is based on timetables that, unfortunately, are subject to an infinite series of delays. But governments and space officials are working on specific projects that should be completed, even with these delays, by predictable dates. Research is also progressing on the foundations of space projects for the more distant future. Scientists can predict, within reason, what the possibilities and limitations of space will be.

Countdown to A.D. 2000

1983

Watch for these developments in the final months of 1983.

• President Reagan's "Star Wars" speech in early 1983 simply made public a kind of high-tech war that specialists have discussed for years. Some reports state that the Russians may have working particle beam weapons by the end of 1983. These weapons shoot bolts of pure energy that move at close to the speed of light in a straight line. Any object that gets in the way is blasted by the full force of millions of volts, enough to destroy satellites or explode ballistic missiles.

• American dental researchers are closing in on a treatment that eliminates the corrosive action of bacteria in the mouth. An experimental vaccine announced in 1983 makes tooth decay virtually impossible. To counter the loss of business formerly generated by tooth decay, dentists have already begun to develop new services, such as tooth painting, which makes teeth perfectly, lastingly white.

• Artificial fertilizations abounded in 1983, making it the "year of the test-tube baby." The most spectacular birth to date in the United States has been the birth of test-tube twins on Long Island, near New York City, early in the year. Human embryos frozen in special cold storage facilities during the early 1980s may soon be revived and implanted in willing donor-mothers. Australia leads this research.

• Beginning in 1983, the Persian Gulf region entered a period of extremely high earthquake risk, based upon the past pattern of tremors in the area. Some scientists fear that Iran may suffer its worst quake of the century before the end of the year. Such a disaster could further destabilize this already tumultuous region, shatter the reign of the Ayatollahs, and provide the Soviet Union with an excuse to enter Iran. It could be the most politically significant natural disaster of our time.

• As 1983 ends, it appears that Acyclovir provides the basis for an effective treatment of genital herpes. Earlier in the year, researchers reported the anti-viral drug as effective at eliminating symptoms during each recurrence of the disease, although the drug couldn't prevent the recurrences. The incidence of herpes rose to epidemic levels during the 1970s and 1980s. Because it is a viral infection, it resists all vaccines and antibiotic medications. So feared has herpes become that social scientists predict it is fostering a return to fidelity in sexual relationships and a decline in promiscuity. Acyclovir may reduce this trend.

• Less sanguine news surrounds another recently discovered health threat. AIDS—acquired immune deficiency syndrome—continues to defy researchers throughout 1983. This vicious disease strips the body's immune system of the ability to fight infection. Its victims die under an onslaught of ills. First discovered among the gay and Haitian communities, AIDS is spreading gradually into the general population. No effective treatment for AIDS has yet appeared. Leading medical commentators, such as Dr. Lewis Thomas, believe that isolating the cause of AIDS will lead to understanding the intricate factors that cause cancer.

1984

• Science fiction fans and literary buffs ring in the new year with readings and re-enactments of George Orwell's novel *1984*. Published in 1949, the book foretold a world split into three totalitarian superstates ruled by media-mythologized demagogues. Orwell's fiction seems eerily true in 1984. Political "double-think" and the technology of communications have progressed to the point where many people feel their decision-making powers and privacy have been eroded.

• Killer hurricanes historically have occurred approximately once every fifty years. These awesome storms are far more devastating than annual hurricanes. Some meteorologists believe that such a hurricane may strike in 1984. Cuba could be ravaged, while some populated islands off the coast of southern Florida could be destroyed.

• A total solar eclipse can be viewed on November 22 from the remote jungles of New Guinea or in the south Pacific. The eclipse will last one minute and fifty-nine seconds.

• In 1984, NASA uses the space shuttle as the launching pad for *Galileo*, a space probe designed to penetrate the dense atmosphere of Jupiter. The ship will plunge down to a level in the Jovian atmosphere where pressures are ten times those on Earth and will then orbit through the murk of compressed, frozen gases for some twenty months.

Centenary Celebrations

● Invention of the modern bicycle.

● Invention of the fountain pen.

● Invention of the electric trolley car.

● Discovery of the sulfate process for making paper.

1985

● NASA launches the giant space telescope from the space shuttle. This massive array of mirrors and sensors provides a cosmic view free from atmospheric distortions that limit the performance of terrestial telescopes. The telescope will orbit 600 kilometers above earth at a speed of 29,000 kilometers per hour. By scanning an expanse of space 350 times greater than previously possible, the telescope will provide critical data for determining the structure, origin, and eventual fate of our universe.

● Halley's comet veers toward earth. Perhaps the most famous of all comets, it was the first to have its return predicted—by the man after whom it was named, Great Britain's second Astronomer Royal, Edmond Halley. The comet, sometimes called the Star Dragon, has been traced farther back in history than any other comet, and its 1985/1986 appearance is the first since it arced across the night skies of 1910. Halley's comet will be most clearly seen in the last two months of this year. The Soviet Union, Japan, and France, but not the United States, plan to send spacecraft to fly by or rendezvous with the comet.

● Late in 1985, the European Space Agency launches *Giotto*, an intercept satellite that will measure the composition of Halley's comet and will try to get clear images of the shape and density of the comet's solid core.

● Computerized expert systems are in operation in many fields, such as weather forecasting and medical diagnostics, having gained experience and efficiency for several years. Some of these computers are being put to work on the task of developing a new generation of expert systems that can develop their own rules in diverse fields of knowledge. Organizations such as Data General, the Heuristics Laboratory at Stanford University, and the Artificial Intelligence program at M.I.T. are at the forefront in this field.

• The long awaited male contraceptive pill finally makes its way to market. Developed by researchers at Vanderbilt University, the pill contains a hormonal inhibitor that blocks testosterone production, dropping sperm counts to zero. The pill also contains ingredients that maintain male sex drive in the absence of testosterone.

• The Space Age reaches Lilliput. The tiny nation of Luxembourg launches *Luxsat*, a direct-to-home broadcast satellite. By 1985, DBT's, as these orbiting communications platforms are known, are being used by dozens of countries to beam hundreds of programs and information services directly into citizens' homes from space.

• A new form of medical scanning, nuclear magnetic resonance, establishes itself as a medical standard in 1985. By measuring and displaying tiny magnetic shifts that occur in the breakdown of biochemical compounds, this system can see small variations in soft or hard body tissues that x-rays never could. The new system surpasses the capabilities of the CAT scan used widely since the late 1970s. In 1985, according to the Health Care Financing Administration, some 1,500 NMR scanners, each costing $750,000, will be in use in the United States.

• A pair of Venera spacecraft are sent into orbit jointly by France and the USSR. The unmanned probes are headed toward Venus, which they will explore in greater detail than ever before. In 1986, one of the ships will veer off to intercept Halley's comet as it gets ready to swing around the sun.

• In 1985, the average cost of making a motion picture tops $10 million for the first time. Audiences, far more willing to watch 100-channel satellite broadcast systems and videodisc interactive programs at home, go only to movies that offer spectacular effects. Fewer movies are being made, and they are enormously expensive.

1986

• Industrial efforts to stimulate vastly expanded production of coal in the United States are in high gear. As a result of plans laid out in the late 1970s, the United States' long-term energy shortage has begun to ease. Popular opposition to building new nuclear power-generating plants reaches a political crescendo now, since coal is reclaiming its position as America's leading source of energy.

• On January 24, the robot spacecraft *Voyager 2* reaches the planet Uranus. The spacecraft's camera bank provides superb photographic coverage of Uranus's hemispheres, the chain of nine narrow rings, and all five of its presently known moons. During this brief fly-by, *Voyager 2* will uncover an enormous quantity of data about Uranus.

• Comet Kohoutek returns. This comet was discovered by Lubos Kohoutek in 1973 at the Hamburg Observatory in West Germany. The comet was supposed to make a spectacular appearance to earth viewers in 1975, but did not live up to its promise. Astronomers believe that each time a comet comes close to the sun, it loses some of its composition. As a result, Kohoutek's 1986 visit should be even less spectacular, and some astronomers suspect the comet may have simply faded away in deep space.

• A fully operational collision avoidance system is put on the market for airplanes, boats, trucks, and other commercial vehicles. The system uses sensors strategically placed on various parts of the vehicle that feed information about the surroundings to a high-speed microprocessor control inside. Whenever the carefully programmed computer determines that a collision is imminent, it assumes control of the vehicle, makes immediate contact with the microprocessor of the other vehicle, and works out the best plan either to reduce injuries and damage or to avoid the accident altogether.

• Dr. John Lilly hopes that his Project JANUS will succeed in establishing reliable human-dolphin communications by 1986. His Joint Analog Numerical Understanding System uses minicomputers to translate the air-carried vocalizations of humans into water-borne sonar pulses that dolphins can sense, and vice versa. Dr. Lilly is aiming toward creation of a sixty-four-sound "alphabet" that allows the two species to begin a dialogue.

• One endangered species that will probably be gone from the world by 1986 is the emperor. Human empires have gradually dwindled. When Africa's Jean-Bedel Bokassa was violently ousted from his jerry-built Central African Empire in 1979, only one emperor remained on earth—elderly and frail Hirohito of Japan. With his eventual death, emperors will vanish into human history.

1987

• The European Space Agency launches *Hipparcos*, the High Precision Parallax Correcting Satellite, which will measure the relative positions and motions of some 10,000 heavenly bodies more precisely than ever before. Information from the satellite will make possible the most accurate star map in history and could help researchers gain a more complete understanding of quasars and other space oddities.

• By this year, a computer chess champion should emerge. In the early eighties, computers were already beating competent players with ease and were beginning to challenge the prodigious skills of masters. The linkage of high speed calculation, vast memory, and an expert system program that can learn from its mistakes, much as a chess master does, makes development of a true computer chess master merely a matter of engineering.

• Cancer chemotherapy shifts by 1987 from injections and implants to the use of "smart spheres," microscopic, perfect spheres coated with monoclonal antibodies that will react only in the presence of cancer cells. The spheres float harmlessly through the patient's body until they find the tumor. Then they rush forward and adhere to it like iron filings caking on a magnet. The cancer is choked off because its chemical reactions are blocked by the spheres. No healthy cells are affected.

• Products derived by genetic engineering are filling the drugstore shelves of 1987 with a variety of pharmaceuticals, so potent and so lacking in side effects as to make traditional pharmacology seem like witch doctoring. By prudently snipping and combining the most effective strands of various compounds, scientists create drugs like MSH/ACTH, which enhances memory, and Factor S, which gently moves the body through the chemical sequences that unfailingly produce deep, refreshing sleep.

• The DNA tinkerers of 1987 are also working to prevent disease by fixing the cellular genetic defects that lead to chronic problems such as arthritis and diabetes. In the future, instead of waiting for symptoms to appear, doctors will examine the gene structures of patients' vital body systems as part of regular preventive check-ups. Any tell-tale genetic inconsistencies will be eliminated by removing some of the patient's cells, inserting new genetic information and returning the cells to the body. Among the information added to the cells will be instructions for "teaching" surrounding cells to repair their own genes. The patient's disease will be cured even before he gets it.

• Environmentalists fear locusts will continue their cycle of proliferation, devastating crops in many regions of the United States. Every seventeen years, one breed of locusts explodes in population and wreaks havoc on farms and suburban gardens. Efforts to control the insect's reproductive cycles have often resulted in more severe environmental disasters. In 1987, scientists and agronomists may face yet another locust plague with little scientific recourse.

• The cost of controlling American pollution has doubled since 1978. More than $94 billion is spent to keep a cap on filth in 1987, compared with just $45 billion nine years earlier.

Centenary Celebrations

• Development of automobile gasoline.

• Invention of the kinetoscope.

• Invention of monotype.

• Invention of celluloid photographic film.

1988

• Mars is at its closest point to earth during 1988. Mars's orbit is rather eccentric, bringing it markedly closer to Earth every fifteen or seventeen years. Its close position allows extremely good viewing by amateur astronomers, particularly south of the equator.

• Japan, attempting to catch up in space technology, announces plans to launch a Japanese astronaut into earth orbit, using its own vehicle and launch system. NASA officials have kept a close eye on Japanese endeavors and cite 1988 as Japan's year to become the fourth member of the "Space Club," after China, the United States, and the Soviet Union.

• The increasingly crowded purviews of space surrounding earth are beginning to resemble New York's rush hour. The problem is so bad that several satellites have been knocked out of commission by broken-down space junk from the early days of the space age. Governments begin to discuss the necessity for parceling near-earth space and establishing some kind of formal control system to alleviate the traffic jam in orbit.

• The biggest winners in terrestrial business this year are enzymes. Technologies first used in the early 1980s are now spewing out synthetic cloth, specialty fuels, mock plastics, and hundreds of other products once entirely derived from fossil fuels. So overwhelming is the economic superiority of enzyme processing as a chemical synthesis system that it has become the fastest growing industry on earth. The size of the business is still relatively small (less than $1 billion), but five years earlier it had been almost zero. By the turn of the century, enzymes should have produced several "Fortune 500" companies.

1989

• On August 24, *Voyager 2* arrives at Neptune, three years after its fly-by of Uranus. The unmanned spacecraft will dive over Neptune's north pole, 7,500 kilometers above the planet's cloud tops. Five hours later, *Voyager 2* will be in position for a close encounter with Triton, Neptune's largest satellite. Scientists at the Jet Propulsion Laboratory in Pasadena, California, (*Voyager*'s data-receiving station on earth) are anxious to find out whether the huge moon Triton resembles Saturnian or Jovian moons and whether it possesses an atmosphere. After the Neptune rendezvous, *Voyager 2*, like its twin, *Voyager 1*, will leave the solar system at just over sixteen kilometers per second. At this speed, 358 millenia will pass before the robot scout ship will fly within one light-year of Sirius, the brightest star in earth's sky.

• Two decades of meteorological data collection by satellites have begun to improve weather forecasting significantly by the close of the 1980s. With increasingly sophisticated satellite weather monitoring, thirty-day global forecasts can be expected soon to achieve an accuracy rate of 80 percent.

• Coastal erosion becomes more noticeable in many areas. At the close of the decade, shifts along America's eastern shoreline have reduced the size of North Carolina's Outer Banks by more than 10 percent since 1970. Seaside casinos in Atlantic City are finding their foundations eroded as the sea encroaches on coastal barrier islands, such as the one upon which Atlantic City rests.

1990

• Wrist televisions are the consumer rage this Christmas, as popular as the Walkman headset of the early 1980s. They are inexpensive and offer hundreds of channels through the abundant satellite communications systems in earth orbit. Portable televisions supplement the stationary telephone and video display terminal as primary forms of communication.

• Deserts in the southwestern United States, northern Africa, and other arid areas continue to spread without constraint. Each year they overtake an area the size of Massachusetts. Agronomists fear that these expanding deserts will encroach upon enough valuable farmland to hamper severely the world's ability to feed itself. Throughout history, one-half to two-thirds of earth's arable topsoil has been lost to deserts. We continue to lose topsoil at the rate of one truckload per second. Agronomists propose chemical applications and extensive irrigation as possible solutions to the problem, but by 1990 the devastating process of desertification may be too severe to halt.

• A total solar eclipse, visible from Finland, the Soviet Union, and the entire United States, occurs on July 22. It lasts just two minutes and thirty-three seconds.

• The typical American family's income exceeds $20,000 for the first time. In 1980, it was $15,500. However, because of inflation, the lifestyle of most Americans will not improve much through this increase.

1991

• The first commercially viable computer system that is completely conceived, designed, and manufactured by other computers and robots appears on the market. A vast storage and retrieval network for amassing incredible amounts of fast-moving repetitive information, such as weather data, the computer has become feasible because cybernetic workers can construct its intricate framework faster and more accurately than humans, who would be bored by the task.

• EMV Associates, a Maryland research firm, has set 1991 as the target date for development of an implantable brain electrode. This tiny electronic chip would interlace with brain nerve endings and produce a natural electronic interface within an individual. Through this connection, a computer could transmit pictures and data directly into the human brain.

• The number of traditional family farms operating in America drops below 1 million for the first time in 1991. The economics of scale have taken over farming in America. Only huge combines with the latest in laser crop control, genetically engineered crop strains, and robot-controlled farm machinery can compete effectively. There are slightly more than 900,000 family farms in 1991. In 1930, there were 6.5 million; in 1970, 3 million.

• On the fiftieth anniversary of the Japanese attack on Pearl Harbor, which occurred on December 7, 1941, American and Japanese officials renew their bonds of post-war friendship. American survivors of the attack and Japanese veterans of the air assault meet at the harbor for one of the most unusual war reunions ever planned.

Century Celebrations

• Development of steel alloy.

• Invention of the submarine.

• Invention of the automatic telephone.

• Invention of the zipper. Avant-garde clothes designers, however, predict that the zipper will be on the way to becoming a collector's item because of several new fastening devices and glues.

1992

• This year marks the 500th anniversary of Christopher Columbus's arrival in the New World. Seaside extravaganzas take place along the American coast during October, making this the biggest national celebration since the 1976 Bicentennial festivities. The Flat Earth Society pickets the White House, protesting the commemoration.

• American physicists anticipate that by 1992, the first successful fusion reactor system will be demonstrated at the Plasma Physics Laboratory of Princeton University. Nuclear fusion is a complex process that fuses the nuclei of the hydrogen gas molecules deuterium and tritium. The result is a massive dose of energy, with relatively little radiation. This energy can supply electricity or generate thrust for a starship. It will most likely become the ultimate principal energy source for earth's needs. In the twenty-first century, fusion plants will operate both on earth and in orbit.

• In Japan, approximately 10 percent of the gross national product will be produced this year without the aid of human hands. As Japanese workers watch from the control room, robotic laborers perform such repetitive processes as electronic component assembly. Several Japanese factories are totally run by robots, who handle every facet of production from processing incoming orders to loading finished orders onto trucks.

• The number of American homes with television sets tops 100 million. The growth of cable, satellite, and interactive video have made television an infinitely more alluring communications medium than it was in the 1980s. Entertainment programming represents a small portion of on-the-air fare; training, education, documentaries, and simulations have grabbed a dominant share of the airspace.

• A programming language is developed for microcomputers that allows users to communicate with the machine in English. People can now converse with their computers, which can, in turn, respond through electronic voice circuits. Being able to talk to a computer in ordinary language instead of through an artificial programming language represents a significant milestone in the development of computer adaptability and intelligence.

Centenary Celebrations

• Invention of the addressograph.

• Invention of the electric automobile.

• Invention of the alternating-current electrical motor.

• Discovery of acetylene gas.

1993

• By 1993, cosmologists hope to have gathered enough information about the universe's structure and composition to determine whether it will expand endlessly or will eventually begin to contract. Since the launch of the space telescope, scientists have been mapping the universe's supply of hydrogen, the most abundant element. If enough hydrogen is found, its weight will force the universe's expansion to slow and its subsequent contraction to begin. If the supply of hydrogen is less than anticipated, the universe may continue to grow forever.

• Brazil's space program, fueled by one of the fastest growing economies on earth, employs some one thousand scientists and has a budget of $1 billion in 1993, with four major satellites in orbit. Brazil's emergence as a dominant space power heralds the growing technological sophistication of Latin American nations.

• The Geminid meteor shower on December 12 is one of the more brilliant showers of the year. Meteors are particles of interplanetary material, usually no larger than grains of sand, that burn up as they enter earth's atmosphere. Typically traveling at thirty kilometers per second, meteors glow and vaporize as they cause brief flashes across cloudless night skies. The Geminids are best visible after midnight in the northern hemisphere, where skywatchers can see as many as fifty-eight meteors per hour.

• Metallurgists and engineers, long toying with the so-called memory metal Nitinol and similar alloys, begin to achieve commercial success by 1993. By applying heat to dents, bends, and warps in memory metal, scientists may be able to snap it back to its original shape. The most obvious advantage of memory metal is that banged-up metallic objects like automobiles do not have to be scrapped but can be recycled easily, thereby lessening the demand for raw mineral resources. If the production of memory metal does indeed succeed, it may still be some time before the new process has a significant impact on worldwide demand for processed metals.

• A team of American military pilots sets a new speed record for an around-the-world trip. Leaving from White Sands Missile Range in New Mexico, the group races around the the globe in just under 24 hours. This marks the first time, except for space flights, that the globe has been circumnavigated in less than a day.

1994

• According to meteorological patterns, the twenty-two-year drought cycle will return to the Great Plains of the United States in 1994. This agriculturally rich area, which produces a major portion of the world's food supply, suffered its worst drought in the mid-1930s when the region was nicknamed the Dust Bowl. The 1994 drought, agronomists and meteorologists predict, will not be as severe, but it could create an inflationary surge in farm produce prices and a shortage of grain shipped to other nations, particularly affecting major importers like the Soviet Union.

• Routine access to near-earth orbit by the space shuttle costs less than ten dollars per pound (1981 dollars) in 1994, as predicted by NASA's cost-analysis projections in the early 1980s. Even at this low price, several private corporations probably offer better bargains. But the increasing demand for "orbit access" by industry, the emergence of a space tourist industry, and the needs of the United States Defense Department provide sufficient business for many shuttles.

• Scientists create compounds that can carry electricity without resistance at ordinary temperatures. Called room-temperature superconductors, these materials can save more than 15 percent of American energy production without requiring any new plants to be built. In the past, electricity was wasted to overcome the natural resistance in power lines. Superconducting power lines conserve all the electricity put into them, resulting in an enormous savings. Room-temperature superconductors also have applications in appliances and computers.

• A melody derived from a computer music-generation program reaches the top of the pop music charts. Unlike the synthesizer and computer music melodies of the 1980s, this song isn't created by a human composer working through a computer-controlled instrument; the computer itself crafts the melody, feeds it through the instruments, and records it. The first human to hear it is the director of the lab where the computer works.

• The first permanently manned space station goes into operation in orbit. It is served by monthly shuttle flights for supplies. Standard tour of duty is ninety days in orbit. The crew consists of nineteen: two chemists, two biologists, three engineers, two physicists, two botanists, three astronomers, one physician, two astronauts, and two construction and maintenance engineers. The purpose of the lab is to conduct experiments and collect data to lay the foundation for science and industry in space.

1995

● Advances in genetic engineering may allow parents to choose the gender of their child before conception. Underdeveloped or over-populated nations, such as China and India, could use such techniques for population control. A significant change in gender ratio could occur in societies where male children are preferred to females. This would reduce the number of babies the next generation could produce.

● Measles, the childhood scourge that once killed some 1.5 million youngsters annually and made uncounted millions of others miserable, should disappear by 1995. America expects its last case of indiginous measles in 1983, according to the National Institute of Health. A world-wide program of scrupulous vaccination will wipe out the disease eve-rywhere shortly thereafter.

● Airplanes, spacecraft, submarines, and other largescale commer-cial vehicles are equipped with human-machine interfaces by 1995. These electronic networks allow the machine and its human operator to trade information and impulses as quickly as the brain communicates with nerves. The pilot can ''see'' what his gauges are looking at; the equipment can ''feel'' his response. Remote sensing apparatus—links between planetary exploration drones, and command module crews for example — allow humans to explore with their own senses places they have never been physically.

● The first U.S. military outpost in space is launched. It has several planned purposes: to protect American space platforms from attack or accident; to help train astronaut-soldiers for future outposts in space; to locate and remove old, nonfunctioning satellites. The outpost has a crew of four on a 120-day rotation. The equipment includes sophisticat-ed communications and photo reconnaisance gear, laser and particle-beam weapons, and small rockets. The outpost performs numerous maneuvers on its first flight, including docking with the American space station. The space shuttle also stops here on its monthly trips.

● 1995 may see the first computer that reliable scientists feel may qualify for the designation ''intelligent.'' The self-teaching computer will produce a new theorem that goes beyond any information it was fed and will defend its findings with a ferocity that implies a kind of personal pride in its work.

• This year marks the fiftieth anniversary of the signing of the United Nations charter. United Nations officials have indicated that by 1995, their headquarters will have moved from New York City to Geneva, Switzerland. The influence of the Third World and other developing countries in the United Nations will increase greatly in the years to come.

Centenary Celebrations

• Invention of the diesel engine.

• Invention of radio signals.

• Invention of the photoelectric cell, an integral part of changing solar energy into electrical energy.

1996

• The largest volcanic eruptions in recent centuries have occurred in Indonesia. Geologists predict that the trend will continue with a major explosion on the island of Krakatoa, where a volcano will erupt either before or in 1996. Krakatoa was the scene of major destruction on August 27, 1883, when an 800-meter-high volcano collapsed to -300 meters (below sea level), leaving only a small portion of the island above the sea. Geologists fear that when the volcano erupts again, it will obliterate any presence of the island.

• NASA officials hope to launch a manned expedition to Mars by the end of the year. The spacecraft will be an updated version of the Apollo models that were sent to the moon in the 1960s and early 1970s. One part of the craft will remain in Mars orbit, while the other portion will land on the planet. The mission will resolve questions about Martian life that were left unanswered by the *Viking* robot probes that landed on the planet two decades earlier. Most scientists believe the manned expedition will only confirm what the *Viking* probes suggested: there is no life on Mars. However, NASA officials hope some evidence may be found to support the theory that there were once, tens of thousands of years ago, some Martian forms of life.

• By 1996, the artificial womb should be widely available for women who can't otherwise carry a child. A human embryo will be implanted in a laboratory device and will be allowed to develop under conditions that simulate the mother's womb.

• Space industry has soared beyond $2 billion per year, aided by a booming business in ultra-pure semiconductors. Space has become the Silicon Valley of the 1990s. Space business, worth only $500 million in 1990, has quadrupled in six years.

Centenary Celebrations

• Development of the first experimental airplane.

• Invention of the electric stove.

• Invention of high-frequency wireless telegraphy.

1997

• Psychiatrists and neurochemists succeed in exerting chemical control over the unhealthy brain. By subtly altering an individual's brain chemistry, scientists can now effectively treat schizophrenia and other serious mental problems.

• Two United States communications satellites disappear within a few months. The government suspects, but cannot prove, that the Soviet Union has used its killer satellites to destroy the American orbiters. Killer satellites will use either lasers that can blind another orbiter's electronic circuits or explosives that will blast the opponent's system into space junk. America has long since deployed killer satellites of its own, and U.S. retaliation against Soviet orbiters could set off the first armed conflict in space.

1998

• The modern nation of Israel turns fifty in 1998. Although political prognosticators differ on what the size and boundaries of the Jewish nation will be, most agree that the war-torn nation will continue to exist in some form.

• Construction of America's first solar power-generating plant in earth orbit could be completed by this year. Assembled by shuttle and space station crews, this facility is the first of many planned to help alleviate the energy woes of the United States.

• This year for the first time, more than half the world's population lives in urban areas. In 1920, just 19 percent of the world's people lived in cities. The trend toward increased urbanization should continue well into the twenty-first century.

Centenary Celebrations

• Invention of photographic paper.

• Invention of the recording telephone.

• Discovery of spinal anesthesia.

• Discovery of uranium.

1999

• Popularly considered the last year of the century (in fact, the century ends on December 31, 2000), 1999 is seen as a time of omens, portents, and foresights. Superstitious people fear that the last day in December will bring Armageddon, the cataclysmic end of the world. More optimistic individuals view the historic occasion as the dawning of a new era.

The passage from one millenium to another is an extraordinary event that may spark controversy between the religious and scientific communities. The believers of many faiths throughout the world, the educated and ignorant, the rich and poor, may use scientific data to support the interpretion of signs from religious texts predicting imminent doom. Scientists, some religious leaders, and government officials may launch campaigns of education and appeasement to calm the general public, but psychologists predict that many people will complain of violent dreams depicting scenes of disaster.

Survivalism may reach its zenith, with many families building survival shelters in their backyards and urban residents demanding more and
better fallout shelters from their city governments. Hoping that the
anticipated destruction may not reach the more remote regions of
earth, cults and religious colonies may be established near the poles
and in the far corners of the planet, imitating the behavior of the
Puritans who settled Massachusetts nearly 400 years before. Expect the
most affluent of the doomsayers to purchase habitats on orbiting space
stations, serene in their belief that the earthly catastrophe will pass
them by. Even eschatological skeptics may feel some anxiety and
urgency as the millenium draws to a close.

• Pluto regains its position as the ninth and outermost planet in the
solar system in 1999. This remote planet has a peculiar orbit that periodically brings it closer to the sun than Neptune. Since January 1979, Pluto
has actually been the eighth planet from the sun.

• Geologists believe that earthquakes may strike the western coast
of South America in approximately 1999. The Andean region has a
long, unhappy history of severe quakes and experts feel that another
major quake will be overdue by the end of the century.

• The Leonid meteor showers arrive this November. This unpredict-
able periodic display is sometimes spectacular, yet sometimes quite
uneventful. In 1966, the showers were spendid, and astronomers hope
that this year's display matches that show.

• On December 31, 1999, the United States, after close to a century
of control of the Panama Canal, transfers title of the canal to the Pana-
manian government.

• Extravagant and elaborate New Year's Eve celebrations are
organized throughout the world. No one will want to miss the exact
second when, according to popular belief, modern man passes into the
third millenium.

Centenary Celebrations

• Invention of the magnetic tape recorder.

• Invention of the wireless telephone.

• Invention of the gas turbine.

The Turn of the Century

The year 2000 is a milestone. World's fairs, national festivities, and centenary commemorations will abound. The beginning of the new century marks a time of renewed commitment to good deeds, such as ridding the world of poverty, starvation, war, and hatred. The Pope will outline the Roman Catholic Church's objectives for the twenty-first century, these most likely being a renewal of faith in God and general salvation for mankind. The United Nations will probably announce similar goals. Individual governments no doubt will promise miraculous progess and benefits for the average man by the century's end. In any case, the year will be a hopeful one, imbued with excitement and a renewed sense of beginning.

• By 2000, over one thousand people live and work on the moon, a slight majority of them female, according to NASA predictions. A more disturbing statistic projected by the United Nations is the estimate that 600 million people will live in abject poverty in 2000, unable to provide for their own subsistence.

• The World Wildlife Fund believes that the following animals are among those most likely to vanish by the year 2000:

Madagascar sea eagle
Imperial woodpecker
Mauritius kestrel
Japanese crested ibis
Mauritius parakeet
Chatham Island black robin
Kauai o'o
Marianas mallard
California condor
Iriomote cat
Javan rhinoceros
Red wolf
Mesopotamian deer
Central African mountain gorilla
Wild Bactrian camel
Aye-aye
Giant panda
Gray whale
Indus dolphin
Mediterranean monk seal
Mariana flying fox

• Magnetic-levitation trains developed by Japan, France, and Germany over the past twenty years now operate extensively in those countries. Capable of speeds up to 700 kilometers per hour, these supertrains are exclusively used for long-range, intercity travel. Other proposals on the planning boards include building train lines under the English Channel, the Mediterranean Sea, and the Atlantic Ocean.

• Reference books and highly illustrated manuals have finally become too expensive to produce as books. Instead, they are available more cheaply in electronic forms or on laser videodiscs. When a person needs to refer to one of these books, he programs his question into his videodisc player or computer microprocessor, and the required section appears on his video screen.

• Sociologists believe that enough people will be present in space by 2000 to make a major space crime predictable during this time. Crime, the blight of modern urban civilization, will spread beyond the confines of earth. This space incident would provide the first legal precedent for a criminal justice system for space. At first, the existing laws of the various nations operating in space will apply, however unsuitably. Eventually, lawyers and judges from around the world will have to convene to develop a separate code of space law.

• Signs of extraterrestial life are yet to be detected. Cosmologists may have to accept the notion that humans are the only intelligent life forms in this area of the galaxy.

• The "beat" generation of the 1950s is now in its seventies. The hippies of the 1960s are reaching retirement, telling their grandchildren tales of sexual liberation and anti-war struggles.

• Some scientists cite 2000 as the approximate year when the carbon dioxide "greenhouse" effect will be recognized as having raised global temperatures significantly. Some environmentalists predict that CO_2 pollution will create a canopy over the earth that will prevent heat from radiating into space. Most experts doubt that this effect will occur. Instead, many scientists are worried about a widespread, gradual cooling trend that could take hold by this year. If earth is indeed cooling, this climate change could signal the eventual onset of a new Ice Age that would slowly freeze much of the populated world by the year 12,000.

• The gap between the world's richest and poorest nations is increasing alarmingly. In 1975, the per capita income of a citizen in the world's poorest country was only $4,000 less than that of a citizen in the richest country. In 2000, this gap is $8,000.

• Almost 1,000 billion barrels of the world's original supply of 2,000 billion barrels of petroleum has been used up, almost half of that within the last twenty-five years of the twentieth century.

• The intricacies of the human genetic code should have been unraveled by this year. Researchers will have located each of the approximately 100,000 genes that make up a human chromosomal set. They can snip out defective strands and replace them with genes containing proper instructions.

• California is expected to be struck by a devastating earthquake before this year. The San Andreas fault that zig-zags from San Francisco south past Los Angeles has been under steadily increasing stress. A break in the pressure has been overdue, from the geological point of view, for years. Most experts will be shocked if 2000 passes without the quake's violent arrival.

• Fourteen nations possess nuclear weapons in 2000, including a number of countries representing the Third World. The nations most likely on the list are the United States, the Soviet Union, China, Britain, France, India, Iraq, Libya, South Korea, Taiwan, Pakistan, Brazil, South Africa, and Israel.

• Five countries or political groups now have weapons in outer space. They are the United States, the Soviet Union, East Germany, China, and the European Space Agency.

• A pound of hamburger that cost $1.99 in 1980 costs $10.50 in 2000 (assuming a steady rate of inflation). At the same rate, a secretary who made $6,000 in 1980 will take home $45,000 this year.

• There are 50 percent more cars on American roads than there were in the early 1980s. These automobiles are smaller and more efficient than those of twenty years ago, and air pollution has dropped from nearly 70 million tons a year to 27 million tons.

• Mexico City becomes the first metropolitan area with over 30 million people. The city is rife with poverty, since Mexico's capital has always been a mecca for the poor of the entire country.

Decade by Decade
to 2050

What will happen in the first half of the twenty-first century cannot be easily predicted year by year. A more accurate approach is to examine the half century by decades. If an event is certain to occur in a particular year, it is noted as such.

2001-2010

• World population surpasses 6 billion people. The number may begin to stabilize if contraception programs and increased education take hold in underdeveloped countries.

• Advanced electronics and sophisticated computers account for 90 percent of all communication. High technology may be used to revive and enhance traditional cultures around the world. Computers, rather than impeding literacy and destroying folklore, may actually revive and transmit native languages, customs, and literature. Although English will remain the prevalent global language, the need for an international computer language will become a pressing concern.

• Full-immersion video rooms provide a new form of home ambience. At the touch of a button, people can surround themselves with a tropical rain forest, a coral reef, a Saturnian landscape, or a 360-degree scene from the latest action-packed digital movie. These environments are formed by optical laser images projected onto the walls and ceilings.

• The first commercial vehicles powered by hydrogen are put on the market. Many scientists believe that hydrogen by this decade will become a viable energy source. Invented in the 1940s by the Germans and pioneered in the 1960s by a far-sighted entrepreneur, Roger Billings, the method of converting gasoline engines to hydrogen engines could be routinely performed at neighborhood hydro-stations. Hydrogen's appeal as a fuel source lies in its high efficiency, its abundance as a resource, and its waste product: plain water. Some people may have chuckled when they first saw Billings drink his car engine exhaust in the 1970s, but no one is guffawing now. Hydrogen may become the most popular small-scale energy source in the future.

• The frequency of volcanic activity in the Pacific Northwest of the United States suggests that this area may suffer more violent eruptions in the near future, similar to the Mount Saint Helens disaster of May 18, 1980. The entire Cascade Range has volcanic potential, but the likeliest sites for problems are the major peaks: Mount Baker outside of Seattle, Mount Ranier in southwestern Washington, and Mount Hood near Portland, Oregon.

• The fiftieth anniversary of the birth of the Space Age arrives in 2007. On October 4, 1957, the USSR startled the world by launching Sputnik, a crude radio transmitter barely larger than a football.

• A small, floating city may be built on the high seas, supported by underwater mining rigs. The community could be the first of a new wave of boom towns, similar to those that sprang up in the American West and Alaska around gold and silver mines. These ocean cities may also be dismantled and put up at new locations.

• Equatorial countries will benefit in a unique way from space industrialization due to their prime location for commercial rocket launches. These poor nations will capitalize on their sudden resource—geographical position—to vitalize their moribund economies. They will be among the biggest beneficiaries of the growing business of space manufacturing.

Centenary Celebrations

• Launch of the first rigid, dirigible airship in 1901. Airships may stage a comeback during the dirigible's centennial as heavy-duty transport machines to carry loads from inaccessible areas. Timber from northern and western Canada could be shipped in this manner.

• Discovery of adrenalin in 1901.

• Invention of the radio telephone in 1902.

• Commemorations of the world's first successful flight in a powered aircraft take place at the original site, Kitty Hawk, North Carolina. Merely one hundred years ago, in 1903, the Wright Brothers flew their primitive craft a few feet above the ground.

• Formulation of the theory of relativity in 1905.

- Invention of the electric washing machine in 1907.

- Invention of the vacuum cleaner in 1907.

- Invention of the radio amplifier in 1907.

- Invention of the gun silencer in 1908.

- Invention of the fused, bifocal lens for eyeglasses in 1908.

- Discovery of cosmic rays in 1910.

2010-2020

- Genetic engineering may make possible the creation of babies with certain characteristics specified before conception. Blue eyes, operatic voices, and other popular traits will be codable into human cells. However, it is likely that legal, ethical, and moral disputes will prevent the program from achieving broad acceptance—at least on the record.

- Terraforming, the changing of an alien environment to support human life, may begin during this decade, perhaps with experiments on Mars. A permanent colony that could subsist on Martian resources would be the long-term goal, but the immediate objective would be fostering organic cell growth in a Martian environment. Venus may be chosen instead, however, because Mars is too small to hold a breathable atmosphere.

- Population growth in space:

Population	2000	2010	2020	2030
Men	125	500	900	2000
Women	155	575	1000	2200
Children	1	12	50	150

These figures are based on projections made of possible space missions outlined by NASA and independent futurists in the early 1980s.

After 2030, the human population in space will be multiplied by four every ten years if current projections prove accurate.

• In 2017, a total eclipse of the sun is visible to people living in North America.

• Two thousand thirteen marks the fiftieth anniversary of the assassination of President John F. Kennedy. The generation that idolized the fallen leader is now elderly, and the exploits of the Camelot era are remembered primarily by historians.

• The first breed of dog created through genetic engineering techniques is recognized by the American Kennel Club during this decade.

• Major resource shortages similar to the energy crisis of the last century may arise. Shortages of materials like mercury, copper, tin, silver, and cadmium are likely to arise. Even with extensive mining of subocean areas, minerals could run short by this decade. Industrial spacecraft, however, will be used to mine the asteroid belts, where useful minerals are abundant. Space-mining engineers may even try to capture a huge asteroid in space and haul it back to earth orbit, rather than send vehicles to mine it in space. Huge profits may result from such an entrepreneurial mission.

• Nuclear fission plants on earth will be phased out or simply shut down. The first space fusion reactor could be operational.

• The United Nations sets up a central computer at its headquarters. UN officials say the international mega-computer will be capable of processing data for the entire world. Its main function will be to serve as a central dispensary of scientific, financial, and cultural information. United Nations administrators hope the computer will encourage all nations of the world to look to the institution for help in solving their problems, thereby creating a greater influence for the UN in global affairs.

• When the twenty-two-year drought cycle makes its regular visit to the American Great Plains during this decade, new high technology protection systems, such as laser ground water management and sophisticated cloud seeding, will ameliorate the effects. The drought will have scant commercial impact.

• In 2011, the world celebrates the fiftieth anniversary of the first manned space flights. In April, 1961, the Soviets sent Yuri Gagarin aloft, and the Americans launched Alan Shepard, Jr. in May. Commemorative exhibitions travel around the United States throughout the year. Crowds marvel at the primitive, tin-can spacecraft of the pioneer days. Later in the decade, in 2019, the fiftieth anniversary of America's first moon landing is commemorated. "The Year of the Moon" is declared and special missions are launched from orbiting space bases to bring humans to the moon for the first time since the end of the Apollo program.

• Life expectancy for Americans surpasses eighty years during the decade from 2010 to 2019. An American born in 2019 can expect to live a very long time, possibly even to 120 years, the span the Bible mentions as the ideal length for human life.

• Nations belonging to the atomic club by 2020 are the United States, the Soviet Union, China, Britain, France, India, Iraq, Libya, South Korea, Taiwan, Pakistan, Brazil, Argentina, Saudi Arabia, South Africa, Israel, Nigeria, Iran, West Germany, Cuba, Venezuela, Italy, Zaire, Spain, Indonesia, and possibly even Japan. The large number of countries with atomic weapons could make some kind of nuclear incident unfortunately inevitable.

Centenary Celebrations

• Invention of the hydroplane in 1911.

• Invention of cellophane in 1911.

• Invention of the gyrocompass in 1911.

• Discovery of isotopes in 1912.

• Discovery of vitamin C in 1912.

• Invention of the geiger counter in 1913.

• Development of atomic numbers in 1913.

• Discovery of vitamin A in 1913.

• Invention of the military tank in 1914.

• Invention of the neon lamp in 1915.

- Invention of stainless steel in 1916.

- Discovery of vitamin B in 1916.

- Invention of the mass spectroscope in 1918.

- Development of synthetic quinine in 1918.

2020-2030

- The last American veteran of World War II dies during this decade, at an age exceeding 100 years. With his passing, the central conflict of the twentieth century passes into the realm of history.

- An atmospheric cooling trend, if it ever comes about, would be confirmed in this decade. A steady decline in winter temperatures would provide the clues. Climate theorists speculate that the advent of such a new Ice Age may occur because of minute changes in the tilt of earth as it orbits the sun. The historical record of earlier Ice Ages supports this astronomical theory. No decisive action could take place during this decade, but people will accept the fact that another Ice Age is coming, since it won't arrive for a few thousand years and requires no immediate response.

- Tests continue on long-range propulsion systems that attain speeds just below the velocity of light in anticipation of manned travel to Alpha Centauri. A robot probe now dispatched to the system will take up to fifty years to send back information on possible destinations for manned craft. It will be many decades before man can travel out of the solar system.

Centenary Celebrations

- Invention of the push-button elevator in 1922.

- Discovery of insulin in 1922.

- Invention of the wind tunnel in 1923.

- Discovery of carbon oxides in 1925.

- Invention of electronic television in 1927.

- Invention of the talking movie in 1927.

- Invention of teletype in 1928.

- Invention of the iron lung in 1928.

- Invention of the automatic airplane pilot in 1929.

- Invention of the rocket engine by Robert Goddard in 1929.

2030-2040

- The medieval prophet Nostradamus (1503-1566), whom many people throughout history have called the greatest "seer" of all time, cites 2038 as the end of the world. His eschatological prediction is based on astrological calculations that civilization will abruptly end when Easter falls on April 25. But Easter has already occurred on that date four times since Nostradamus made his prediction, most recently in 1943, and man is still alive. Few give credence to the 2038 prediction.

- New tools available to archaeologists by the middle of the twenty-first century revolutionize their search for the past. Devices that trace faint nuclear echoes of buried structures are used to unlock clues to the locations of long-lost cities and temples. Deep-ground mapping with machines similar to human CAT scanners help in the search for the bones of prehistoric man. Ocean-bottom exploring modules find answers to settle the long-standing arguments about the existence of Atlantis and other sunken civilizations.

- Fashion experts predict that the most sensuous human bodies will still be thin; the large hips and thighs popular with women in the late ninteenth century will not come back into style. Natural fibers in fashion, such as cotton and wool, will become less common. People may treat handmade natural clothes as family heirlooms. However, the technology behind synthetic fabrics will have progressed to the point where most clothes will be synthetic.

- Extensive irrigation in the midwestern United States continues to consume more water than can be replaced by rainfall. This steady loss of water significantly reduces the output of American farmers, a situation that reaches crisis proportions during this decade. Conservation and strict enforcement of water-consumption limits may have to be implemented to stabilize the overall agricultural system in the United States.

Centenary Celebrations

• Development of high-octane gasoline in 1930.

• Invention of synthetic nylon in 1930.

• Invention of the cyclotron in 1930.

• Invention of the electronic microscope in 1931.

• Invention of the electric razor in 1931.

• Invention of synthetic resin in 1931.

• Discovery of the neutron in 1932.

• Discovery of the positron in 1932.

• Invention of the coin-operated washing machine in 1934.

• Development of the lobotomy in 1935.

• Discovery of cortisone in 1936.

• Invention of xerography in 1938.

• Development of electroshock treatment in 1938.

• Invention of the automatic-sequence computer in 1939.

• Invention of the helicopter in 1939.

• Development of the theory of uranium fission in 1939.

2040-2050

• Earthquake prediction becomes reliably accurate by this decade. Geologists may master the technique of earthquake prevention by injecting huge amounts of water into wells along faults in the earth.

• The 100th anniversary of both the end of World War II and the atomic bombings of Hiroshima and Nagasaki occurs in 2045. Unfortunately, war is still common by this time, and the 1945 bombings have been supplanted by more recent nuclear incidents. Still, the commemoration is marked solemnly around the world and becomes the focus of great hope for the second half of the twenty-first century.

• Skyhooks—elevators run on cables connecting satellites with various space bodies—may be constructed for Earth's moon, Jupiter's Ganymede, and Saturn's Titan by 2050. A satellite carrying a cable-making machine could construct a cable strong enough to support its own weight and extend to the surface of the particular moon. For balance, the satellite would extend another cable out into space. Gravity and centrifugal force would hold the satellite in a stable orbit and keep the cable exactly vertical. On such cables, passenger and cargo carriers could move up and down at high speeds. First theorized by Soviet space pioneer Konstantin Tsiolkovsky more than a century ago, these skyhooks will eventually permit practical and cheap transportation into space. Such possibilities would be especially alluring to the companies with mining interests on the various moons. However, a skyhook for earth is technologically still out of reach because of the immense strength required of the cable in so powerful a gravity field.

• A method for sustaining human brains outside the body is perfected. Complex circulatory systems are used to maintain a brain in full health in the lab. At first this procedure will keep a brain alive until a host for it can be found. Eventually, brains will be hooked to sensory systems and communications circuits and will live out independent lives without bodies.

• The population of outer space exceeds 7,500 people.

• *Pioneer 10*, now some 40 billion kilometers from the sun, might be intercepted by another civilization. The spacecraft was constructed for extremely long life, and it carries a plaque designating its origin. It will be the first earth craft to leave the solar system and travel into other parts of the galaxy. Before this happens, some scientists think that *Pioneer 10* may be discovered and intercepted by an alien race. NASA scientists hope that such aliens will be able to decipher the message from earth shown on page 292.

At top left is a representation of the basic laws governing the most abundant atom in the universe, hydrogen. Scientists predict that its structure will be recognizable to physicists from other civilizations. The hydrogen diagram is the key to deciphering other parts of the message. The

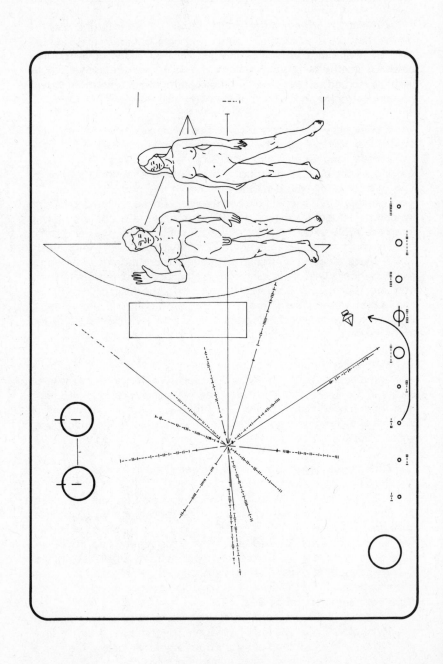

radial pattern at left-center is a depiction of how the earth's galactic position might be viewed from other parts of the galaxy. The pattern also indicates when the spacecraft was launched. At the bottom of the picture is a schematic solar system, indicating earth's position more accurately. The message is completed by a man and a woman, drawn to scale with *Pioneer 10*, so that aliens will be able to determine our size.

Centenary Celebrations

- Invention of aerosol spray in 1941.

- Invention of the electron spectrometer in 1944.

- Invention of the transistor in 1947.

- Invention of the long-playing record in 1948.

- Invention of the Polaroid Land camera in 1948.

Art and Photo Credits

Artwork by Margaret Richichi

Photo research by Hildegard Kron

Cover Photograph by Dan Morrill

Photos: Chapter 1 -- Helmut Wimmer; Chapter 2 -- Dan McCoy/Rainbow; Chapter 3 --
           Dan Morrill; Chapter 4 -- Don Dixon; Chapter 5 -- Alain Nogues/Sygma; Chapter
           6 -- Malcolm Kirk; Chapter 7 -- Bill Longcore; Chapter 8 -- Dan Morrill

Space artwork courtesy of NASA; Extent of New Madrid Quake courtesy of Midwest
Research Institute

INDEX

veterans, 288
Wright Brothers, 284
Wrist television, 270
Wyatt, Richard, 103-104

X

Xerography, 290

Y

Yankee Group Researchers
 (Massachusetts), 208

Yannis, Ioannis, 93
Yenesi River, 27
Yugoslavia
 population of, 241

Z

Zaire
 population of, 241
Zero Population Growth, 255
Zipper, 271

WORLD ALMANAC PUBLICATIONS
200 Park Avenue
Department B
New York, New York 10166

Please send me, postpaid, the books checked below:

☐ THE WORLD ALMANAC® AND BOOK OF FACTS 1984 . . . . . . $4.95
☐ THE WORLD ALMANAC BOOK OF WORLD WAR II $10.95
☐ 101 LISTS: HOW TO DO PRACTICALLY EVERYTHING FASTER,
   EASIER, & CHEAPER $4.95
☐ THE WORLD ALMANAC DICTIONARY OF DATES. $8.95
☐ THE SNOOPY COLLECTION $9.95
☐ THE LAST TIME WHEN $8.95
☐ WORLD DATA $9.95
☐ THE CIVIL WAR ALMANAC $10.95
☐ THE OMNI FUTURE ALMANAC $8.95
☐ THE LANGUAGE OF SPORT $7.95
☐ THE COOK'S ALMANAC. $8.95
☐ THE GREAT JOHN L $3.95
   WORLD OF INFORMATION:
☐ MIDDLE EAST REVIEW 1983. . . . .$24.95
☐ ASIA & PACIFIC 1983 . . . .$24.95
☐ LATIN AMERICA & CARIBBEAN. $24.95
☐ AFRICA GUIDE 1983. . . . .$24.95

(Add $1 postage and handling for the first book, plus 50 cents for each additional
book ordered.)
Enclosed is my check or money order for $_____

NAME_____

ADDRESS_____

CITY_____ STATE_____ ZIP_____